# ZUMÁRRAGA

### AND

## The Mexican Inquisition

### 1536 - 1543

Richard E. Greenleaf

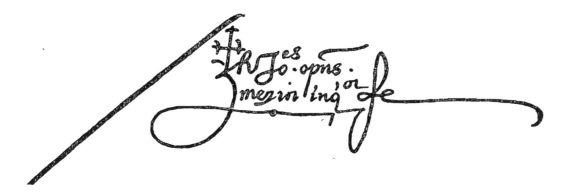

1961

ACADEMY OF AMERICAN FRANCISCAN HISTORY

WASHINGTON 14, D. C.

PRINTED IN THE UNITED STATES OF AMERICA
BY THE
WILLIAM BYRD PRESS, INC.
RICHMOND, VIRGINIA

Fray Juan de Zumárraga

## DEDICATION

*This book is dedicated to my parents, Frank Oliver Greenleaf and Grace Poindexter Greenleaf, with love and appreciation.*

# Preface

The purpose of this study is to investigate the inquisitorial activities of Don Fray Juan de Zumárraga, first Bishop and Archbishop of Mexico, 1528-1548. Zumárraga served as Apostolic Inquisitor in the bishopric of Mexico from 1536 to 1542, when he was superseded in that office by the Visitor General, Francisco Tello de Sandoval, largely because he had relaxed Don Carlos, the cacique of Texcoco, to the secular arm for burning, an act regarded as rash by the authorities in Spain.

Throughout this essay an attempt is made to relate the Inquisition to the political and intellectual life of early sixteenth-century Mexico. Zumárraga is pictured as the defender of orthodoxy and the stabilizer of the spiritual conquest in Mexico. The relationship of the individual and of society collectively with the Holy Office of the Inquisition is stressed.

With the exception of background materials, this study is based entirely upon primary sources, trial records which for the most part have lain unstudied since the sixteenth century. In all, two years of research in the Ramo de la Inquisición of the Archivo General de la Nación in Mexico City were consumed in ferreting out these materials. Subsidiary investigations in other sections of the Mexican archives were made in order to place the Inquisition materials in their proper perspective.

Secondary materials of two types were used. Studies dealing with the Mexican Inquisition by Don José Toribio Medina and Don Joaquín García Icazbalceta were examined very carefully and their conclusions were checked with actual archival materials. To some extent this author has disagreed with the two masters and has offered corrections and revisions. Other secondary materials dealing with archaeology, ethnohistory, Mexican history, and Christian and non-Christian theology were consulted.

Although some preconceived ideas are impossible to avoid, the author of this study has attempted to be scrupulously objective. He has not been polemical. For each interpretation offered there are documentary sources.

The initial chapters of the work that follows are introductory. Chapter I is a pioneer history of the episcopal Inquisition in Mexico from 1522 to 1571. Zumárraga's inquisitorial ministry is placed in its proper perspective. Inquisitorial procedures are examined. Medina and

García Icazbalceta are cited with frequency but within the interpretations arrived at by the author's own researches. Chapter II investigates Renaissance utopianism in Mexico during the period of the conquest and the intellectual fiber of Zumárraga the Inquisitor. Chapters III and IV deal with the Indians and the Inquisition and exemplify the conflict between the tenets of humanism and established orthodoxy. Chapter V is a treatment of Zumárraga's dealings with the Lutherans and other heretics, while chapter VI narrates his campaign against the *Judaizantes*. The Holy Office's preoccupation with blasphemy and the morality of the colonists is analyzed in Chapter VII. Sorcery and superstition are the concern of Chapter VIII. The concluding chapter investigates Zumárraga's special jurisdictions as Inquisitor. Conclusions on Zumárraga and the Mexican Inquisition and a bibliography follow Chapter IX.

It is a difficult task to offer adequate thanks to the many individuals who have given so freely of their time while this study was in progress. The Rotary Foundation of Rotary International made possible a year of research and advanced study in Mexico. The staff of the Archivo General de la Nación in Mexico City lightened my task by its kindness in helping me to locate materials and allowing me to microfilm them. I am indebted to John E. Longhurst and Miguel Jorrín of the University of New Mexico who read, edited, and criticized the manuscript.

Miss Eleanor B. Adams, Research Associate in the Department of History at the University of New Mexico, gave me her kind encouragement and professional advice both in Mexico City and in Albuquerque while my research was in progress. President Paul V. Murray of Mexico City College and Dean Lorna Lavery Stafford of the Mexico City College Graduate School encouraged me to do further research and publish and saw to it that I had time off from my academic responsibilities for this purpose.

My greatest debt is to France V. Scholes, who as professor, chairman of my doctoral committee at the University of New Mexico, and my mentor in paleography, has sharpened my perceptions and deepened my knowledge of Mexican history in countless ways. He is truly, as the Mexicans call him, "el decano de los investigadores."

Mexico, D. F.                                    RICHARD E. GREENLEAF
*May, 1960*

# Contents

# Illustrations

### FACSIMILE SIGNATURES

Joannes Episcopus Mexici, Inquisitor
Zumárraga's signature as inquisitor
TITLE-PAGE

Rafael de Cervanes
Fiscal of the Holy Office
PAGE 25

Miguel López de Legazpi
Secretary of the Holy Office and Leader
of the Expedition to the Philippines
PAGE 75

ZUMÁRRAGA AND THE MEXICAN INQUISITION
1536-1543

CHAPTER I

# The Functioning of the Holy Office of the Inquisition in Mexico from 1522 to 1571

I. *The European Background*

The purpose of the Inquisition was to preserve the supremacy of the Roman Catholic faith and dogma against individuals who held heretical views or were guilty of actions showing lack of respect for religious principles. The term Inquisition usually implied a special ecclesiastical institution which combated and disciplined those who sought to undermine the faith.[1] Although the practice of punishing heretics had existed from antiquity, the Inquisition as an institution was founded in the third decade of the thirteenth century. Prior to that time the bishops had jurisdiction over faith and morals in their dioceses, and civil authorities also tried cases of heresy and immorality.

The thirteenth century brought to a culmination the wide revival of the ancient Manichean doctrines that had begun to menace the Christian monolithic structure. To meet this challenge Pope Gregory IX founded a monastic Inquisition in 1231. The Pope utilized many of the imperial decrees of Emperor Frederick II in establishing his institution, and he appointed friars from the Dominican and Franciscan Orders as the first inquisitors.[2]

[1] Joseph Blotzer, "The Inquisition," *The Catholic Encyclopedia* (New York, 1910), VIII, 26. Specific bibliography on the Inquisition will be noted throughout this chapter.

[2] An invaluable orthodox source on the evolution of the medieval Inquisition from civil practice is Elphege Vacandard, *The Inquisition; A Critical and Historical Study of the Coercive Power of the Church*, trans. from 2d ed. by Bertrand L. Conway, C. S.

P. (New York, 1926), especially pp. 75-84. A prime source for the episcopal Inquisition at the time of Innocent III (1198-1215) is *Literae apostolicae diversorum romanorum pontificum, pro officio sanctissimae inquisitionis, ab Innoc. III* (Rome, 1579). Despite a strong bias Henry C. Lea's, *The Inquisition of the Middle Ages* (3 vols.; London, 1909) is indispensable for a study of the Inquisition of this era. Shorter treatments are Alpheus H. Verrill, *The*

3

The sixteenth century produced a fanaticism in religious affairs. Orthodoxy was gravely imperiled and drastic measures were used in Spain and elsewhere to eradicate the new doctrines of the Reformation. Heresy in itself was not the major problem; rather it was the suppression of heretics who were leading others into error. The line between heresy and treason became very vague, and since heretics robbed the community of its faith, sacraments, and spiritual life, it was deemed just to execute them as traitors and fomentors of social revolution.

Although there were few Lutherans in the Iberian peninsula, it was Luther who was regarded by the Inquisition as the great enemy of Spanish society. Many liberal and reform-minded Catholics were branded as Lutherans, and the Spanish mystics and Erasmists, who were on the fringes of orthodoxy, were suppressed. Furthermore, the Spanish Church of the sixteenth century undertook to supervise very closely all phases of individual Catholic life, especially morals, because it was felt that minor deviations from orthodox moral conduct created a climate in which major heresy might thrive.

It was this background to which the Mexican Inquisition owed its origin.

## II. *The First Decade of the Mexican Inquisition: 1522-1532*

Spain's claim to territorial dominium in the New World was based upon the bull *Inter caetera* issued by Pope Alexander VI on May 4, 1493.[10] This bull in effect divided the Americas between Spain and Portugal but had as its primary aim the propagation of the faith in the newly discovered lands. By their acceptance of the papal decree the Catholic Kings assumed the arduous role of missionary to the Indian and defender of orthodoxy in the vast new realms. The empire clergy were charged to take special care in causes of faith as well as to set a good example for Indians and Christians alike, and should they find heretics, to prosecute them.

We have no available data on the first three decades of the Inquisition in the Indies, but contemporary records lead one to believe that un-

to escape the secular disabilities that were destined to be placed upon the infidel. The Moriscos continued to live peacefully in Granada as pseudo-Christians until the Holy Office moved against them in the early seventeenth century. Henry C. Lea's *The Moriscoes of Spain: Their Conversion and Expulsion* (London, 1901), is the authoritative study of the Inquisition and the Moriscos. On the expulsion and sufferings of the Jews, see Lea, *The Spanish Inquisition*, I, 81-143, and Nicolás López Martínez,

*Los Judaizantes castellanos y la Inquisición en tiempo de Isabel la Católica* (Burgos, 1954).

[9] The term applied to Jewish pseudo-converts to Catholicism who were discovered practicing and teaching the old religion.

[10] Francisco J. Hernáez, *Colección de bulas, breves, y otros documentos relativos a la iglesia de América y Filipinas* (2 vols.; Brussels, 1879), I, 12-14.

til 1519 inquisitorial activities had little or no significance.[11] There was no organized Inquisition and in the early years there were no bishops and hence no inquisitors as ecclesiastical judges ordinary. In addition there is a confusion as to the chronology on the installation of the first bishops.[12]

Since the episcopal Inquisition had ceased to exist in Spain, and no tribunal of the Holy Office existed, it was deemed necessary again to make use of bishops in coping with heresy in the Indies. On July 22, 1517, Cardinal Ximénez de Cisneros, Inquisitor General of Spain, expressly delegated inquisitorial powers to all bishops of the Indies to deal with European Catholics guilty of misconduct, especially Jews and Moors who were converted.[13] Two years later, on January 7, 1519, the incumbent Inquisitor General, Alonso Manrique, delegated authority to the Bishop of Puerto Rico, Alonso Manso, and to the Vice-Provincial of the Dominican Order in the Indies, Fray Pedro de Córdoba, to establish Inquisitions.[14]

Both Manso and Pedro de Córdoba had been in the Indies for perhaps a decade prior to receiving the delegation of inquisitorial powers from Spain. We have no records to indicate that they exercised such powers previously.[15] García Icazbalceta indicated that Pedro de Córdoba held the office of Commissary of the Holy Office until his death in 1525,[16] a statement which is substantiated by Medina who places the date of Córdoba's death as June 30, 1525, but who admits that the date is open to disagreement.[17]

There is no doubt that the first clergy who came to Mexico with

[11] José Toribio Medina, *La primitiva inquisición americana (1493-1569)* (2 vols.; Santiago de Chile, 1914), I, 83-87; hereafter cited as Medina, *Inquisición primitiva.*

[12] *Ibid.*, I, 73 *et passim;* Clarence Haring, *The Spanish Empire in America* (New York, 1947), pp. 182-185, gives a brief history of the first bishoprics based upon recent research.

[13] This document is printed in Medina, *op. cit.*, II, 69-70.

[14] Medina, *Inquisición primitiva*, I, 76: ". . . Don Alonso Manrique, Cardenal de Tortosa, inquisidor general, en 7 de enero de 1519, designó a Manso, conjuntamente *simul et solidum* con Fray Pedro de Córdoba, vice-provincial de la Orden de Santo Domingo de las Indias, por inquisidores apostólicos en todas las ciudades, villas y lugares de ellas é islas del Mar Océano, dándoles a la vez, facultad para nombrar notario, alguacil, fiscal, y otros oficiales que fuesen necesarios." The entire text is printed in *ibid.*, II, 5-6. Charles V confirmed this delegation on May 20, 1519.

[15] Pedro de Córdoba arrived in Santo Domingo in September of 1510 to found the Dominican Order in America. Conway indicates that due to his fervent preaching on behalf of the natives, the conquistadores grew angry with him, and he returned to Spain to lay the matter before his provincial. G. R. G. Conway, "Hernando Alonso, a Jewish Conquistador with Cortes in Mexico," *Publications of the American Jewish Historical Society*, XXI (1928), 16. There is some question as to when he began to use his power because we do not know full details on his travels to Spain or when he returned to Santo Domingo. Medina, *op. cit.*, I, 95-97. Manso had similar altercations with the Spaniards over encomiendas and personal tithes. He returned to Spain, later to return to Puerto Rico as inquisitor. *Ibid.*, I, 73.

[16] Joaquín García Icazbalceta, *Bibliografía mexicana del siglo XVI* (México, 1954), p. 451.

[17] Medina, *op. cit.*, I, 97.

Cortés carried with them inquisitorial powers. The first trial of the Mexican Inquisition dates from 1522, a trial of an Indian, Marcos of Acolhuacán, for the crime of concubinage.[18] Additional evidence that an Inquisition operated early in Mexico is to be found in two edicts issued in 1523. The first of these was directed against heretics and Jews, but the second was so comprehensive that it was aimed at every person who in word or deed did things that seemed sinful.[19]

The first friar with specific inquisitorial powers in Mexico was the Franciscan, Martín de Valencia.[20] How he assumed the office of Commissary of the Holy Office is not clear. With the death of the Dominican prelate in Santo Domingo in September of 1525, the history of inquisitorial authority became very obscure.

After the magnitude of the mainland conquest became evident to the conquerors themselves and to the crown, a necessity arose for a vast army of clergy to carry on the spiritual conquest. Cortés felt that this undertaking should be given to the regular clergy. He asked the king in his *carta de relación* of October 15, 1524, not to send bishops to New Spain because of their tendency to pomp, formalism, and materialism. Rather, he asked that large numbers of friars be sent with extraordinary powers.[21]

The Franciscan Order had anticipated this request of the conqueror by several years. There was a shortage of secular clergy, making it necessary for the mendicant orders to bear the burden of missionary activity all over the world. In view of the fact that the regular clergy normally did not enjoy full privileges in administering the sacramental rites of the Church, the Franciscans appealed to the pope for extraordinary powers. Pope Leo X on April 10, 1521, issued a bull in which he granted to the Order the right to perform as secular clergy in areas where there were no priests or bishops.[22] His successor, Adrian VI, by the bull *Exponi nobis* (known as the *Omnímoda*) of May 10, 1522, extended these privileges to all of the Orders. This bull authorized prelates of the Orders in areas where there was no resident bishop or where he was two days distant to exercise almost all espiscopal powers except ordination.[23]

[18] The *proceso* has disappeared from the Archivo General de la Nación [hereafter cited as AGN], Ramo de Inquisición, Tomo I, expediente 1. It is listed in the *Catálogo de Inquisición*, Tomo I, página 1.

[19] Unfortunately these two edicts have disappeared from the AGN but the *Catálogo de Inquisición*, Tomo I, página 1, yields the following data: "1523: Primer Edicto contra herejes y judíos-Falta en el Tomo con huellas de haber sido cortado-México, No. 2; 1523: Segundo Edicto publicado en México contra toda persona que de obra o palabra hiciere cosas que parezcan pecado—Falta en el Tomo con huellas de haber sido cortado—México, No. 3."

[20] Medina, *op. cit.*, I, 104 ff.

[21] Cited by Medina, *op. cit.*, I, 129-130.

[22] The bull is reproduced by Medina, *op. cit.*, II, 74-79.

[23] Medina, *op. cit.*, Document XXI, part 6, 83-92; Hernáez, *op. cit.*, I, 382 ff. Spanish canon lawyers of the 1560's upheld the interpretation that the bull *Omnímoda* gave

Fray Martín de Valencia, O.F.M., of the famous *Los Doce* Franciscans, arrived in Mexico May 15, 1524,[24] and he exercised the office of Commissary of the Holy Office of the Inquisition. The origin and termination of Valencia's authority has caused some controversy among Mexican historians of the conquest period. Both García Icazbalceta and Medina, using Remesal[25] as their source, contend that while he still lived Pedro de Córdoba delegated his power as Commissary to Martín de Valencia when the latter passed through Santo Domingo on his way to Mexico, but that the Córdoba delegation stipulated that Valencia should hold the office only until there should be a Dominican prelate in Mexico.[26] The Remesal thesis that the commission was given only to the Dominican prelates to wage inquisitorial activities and that only because a Dominican prelate was lacking did the Franciscan Valencia receive this power is contradicted by another Dominican chronicler of the sixteenth century, Agustín Dávila Padilla,[27] whose writings antedate Remesal and use simple resort to *Omnímoda* to establish Valencia's authority which he later surrendered to the Dominican prelates.[28]

The crux of the controversy was who assumed Pedro de Córdoba's power as Commissary in Santo Domingo after his death. Dávila Padilla and Henry C. Lea[29] contended that the Audiencia of Santo Domingo actually assumed the office until there was another delegation from Spain. Lea insists that the Audiencia either confirmed or reappointed Valencia as Commissary,[30] while Ibáñez contends that the power lapsed completely and could not be exercised by anyone until the crown and Inquisitor General made a new delegation.[31]

---

Order prelates the right to establish Inquisitions. See France V. Scholes, "Fray Diego de Landa and the Problem of Idolatry in Yucatan," *Cooperation in Research* (Washington, D. C., 1938), pp. 585-620.

[24] Medina, *op. cit.*, I, 104.

[25] Antonio de Remesal, *Historia de la provincia de San Vicente de Chyapa* (Guatemala, 1932), Lib. II, Cap. II.

[26] Joaquín García Icazbalceta, *Obras* (10 vols.; México, 1896-1899), I, 272; also *Bibliografía*, p. 452; Medina, *op. cit.*, I, 104-107.

[27] Agustín Dávila Padilla, *Historia de la Fundación y discurso de la provincia de Santiago de México, de la Orden de Predicadores, por las vidas de sus varones insignes y casos notables de Nueva España* (Madrid, 1596), Lib. I, cap. 12.

[28] ". . . que Fr. Martín de Valencia resolvió transmitir al dominico Fr. Domingo de Betanzos, como lo verificó, 'el oficio que administraba de comisario de la In-

quisición, por autoridad apostólica' porque no había entonces obispo en esta tierra, y por una bula de Adriano VI tenía los casos episcopales y comisión apostólica para los del Santo Oficio de la Inquisición el prelado de San Francisco, con declaración del mismo pontífice, que le pudiese dejar al prelado de la orden de Predicadores que en esta tierra asistiese." *Ibid.* It appears that there was a general confusion on the point that the *Omnímoda* bestowed inquisitorial powers on prelates of all of the Orders in the prescribed circumstances.

[29] Henry C. Lea, *The Inquisition in the Spanish Dependencies* (New York, 1908), p. 196.

[30] *Ibid.*

[31] Yolanda Mariel de Ibáñez, *La Inquisición en México durante el siglo XVI* (México, 1945), pp. 65-66, using Remesal comes to this conclusion: "En 1526 llegó Fr. Tomás Ortiz con los primeros dominicanos y quedó como inquisidor, pues in-

Whatever the truth about the delegation of authority in Santo Domingo may have been,[32] it is obvious that the bull *Omnímoda* bestowed inquisitorial powers on Martín de Valencia whether he or his colleagues in the New World were cognizant of it or not.[33]

We know very little about the inquisitorial activities of Fray Martín de Valencia, the first Franciscan prelate in Mexico. It is known from early research by García Icazbalceta and the recent study of Gibson that Martín de Valencia did mete out capital punishment.[34]

Martín de Valencia had some rather obscure but very interesting instructions which brought him into conflict with the civil authorities. He claimed that his credentials endowed him with civil and criminal jurisdiction as well as ecclesiastical. From March through July of 1525 Fray Martín clashed with Cortés' deputy, Gonzalo de Salazar, and the cabildo of Mexico City over the question of civil and criminal jurisdic-

---

forma Remesal que al llegar a la Isla Española, la Audiencia le dió nuevos despachos del Comisario de la Inquisición así para quien lo sucediese como prelado de Santo Domingo . . ." Medina, *op. cit.*, I, 114, and II, 31-32, disagrees with this interpretation, leaning toward the idea that Córdoba delegated the authority to Valencia while he still lived.

[32] Subsequent investigations in archival materials are apt to clear up this point.

[33] García Icazbalceta, *Bibliografía*, p. 452, erred when he made the following statement: "La verdad es que si Fr. Martín de Valencia tenía ese oficio por autoridad Apostólica, no le venía de la famosa Bula llamada Omnímoda, sino de algún otro documento que no conozco, porque en esa Bula no consta tal comisión." An acquaintance with the Yucatecan idolatry trials of Diego de Landa would have led García Icazbalceta to the correct conclusion. In *loc. cit.* García Icazbalceta concluded that both Orders were meant to have jurisdiction in Inquisition matters, because Sebastián Ramírez de Fuenleal, Bishop of Santo Domingo and President of the Audiencia of Mexico, had said the following in a letter to Charles V, dated April 30, 1532:

Los religiosos de estas órdenes de Santo Domingo y San Francisco tienen un Breve de Adriano por el cual *los frailes* de ambas órdenes han pretendido ser obispos y aun tener veces de Pontífices . . . y por virtud de él han procedido en casos de herejía, y han proveído de alguacil con vara y título de alguacil de la Inquisición, y han tenido

notarios, *y han sentenciado a quemar y reconciliar y penitenciar algunos.*

This letter should have led García Icazbalceta to the conclusion that the bull *Omnímoda* gave an implied grant of inquisitorial power.

[34] Icazbalceta based his statement on an ancient Tlaxcalan manuscript which he did not identify:

Por oscuridad y falta de puntuación en el manuscrito, se duda si los reos ejecutados por medio de la horca fueron tres ó solo uno. Ateniéndonos a lo más favorable, contaremos uno. Hemos de suponer que Fray Martín no daría la sentencia, ni menos la ejecutaría; haría *la relajación* como comisario del Santo Oficio, y lo demás, sentencia y ejecución, correría por cuenta del *brazo seglar*, según costumbre.

García Icazbalceta, *Bibliografía*, p. 452; *Obras*, I, 271 ff.; see also Mariano Cuevas, S.J., *Historia de la Iglesia en México* (5 vols.; México, 1921), I, 222-223.

Charles Gibson, *Tlaxcala in the Sixteenth Century* (New Haven, 1952), pp. 34-37, gives a detailed account of Fray Martín's punishment of idolaters in Tlaxcala. The executions were four rather than three. The trial of the cacique Acxotécatl for the murder of his Christian son plus idolatry is treated in some detail. Gibson based much of his account on the *Anales antiguos de México y sus contornos*, José Fernando Ramírez, comp., (2 vols., MS in Museo Nacional, México), No. 16, 716 *et passim.*

tion. On March 9, 1525, he had presented his bulls and other credentials to the cabildo and demanded obedience to his instructions. There is evidence that Valencia even delegated the controversial jurisdiction.[85]

On July 28, 1525, the cabildo ordered Fray Martín de Valencia's deputy, Motolinía, to appear before the regidores for a re-examination of the bulls and briefs. Motolinía complied immediately, arguing that they had already been presented March 9, 1525, and repeating Valencia's command that they be obeyed. The regidores studied the bulls and incorporated them into the cabildo records.[86] After consultation with its lawyers the cabildo informed Motolinía that it could find no grant of authority for the Franciscans to wield civil and criminal jurisdiction and the Order was charged to refrain from doing so.

The Franciscan prelate's term as Commissary of the Holy Office came to an end in 1526 when the Dominican Tomás Ortiz arrived to assume the office. Either the Audiencia of Santo Domingo was exercising the deceased Córdoba's powers when it invested Ortiz as Commissary or, as Ibáñez asserted, the king and Inquisitor General sent a new delegation of authority. At any rate the audiencia decided that Valencia's commission should terminate with the arrival of the Dominican prelate.[37] Almost immediately after his arrival in Mexico in 1526, Tomás Ortiz returned to Spain leaving as prelate of the Order and therefore Commissary of the Holy Office, Fray Domingo de Betanzos.[38] Until the middle of the next decade the Dominicans controlled the Inquisition in Mexico.

Betanzos at the close of 1527 tried nineteen blasphemy cases, mostly of flagrant offenders,[39] some of whom were conquistadores. Pursuant to the *Omnímoda*, Betanzos established an episcopal-type Inquisition in Mexico. He was assisted by Sebastián Arriaga as fiscal, Rodrigo de Torres as *calificador*, and the friars Fuensalida and Toribio de Motolinía. The outstanding case of the Betanzos era was that of Rodrigo

---

[85] On July 28, 1525 an *acuerdo* of the cabildo of Mexico expressed concern over this jurisdiction:

A su noticia es venido que Fr. Martín de Valencia, fraile del monasterio de Sr. S. Francisco, é Fr. Toribio de Motolinía, guardián del dicho monasterio, en esta Nueva España, no solamente entiende en las cosas tocantes a los descargos de consciencia, mas entremétese en usar de jurisdicción civil é criminal, é cohiben por la corona de las justicias, que son cosas tocantes a la preeminencia episcopal, no lo pudiendo hacer, sin tener provision de S. M. para ello.

*Primer libro de las Actas de Cabildo de la Ciudad de México,* Edición del "Municipio

Libre," (México, 1889), p. 49; García Icazbalceta, *Bibliografía,* p. 451.

[86] *Primer libro de Actas de Cabildo,* pp. 49-50 reproduces the bulls in Spanish. One of them was apparently the royal pase of the bull *Omnímoda* and was dated in Pamplona, December 12, 1523. It is fairly clear that no one in New Spain had a definite understanding of the earlier papal bulls granting extraordinary powers to the Order clergy.

[37] Medina, *op. cit.,* I, 115; Conway, *op. cit.,* p. 17.

[38] Medina, *op. cit.,* I, 117; Ibáñez, *op. cit.,* p. 66; Cuevas, *op. cit.,* I, 223.

[39] These *procesos* are found in AGN, Ramo de la Inquisición, Tomo I and Tomo Ia. Part of Tomo Ia is no longer extant.

Rengel, a conquistador of eighty years of age who was convicted of being a horrifying blasphemer.[40] The Rengel *proceso* was signed by Motolinía, who apparently was Betanzos' delegate in the latter's absence.

The *procesos* indicate that Betanzos continued to prosecute causes of faith until July 20, 1528, when he left for Guatemala to establish the Order there.[41] His successor was Fray Vicente de Santa María who had come to Mexico with Ortiz in June of 1526 but who returned to Spain with his superior in 1526 for a brief visit. Prior to Betanzos' departure, Santa María had returned to Mexico with the title of Vicar General of the Order, and after the incumbent prelate left, he was elected superior of the convent and therefore Commissary of the Holy Office of the Inquisition.[42]

The Santa María period of the Mexican Inquisition was short but very industrious. We know of at least nine cases that came before the Commissary, two of which ended in burnings at the stake. He tried two blasphemers, one Greek heretic, one sex pervert, one scribe who had encouraged the Indians to practice idolatry, and three Judaizantes. One *denuncia* for sorcery never reached the trial stage. Of the Jews, Hernando Alonso, a blacksmith from the Condado de Niebla in Spain, and Gonzalo de Morales, a trader from Sevilla, were burned. The third Jew, Diego de Ocaña, a scribe, was reconciled.[43]

All of these cases came before Santa María in 1528, and after that date he ceased to function.[44] Medina and Conway suggest that Santa María does not appear to have exercised any authority after 1528 because he was removed from office due to his rash conduct in the burnings of 1528.[45] Perhaps the most valid explanation why the friar-inquisitor ceased to function is found in the fact that the bishopric of Mexico was erected in 1527, and the first bishop, Fray Juan de Zumárraga, as ecclesiastical judge ordinary assumed the position of Inquisitor.[46] At any

[40] AGN, Inquisición, Tomo I, exp. 10. For details see Chapter VII of this study and Medina, *op. cit.*, I, 120, especially note 27.

[41] Cuevas, *op. cit.*, I, 224.

[42] Medina, *op. cit.*, I, 120.

[43] Details on these Judaizante cases are found in Chapter VI of this study.

[44] Medina, *op. cit.*, I, 126. Medina makes an obscure reference to an Oaxaca burning during this era, but he does not cite his source; *ibid.*, I, 127.

[45] *Ibid.*, I, 127-128; Conway, *op. cit.*, p. 17.

[46] The first mainland bishopric was founded in 1519 at Santa María de los

Remedios de Yucatán, whose church was erected in 1526 by the Dominican prelate Julián Garcés at Tlaxcala but whose headquarters were later moved to Puebla de los Ángeles. With the expansion of the conquest and the influx of colonists, a new diocese was created in 1527. The Franciscan Juan de Zumárraga was named bishop, leaving Spain in August of 1528 and arriving in Mexico in early December of that year. Since Zumárraga left Spain without the bulls of consecration and did not receive them until his return to Spain for an audience before the Council of the Indies, some credence may be given to the idea that Santa María may have continued to

rate there are no *procesos* for the interval of 1529 to 1533, and when one of two trials was carried on in 1534, it was signed by Zumárraga as ordinary.[47]

## III. *Juan de Zumárraga as Apostolic Inquisitor: 1536-1543*

Juan de Zumárraga assumed extraordinary inquisitorial functions on June 27, 1535, when Don Alonso Manrique, the Inquisitor General in Sevilla, appointed him Apostolic Inquisitor.[48] Bishop Zumárraga was empowered to establish an Inquisition tribunal, to appoint the necessary officials, to fix salaries, and to remove subordinates at his discretion.[49]

Pursuant to his instructions Zumárraga organized his tribunal and began to function June 5, 1536. On June 6 a solemn procession with music began at the Hospital of Jesus and made its way to the administrative offices of the bishopric. Two musicians who refused to play for the opening of the Holy Office were tried and fined six pounds of white wax to be delivered to the cathedral.[50] An Inquisition jail was established and Zumárraga's staff was ready to proceed. Miguel López de Legazpi,[51]

hold inquisitorial powers until the early 1530's.

[47] The major case was that of Antonio Anguiano, resident of Mexico, for bigamy and/or concubinage, prosecuted by Rafael de Cervanes as fiscal, signed by Zumárraga with Martín de Campos as secretary. AGN, Inquisición, Tomo 36, exp. 1. The other case was tried in Oaxaca, the defendant being Ruy Díaz, a mule driver who had blasphemed. The judge was Juan de Valdivioso. AGN, Inquisición, Tomo 14, exp. 1.

[48] The commission is reproduced in Joaquín García Icazbalceta, *Don Fray Juan de Zumárraga, primer obispo y arzobispo de México*, eds. Rafael Aguayo Spencer and Antonio Castro Leal (4 vols.; México, 1947), III, 71-73; and in Medina, *op. cit.*, II, 35-37.

[49] García Icazbalceta authored the error that Zumárraga never used his office as Inquisitor: "El Sr. Zumárraga nunca usó el título de inquisidor ni organizó el tribunal y ningún indicio había yo encontrado de que hiciera uso de aquel poder, hasta que en las *Noticias históricas de la Nueva España* de Francisco Peralta, escritas en 1589, pero publicadas hace poco, leí la especie de que prendió, procesó y relajó al brazo seglar a un señor de Texcoco, acusado de haber hecho sacrificios humanos, y que el reo fue quemado en virtud de aquella sentencia. Añade el historiador que cuando eso se

supo en España no pareció bien, por ser recién convertidos los indios y se mandó que no procediese contra ellos el Santo Oficio, sino que los castigase el ordinario. El testimonio es singular y de un autor que incurre en notorias equivocaciones al tratar de sucesos anteriores de su tiempo, por lo cual me resistía darle crédito. . . ." García Icazbalceta, *Zumárraga*, I, 202-204. Icazbalceta footnotes the fact that "había sin embargo cárcel de la Inquisición [*ibid.*, III, 211] y alguacil [*ibid.*, III, 219]." Suárez de Peralta's *Noticias históricas de la Nueva España* was published in Madrid, 1878. Icazbalceta refers to page 279. See Cuevas, *op. cit.*, I, 369, note 4, on Icazbalceta's erroneous statement.

There are 152 *procesos* and 30 *denuncias, informaciones, cartas*, etc. in the Archivo General de la Nación, Ramo de la Inquisición in Mexico City for 1536-1543, most of them signed by Zumárraga. It is difficult to see how Icazbalceta missed this group of documents when he knew so much about the Mexican Inquisition of the decade of the 1520's.

[50] AGN, Inquisición, Tomo 42, exp. 3. See also: Medina, *op. cit.*, I, 132; Cuevas, *op. cit.*, I, 368; Ibáñez, *op. cit.*, p. 70. For details of this case see Chapter IX, *infra*.

[51] Later conqueror of the Philippines. See Conway, *op. cit.*, p. 18. Medina, *op. cit.*, I, 133-134.

Martin de Campos, and Diego de Mayorga served as secretaries, and Dr.
Rafael de Cervanes as fiscal.[52] The treasurer, Augustín Guerrero, the
nuncio, Cristóbal de Canego,[58] the *receptor*, Martín de Zavala, the
alguacil, Alonso de Vargas, rounded out the administrative staff. Zumárraga's delegate, or *provisor*, Juan Rebollo, exercised the office of Commissary of the Holy Office when the Inquisitor had to absent himself
from Mexico City. Rebollo was also the official judge who presided at
torture proceedings. Among the interpreters used in Indian cases before
Zumárraga appear the names of some of the most famous friars of
sixteenth century Mexico, such men as Bernardino de Sahagún, Alonso
de Molina, Toribio de Motolinía, Francisco Maldonado, and others.

The Zumárraga period (1536-1543) was the high point of the
episcopal Inquisition. Original research and tabulations by the author
revealed no less than 152 *procesos*, ten *declaraciones*, thirteen *informaciones*, seven *denuncias*, one *averiguación*, and assorted *cartas*, *memorias*,
and *instrucciones*.[54] Of these cases fifty-six were trials for blasphemy, by
far the most prevalent crime; five for Lutheran heresies; nineteen Judaizantes, including twelve investigations; fourteen for idolatry and sacrifice; twenty-three for sorcery and superstition; eight for heretical
propositions; twenty for bigamy; five trials of clergy; and of the total,
nineteen cases involving Indians. The remainder were for miscellaneous
crimes against orthodoxy.

Zumárraga's downfall as Apostolic Inquisitor came about because
of his Indian policy. Not only were there divided opinions on the nature
of the Indian in the 1530's, but there were also those who held that the
Indian as a recent convert to Catholicism should not be subject to the
jurisdiction of the Holy Office. Zumárraga did not hold this view. He
attacked idolatry and sacrifice wherever he found it, and when such
practices were judged to endanger the entire Christianization process,
he relaxed to the secular arm for burning Don Carlos, the cacique of
Texcoco in 1539. Many authorities contended that there was not sufficient evidence against Carlos to merit such a harsh sentence.[55] Zumár-

[52] These officials are a composite list
gathered from the *procesos* of the era
1536-1543. Medina, *op. cit.*, I, 133, erred
when he called the fiscal Cervantes.

[58] Canego served in three capacities according to the individual case, often as
alguacil, but often as fiscal and nuncio.

[54] My figures are at variance with Cuevas,
*op. cit.*, I, 369, who indicates that there
were no less than 131 *procesos*, 118 against
Spaniards and thirteen against Indians. The
Ibáñez count totals 148 *procesos* dealing
with some twenty-three Indians and the re-

mainder with Europeans; *op. cit.*, p. 10.

My calculations are based upon the
*Catálogo de Inquisición* compared with the
actual documents. It should be noted that
although a fairly thorough list is contained
in this index, it is not entirely accurate because *procesos* are lacking which are listed,
and there are other *procesos* contained in
the bound tomos which are not listed in
the index. Unbound materials are not listed
in the index either.

[55] For a detailed investigation of the Don
Carlos case, see Chapter IV of this study.

raga was censured from Spain for having prescribed the relaxation, and he was eventually removed as Apostolic Inquisitor.

The Visitor General Francisco Tello de Sandoval arrived in Veracruz on February 12, 1544, and was received in Mexico City by Viceroy Mendoza, the Audiencia, Bishop Zumárraga, the cabildo, and six hundred gentlemen of the colony on May 8, 1544.[56] He was instructed to make a thorough visitation of the entire Viceroyalty of New Spain and to introduce the New Laws of 1542. As an added task he had instructions to assume the powers of Apostolic Inquisitor over the entire viceroyalty,[57] and the officialdom of Mexico was charged to render him all assistance.[58] He was further especially instructed to investigate the case of the cacique Carlos and to determine what had been done with his estate and his children.

Tello de Sandoval remained in Mexico for only three years (1544-1547) and the burden of his investigatory activities resulted in his neglecting the Inquisition. There were at least thirteen cases before the Holy Office during the Tello period, but Tello intervened in the proceedings only occasionally.[59] When he left Mexico, inquisitorial powers reverted to the bishops or to the prelates of the various Orders who, under the *Omnímoda*, acted as ordinaries. Prior to his departure from Mexico he made a special point of urging the crown to establish a formal tribunal of the Holy Office there.[60]

## IV. *The Montúfar Period of the Episcopal Inquisition*

Alonso de Montúfar, O. P., the second archbishop of Mexico, arrived at his post in 1554 and began his inquisitorial activities in 1556. He carried no direct commission as Apostolic Inquisitor but assumed the jurisdiction as ecclesiastical judge ordinary.[61]

Montúfar was schooled in the legal tradition and he always in-

[56] Medina, *op. cit.*, I, 202-203; Cuevas, *op. cit.*, I, 381.

[57] Vasco de Puga, *Provisiones, cedulas, instrucciones de su magestad, ordenanças de difuntos y audiencia para la buena expedicion de las negocios y administracion de justicia y gobernacion de esta nueva españa, y para el buen tratamiento y conservacion de los Indios desde el Año 1525 hasta este presente 1563* (2 vols.; México, 1878), I, 452-453; Medina, *op. cit.*, II, 53.

[58] Puga, *op. cit.*, I, 454.

[59] Tello's Inquisition had a staff of only one person, the notary, Luis Guerrero, who served without salary. Cuevas, *op. cit.*, I, 381. Guerrero actually tried cases as Tello's delegate.

[60] Cuevas, *op. cit.*, I, 381 cites this letter from AGI, 58-5-8· "Por otras mías, he avisado a Vuestra Alteza la necesidad que hay en esta tierra del Santo Oficio de la Inquisición y ansí ha parecido por experiencia."

[61] The Montúfar period is obscure. There are masses of documents indicating great activity. The increased number of cases dealing with foreigners indicates considerable immigration. Montúfar had been a *calificador* of the Inquisition in Granada, and his major interest had been combating the Reformation apostasies. See Medina, *op. cit.*, I, 263-295 for case listings of the period, but bear in mind that there are many errors in the Medina account.

sisted upon a number of qualified consultants in the operations of his
Inquisition.[62] The major emphasis of his activities was anti-Lutheran, and
he was instrumental in ferreting out the Protestants not only in Mexico
but in Guatemala, Nicaragua, and Yucatán as well. The primary figure
in the Lutheran prosecutions was Dr. Luis de Anguís, Montúfar's vicar,
and a secret spy of Philip II.[63]

Montúfar's first case was against a Genoese, Agustín Boacio, accused of Lutheran ideas on confession and purgatory. He was tried in
Mexico City after being processed in Veracruz by Anguís. He participated in the same *auto* as Robert Thompson. Thompson held certain
Lutheran ideas on images which the Mexican Inquisition was determined
to suppress, and he was jailed for seven months while the trial was in
progress. Thompson abjured his sins, wore the sanbenito, and suffered
banishment to Spain where he married and procured a license to return
to Mexico to make his fortune.[64]

Activities against French and English corsairs characterized the
decade of the 1560's,[65] but there was an increasing number of trials for
heretical propositions not connected with the pirates. Lutherans and
French Calvinists provided the most interesting cases. Naturally as the
population increased owing to the influx of colonists, blasphemy and
bigamy cases also increased. Indians continued to be tried.

Montúfar took it upon himself to deal with certain phases of unorthodoxy among the Mexican clergy of the mid-sixteenth century,
especially those who were dealing with the native populations. Close
scrutiny was given to all works translated into the Indian tongues for
purposes of instruction. Don Vasco de Quiroga, the first bishop of
Michoacán, assisted the Montúfar tribunal in this work. As a result of
the investigations the writings of two of the most famous clergymen of
Mexico became suspect and in two cases condemned, the *Doctrina en
romance* of Juan de Zumárraga, now deceased, and the Tarascan writings
of Father Maturino Gilberti.[66]

The most celebrated trial of a Mexican cleric by Montúfar was that

[62] Montúfar always consulted with the
oidores and the fiscal of the Audiencia
along with other lawyers, jurists, and theologians.

[63] Cuevas *op. cit.*, II, 262; Ibáñez, *op. cit.*,
p. 93.

[64] G. R. G. Conway, *An Englishman and
the Mexican Inquisition* (México, 1927).
Appendix I contains the Spanish transcript
of this trial. Appendix III contains a list of
original documents relating to Englishmen
and others associated with them who were
condemned by the Mexican Inquisition
from 1559 to 1575.

[65] See Julio Jiménez Rueda, *Corsarios
franceses e ingleses en la Inquisición de la
Nueva España* (México, 1945), for an incomplete list of these cases. Parts of this
study are based on Conway.

[66] See Francisco Fernández del Castillo,
*Libros y libreros en el Siglo XVI*, Vol. VI
of the *Publicaciones del Archivo General
de la Nación* (México, 1914), 4-36, for the
Gilberti investigation. See Chapter II of
this study for a fuller description of the
Zumárraga writings. See also Medina, *op.
cit.*, I, 266.

of Dr. Alonso Chico de Molina, the Archdeacon of the Cathedral of Mexico.[67] It was alleged that Chico de Molina had preached a sermon in which there were no less than six propositions deemed heretical, offensive, and scandalous. Molina was intransigent in asserting his orthodoxy. Montúfar commissioned six Dominicans, one Franciscan, and two other theologians, along with two Augustinians to investigate the Molina affair. When they were unable to reach a decision the entire case was referred to the Suprema in Spain which ruled pro-Molina, but whose sentence was lost at sea, causing a seemingly interminable delay in the exoneration of the archdeacon.

Near the end of the Montúfar period two famous conquistadores had altercations with the Inquisition. The first was Diego Díaz del Castillo, corregidor of Tololoapan Yxtalapa in Guatemala and son of Bernal Díaz, for "decir a los indios que no reedificasen las iglesias caídas, por menospreciar al Papa a los obispos y por tratar mal a los clérigos."[68] Unfortunately we do not know the sentence because the conclusion of the *proceso* has disappeared. The second was the centenarian conquistador of Oaxaca, Rodrigo de Segura from Castilla, who had asserted the following: "Jesucristo no había sabido la hora de su muerte sino que un ángel se la vino a decir."[69] Again because the *proceso* is incomplete, we have no inkling of the sentence.

V. *The End of the Episcopal Inquisition in Mexico: The Founding of the Tribunal of the Holy Office, 1571*

It appears that provincial bishops and prelates of monastic houses were zealous inquisitors in the fifteen years preceding the founding of the permanent tribunal of the Holy Office in Mexico. In Oaxaca there were evidences of sixty-three cases[70] while Yucatán boasted more than fourteen cases, New Galicia thirty-nine, Michoacán twenty-eight, and Puebla one. This decade and a half witnessed a growing laxity on the part of the inquisitors in observing the legal rights of their subjects. The abuses in this episcopal and monastic period of the Mexican Holy Office stemmed from the fact that it had no central direction and its provincial commissaries lacked adequate training. This situation was further complicated by a growing civil intervention in Inquisition activities. Three cases in point may be used to indicate these tendencies in the decade of the 1560's:

1) In the opening years of the decade (1560) the Dominican friars in Oaxaca were guilty of excesses and gross illegalities in their dealings

[67] Ibáñez, *op. cit.*, p. 99.
[68] AGN, Inquisición, Tomo 8, exp. 3.
[69] AGN, Inquisición, Tomo 18, exp. 6.

[70] These were *procesos, denuncias,* and *informaciones.*

with the pueblo of Teitipac. Responsible was one Friar Guidielmo who
employed torture on the natives and even staged an *auto-da-fe*. He was
later castigated and relieved of his office by the Order.[71]

2) In the same years the civil authorities in Toluca assumed quasi-
inquisitorial powers. Francisco de Tejera, a Portuguese Jew from Toluca,
was arrested for blasphemy and spitting on a crucifix. He was tried civilly
by the alcalde without benefit of ecclesiastical advice. His sentence was
extremely harsh: thirty days' incarceration, three hundred lashes, and
his tongue was split on both sides.[72] He was later given a spiritual penance in Mexico City.

3) The last and most publicized example of growing irresponsibility
of the inquisitors and their civil colleagues was the idolatry trials carried
on by Fray Diego de Landa, the provincial of the Franciscan Order in
Yucatán.[73] He was assisted by the alcalde mayor of Yucatán, Don Diego
de Quijada, who had already performed inquisitorial investigations on
his own.[74] Rigorous investigations and the widespread use of torture
characterized the Yucatecan trials. The sentences were harsh, and some
Indians committed suicide to escape torture.[75] When the first bishop of
Yucatán, Fray Francisco de Torral, arrived in Mérida August 14, 1562,
Landa's authority under *Omnímoda* came to an end. Torral was convinced that more lenient measures toward the recently converted natives
were advisable and he reversed many of the sentences handed down by
Landa. This was done over the protests of Alcalde Mayor Quijada.

Increased petitions flooded into Spain during the two decades prior
to 1570 urging the crown to establish in Mexico a permanent tribunal of
the Holy Office of the Inquisition subordinate to the Suprema in Spain.
These petitions reflected the inadequacies of the episcopal Inquisition in
action. Clerical abuses of power were the most prevalent complaint.[76]
The growing civil invasion of religious functions in the Inquisition; the
need for centralization of authority; the necessity for an adequately
trained Inquisition personnel; the wide infiltration of heresies debilitating
to religious unity; and finally the increased trade in books condemned
by the Holy Office caused the king and Inquisitor General to consider
seriously the establishment of a separate tribunal in New Spain.

[71] See José Antonio Gay, *Historia de Oaxaca* (4 vols.; México, 1950), I, 629-634, for the story of the auto in Teitipac; Cuevas, *op. cit.*, II, 263.
[72] AGN, Inquisición, Tomo, 18, exp. 6.
[73] It was established by Spanish canon lawyers in the subsequent controversy that Landa legally had inquisitorial powers un-der the bull *Omnímoda* of Adrian VI, 1523. See Scholes and Roys, *op. cit.*, for
more details. Very valuable is France V. Scholes and Eleanor B. Adams, *Don Diego de Quijada Alcalde Mayor de Yucatan, 1561-1565* (2 vols., México, 1938).
[74] AGN, Inquisición, Tomo 32, exp. 11.
[75] Scholes and Roys, *op. cit.*, p. 596.
[76] In addition to the Dominican excesses in Oaxaca and the Landa controversy in Yucatán, Medina, *op. cit.*, I, 484, reviews other abuses.

The Mexican clergy seemed anxious to systematize the inquisitorial power. Fuenleal had tried to convince the crown in a letter of 1532 that there was a need for a tribunal of the Holy Office to combat foreign merchants and corsairs who were coming in increasing numbers to Mexico.[77] The Franciscan Order as a whole made the same request in 1552.[78] The Visitor and Apostolic Inquisitor, Francisco Tello de San-doval, in a letter to Prince Philip dated September 19, 1545, informed the latter of the need in New Spain for a permanent Holy Office.[79] Medina cites additional petitions directed to the crown from all over the Spanish empire which in effect demanded that some action be taken in establishing empire tribunals subordinate to Spain.[80] Lea has taken issue with Medina over the idea that the Mexican clergy wished to be relieved of the inquisitorial responsibility.[81]

The long-awaited reply of Philip II to the pleas of his subjects for tribunals of the Holy Office in the New World came in 1569. On January 25 of that year Philip by royal cedula authorized the creation of two tribunals of the Holy Office in Mexico and Peru.[82] A second cedula of August 16, 1570, defined the jurisdiction of the new tribunals.[83] The Mexican tribunal and the one in Lima had jurisdiction over all inhabitants, including the viceroys, and the entire political machinery of the viceroyalty was charged to assist the tribunal in all ways.

The Inquisitor General of Spain, the Cardinal-Bishop of Sigüenza, Diego de Espinosa, with the king's approval named the former Inquisitor of Murcia, Don Pedro Moya de Contreras, as the first Inquisitor General of Mexico.[84] Licenciado Alonso de Bonilla was named junior in-

[77] Medina, op. cit., I, 483.

[78] Ibid., I, 488.

[79] Cuevas, op. cit., I, 381, cites this letter from AGI, 58-5-8.

[80] Medina, op. cit., I, 496.

[81] "These inquisitorial powers, however, were only enjoyed temporarily by the bishops and when, in 1570, a tribunal was finally established in Mexico, a circular was addressed to them formally warning them against allowing their provisors or officials to exercise jurisdiction in matters of faith and ordering them to transmit to the inquisitors any evidence which they might have or might obtain in cases of heresy. The bishops apparently were unwilling to surrender the jurisdiction to which they had grown accustomed for the command had to be repeated, May 26, 1585." Lea, The Inquisition in the Spanish Dependencies, p. 199, cites Juan de Solórzano Pereira, Política indiana (Madrid, 1647), Lib. III. cap. XXIV, n. 38.

[82] Recopilación de leyes de los Reynos de las Indias (Madrid, 1681), Lib. I, tit. 19.

[83] Medina, op. cit., II, 34-36, reproduces the cédula. See also Ibáñez, op. cit., p. 111. The political jurisdiction of the Mexican body included the Audiencias of Mexico, Guatemala, New Galicia, and the Philippines. The religious jurisdiction included the Archbishopric of Mexico, the Bishoprics of Tlaxcala, Michoacán, Oaxaca, New Galicia, Yucatán, Guatemala, Vera Paz, Chiapas, Honduras, and Nicaragua.

[84] See Julio Jiménez Rueda, Don Pedro Moya de Contreras, Primer Inquisidor de México (México, 1944). On January 3, 1570, Espinosa notified Moya de Contreras of his appointment. Moya at first refused the appointment because of finances and ill-health but with the insistence of the crown and Inquisitor General, he accepted. His commission was dated August 18, 1570. For these and other details, see Lea, The Inquisition in the Spanish Dependencies, pp. 201-203.

quisitor, Juan de Cervantes as fiscal, and Pedro de los Ríos as notary. The staff of the tribunal left Spain in November of 1570, but because of a layover in the Canaries while waiting to join the *flota*, Moya de Contreras did not arrive in Mexico until almost a year later.[85]

Relations between Moya and Viceroy Martín Enríquez were not cordial initially. The viceroy had ordered the people in the towns along the way from Veracruz to the viceregal capital to give profuse welcome to the Inquisitor General and his staff. However, the viceroy himself received Moya and his delegation rather coolly when they arrived. Enríquez was later reprimanded for his conduct.[86] He handed over to Moya the old establishment of the Holy Office, which the latter described as very comfortable.[87]

Two months later the tribunal of the Holy Office began to function in Mexico. On November 2, 1571, a proclamation was posted and read which required the entire populace over twelve years of age to present themselves two days hence at Mass and make the *juramento de la fe* publicly, upon threat of excommunication.[88] On November 4, 1571, the tribunal staged a solemn procession to the cathedral where the ceremony took place.[89]

After the sermon and while the people were still kneeling, the secretary of the tribunal read the king's commands to the viceroy and other secular officials to respect the authority of Moya de Contreras, and he read to the people an edict exhorting them to obey the Holy Office and not to conceal heretical enemies of the faith but to pursue them and denounce them to the Inquisitors "como lobos y perros rabiosos inficionadores de las ánimas y destruidores de la viña del Señor."[90] Lifting their hands, all said, "ansí lo prometemos y juramos."[91] Afterwards, individually, the viceroy and the oidores swore the oath before the missal and the cross, as did other officials.

The ceremony concluded with the reading of the Edict of Grace wherein within a period of only six days self-denunciations were ac-

[85] Lea places Moya's time of arrival in Veracruz as August 18, 1571, and in Mexico City as September 12, 1571.
[86] José Toribio Medina, *Historia del tribunal del Santo Oficio de la Inquisición en México* (México, 1954), p. 38.
[87] *Ibid.*, p. 26.
[88] Lea, *The Inquisition in the Spanish Dependencies*, p. 202; Cuevas, *op. cit.*, II, 266.
[89] Fué desde las Casas de este Santo Oficio, a la Iglesia Mayor de esta ciudad, en medio de el [*sic*] Señor Don Martín Enríquez y el Doctor Villalobos, Oidor Antiguo de la Audiencia Real de México, llevando delante de sí al Lic. Bonilla que llevaba el estandarte de la Fe, en medio de los doctores Puga y Villanueva y demás Oidores, el Ayuntamiento con sus maceros, la Universidad con sus bedeles y gran número de pueblo. En la puerta de la Iglesia estaba el Cabildo y las tres Ordenes.
Quoted by Cuevas, *op. cit.*, II, 266, from the original *relación* of the secretary Pedro de los Ríos.
[90] Medina, *Historia del Tribunal*, p. 40.
[91] *Ibid.*

cepted and pardoned after light penance had been done. Many people came forward and voluntarily confessed; many others were accused before the tribunal of crimes against the faith.

On November 10, 1571, letters were sent from the tribunal of the Holy Office to all areas of the viceroyalty, "commanding them and their officials to take the same portentous oath of obedience."[92] *Familiares*, or Inquisition police, were sent to all provincial areas to enforce the decrees of the Holy Office and to arrest those guilty of unorthodox conduct. *Comisarios* were appointed in provincial areas to investigate cases and gather evidence for the central Tribunal. They also made arrests upon order from Mexico City, but the cases were always tried in the capital.

With the establishment of the tribunal of the Holy Office, the Inquisition settled down to a more permanent and orderly existence in Mexico. The episcopal Inquisition with its many abuses was over; and although the new inquisitors were often harsh in their procedures and sentences, the rule of law prevailed. Father Cuevas has called the period of Mexican history after 1570 one of stabilization because the university was turning out trained men, because procedure was formalized and never deviated from, and finally because the Jesuits came to New Spain in 1571.[93] At any rate authority was centralized, and the Inquisition was cast into the mold that it was to occupy until its abolition some two and a quarter centuries later during the Mexican revolutions for independence.

## VI. *Inquisitorial Procedure*

The episcopal Inquisition in Mexico, and later on the tribunal, functioned on Spanish procedure modified to meet the problems of the New World.[94] In line with the *real patronato de las Indias* the viceroy exercised supervisory power over the Mexican Inquisition and issued instructions to Zumárraga on the procedure of his tribunal. Mendoza especially prescribed the methods of keeping records.[95]

[92] Lea, *The Inquisition in the Spanish Dependencies*, p. 203. See *ibid.*, Appendix XI, pp. 534-535 for this edict.

[93] See Cuevas, *op. cit.*, II, 258-283, for an evaluation of this period.

[94] This section does not contain a detailed treatment of inquisitorial procedure. Rather, a brief summary of a composite inquisition trial is presented. The sum total of the documents of the Zumárraga period were used to frame this picture of the procedure. Obviously both the episcopal Inquisition and the later tribunal operated on the Torquemada instructions somewhat modified. See Tomás de Torquemada,

*Compilación de las instrucciones del Santo Oficio de la Inquisición* (Madrid, 1630) which in turn relies on Nicolas Eymericus, *Directorium inquisitorum* (Rome, 1579). Both of these handbooks were used in manual form prior to their many printed editions. Useful for procedure also are Julio Marín Melgares, *Procedimientos de la Inquisición* (2 vols.; Madrid, 1888) and the treatment of Lea, *The Spanish Inquisition*, II, 457-586; III, 1-229. A more recent, and highly critical, study is Eduardo Pallares, *El Procedimiento inquisitorial* (México, 1951).

[95] These detailed instructions are set

Within the framework of its procedure the Inquisition did not act in an arbitrary but in a very orderly manner. The first step was an Edict of Grace, a public declaration in church on some feast day when it was announced that the crown had established tribunals of the Inquisition. A term of thirty or forty days was granted for voluntary confession, and those who freely confessed were absolved of their sins after doing mild penance. However, the people were called upon to denounce anyone known to be suspect of heresy, under pain of excommunication if they failed to do so.

As procedure formalized in Mexico the Inquisitor or his delegate made a yearly visit to each town in his jurisdiction. This *visita de partido* was the main vehicle in the gathering of evidence. Again the penalty for withholding evidence was excommunication. Three clear and trustworthy denunciations were required before a suspect could be prosecuted.[96] It was always sworn that the informer was not motivated by hatred or vengeance but by a sincere desire to rid himself of responsibility. Many times heretics denounced other people in frantic attempts to get lighter sentences.

After the denunciations had been processed, additional evidence was gathered from various sources and the case was built. The evidence was examined by the *calificadores*,[97] who decided whether heresy was involved or a crime against the faith had been committed. The fiscal then petitioned the court for arrest[98] and after the arrest some of the property of the accused was embargoed. The prisoner was usually tried within eight days after the arrest.[99] He was called before the tribunal for his first audience. There he was questioned about his life history, and he often perjured himself by denying his Jewish or Moorish descent or by denying that members of his family had been tried by the Inquisition.

The prisoner was then given the first of three admonitions. He was

forth in AGN, Inquisición, Tomo 30, exp. O. First there is a *Pragmatico contra los herejes,* and then instructions on how to proceed. After an admonition to keep sources of information secret, Mendoza instructed the inquisitors on the method of processing the accused. A *proceso* was to be formed containing the information on the crime; a petition for arrest by the fiscal was to be included along with what was done with the *reo* after the arrest. The following materials were required: a *limpieza* in verbal form from the accused; the initial interrogatory of the *reo*; the accusation of the fiscal and the *reo*'s reply; the testimonies of the witnesses; the testimony of the *reo*. The *proceso* was to conclude with: the vote and the sentence, for which there was a prescribed form; the mode of dealing with the reconciled; abjuration; the sentence of the obstinate heretic; a note on public execution of the sentence. Finally, Mendoza prescribed certain regulations on the wearing and conservation of sanbenitos.

[96] In the Zumárraga period this provision was not enforced.

[97] Usually friars trained in canon law from nearby monastic houses.

[98] The alguacil and/or nuncio ordinarily performed the arrest. The prisoner was confined in the Inquisition jail.

[99] That is, the *proceso* was begun.

told to search his conscience to see if he could advise the court why he was on trial. He was not told the charge. The fiscal would then gather together the evidence and formulate the charge. The indictment was read to the prisoner, who replied to the charges, and the court appointed a defense attorney. The publication of the witnesses followed: abstracts of their testimony were read but the names were withheld. The accused never faced his accusers and was never told their names. He was given ample opportunity to answer their testimony.

In most cases the evidence was such as to convict or exonerate; in some cases the evidence was trustworthy but insufficient to prove guilt. Two methods were used to get at the truth: the use of *cautelas*, or tricksters, who were often placed in the cell to gain the accused's confidence and get a confession through friendly persuasion, and torture.

Torture was not the usual procedure; it was used only in the most serious cases, those of major heresy. If it was used, it came just before or just after the preliminary sentence. The purpose was to get a confession, for if the *reo* could be brought to confess, he could then be absolved and reconciled with the Church. Physical torture was used with no distinction as to sex, age, or social position, although there were often exemptions due to delicate health. The torture session lasted only one hour, and a *reo* could be tortured only once. Often the torture was "continued" but forced testimony under duress had no validity unless the defendant repeated it in court.

Torture methods in Mexico followed Spanish practice with few exceptions. There was always the admonition to tell the truth and thereby avoid untold anguish. The *reo* was stripped to his underwear, often naked, and strapped upon a table while a cord was wound around his arm from wrist to shoulder. Successive tightening was usually enough to get the confession. A frequent method used was the rack (*el potro*). Again the *reo* was bound on a long table, frequently a stairway, and garrotes were attached to the limbs and were alternately tightened and relaxed during the questioning. Often the water torture was used and combined with the rack procedure. In this case linen was placed over the face of the accused and the water was poured in volume on the linen. This procedure produced the sensation of drowning and proved very effective in securing confessions. One of the more strenuous devices used was the Valencian *garrucha*, whereby the hands were bound with ropes and the body was hoisted and dropped to within a few feet of the floor. This last method was considered extreme, but the Indian in Mexico, especially in Yucatán, resented more being stripped and having hot wax dropped upon the naked body.

After the publication of the witnesses and possible torture of the major heretic, the preliminary sentence was read. It was very often extreme, much more rigorous than the final or definite sentence. It provided another in the series of shocks designed to make the defendant confess, recant, and ask for mercy. Often torture was employed after the preliminary sentence.

In the case of minor heresies or crimes against the faith, sentences were light. Generally the convicted was fined or flogged and had to perform some sort of spiritual penance. Major heretics faced harsh sentences, even to the point of death by burning at the stake. When the defendant confessed major heresy he was reconciled, that is, by the acknowledgment of his guilt and the demonstration of remorse he was united with the Church and allowed to escape the death penalty. He generally had his property confiscated and went to prison for a long period of time.[100] Frequently he was banished from Mexico to serve his sentence in Spain. The sentence of banishment was usually pronounced upon heretics who had attempted to lead others into error, especially foreigners. *Reconciliados* often went to the galleys, but this dreaded penalty was limited in time of service owing to the harshness of the work and the short life expectancy of galleymen.

The sentence of abjuration was pronounced upon the *reconciliado* when the Inquisitor doubted that the prisoner had fully recanted. He often coupled this sentence with flogging, banishment, etc. The most feared sentence was, of course, *relajación al brazo seglar*. The unrepentant or obstinate heretic was remanded to the custody of the civil authorities who meted out the required civil law penalty. In the medieval and early modern periods civil law prescribed burning at the stake for condemned heretics.[101] As a general rule the convict was not burned alive. Eleventh hour confessions did not enable the obstinate heretic to escape the stake. The *relajado* who at the last minute recanted was strangled by the garrote prior to the burning of the cadaver. Furthermore, effigies of escaped heretics were burned so that both Church and state might show their detestation of the offender.

The *auto de fe* was not a mass burning.[102] It was merely an ecclesiastical procession followed by a sermon and an oath of fidelity to the Holy Office. In the Zumárraga period the procession started from the administrative offices of the bishopric and ended in the Zócalo. The

[100] The condemned was allowed to work in prison to support his family. Rarely were married couples separated. Prison was also looked upon as an opportunity to recant and to prevent relapse into error.

[101] Lea, *The Spanish Inquisition*, III, 183-208, discusses fully the body of sub-stantive and procedural law of the Church dealing with relaxation to the secular arm.

[102] See *ibid.*, pp. 207-229, for Lea's description of the *auto de fe* ceremonies from primary sources. See also Turberville, *op. cit.*, pp. 95-96, *passim* and Llorca, *op. cit.*, p. 244, *passim*.

prisoners wore penitential garb, the lesser offenders marching first, the condemned trailing. The Inquisitors, civil officials, the Inquisition police, and others also marched. In the Zócalo the sermon was preached from a special platform and the *juramento de la fe* was repeated by all present. Each sentence was read and each *reconciliado* knelt and received absolution and was reunited with the Church. When the *auto* was over the prisoners were returned to the Inquisition jail, and the next day they began serving their sentences. Civil officials waited to receive the relaxed heretics and took them to the *quemadero*, outside the Zócalo,[103] where they were burned by civil executioners. The clergy were present, but merely as chaplains. All was done in an orderly, non-arbitrary manner.

[103] The *quemadero* in Mexico City was at the present site of the neartheast corner of the Alameda.

# CHAPTER II

# The Intellectual Background of Zumárraga the Inquisitor

I. *The Intellectual Climate of Mexico in the First Half of the Sixteenth Century*

The discovery and colonization of America coincided with the period of the high Renaissance in Europe. Christian humanists[1] and other reform-minded individuals were excited with the idea of a "new world" in which they could apply their theories and construct a perfect Christian society free from the apparent defects of fifteenth and sixteenth-century European society.

These theorists had a relatively simply formula: a return to the basic precepts of Christianity in its pure form, as it existed in the golden apostolic age of the Church. The noble American savage, "blessed by nature, and free from the taint of fraud and hypocrisy,"[2] was to furnish the raw material for the new order, a society which would be built upon the indigenous agrarian collectivism. The upshot of such

[1] Christian humanism belonged, essentially, to the northern Renaissance, Spain included, where the term did not imply amorality or extreme individualism in intellectual activity as it did in Italy, but was linked with piety and public virtue. With these humanists of the northern Renaissance, the Christian world view predominated and Dante's idea of the world empire gained acceptance. The ideal was a fusion of the philosophy of Christ with the moral wisdom of Greece and Rome and the tone was reformistic—new men rather than new institutions. See Franklin le Van Baumer, *Main Currents of Western Thought* (New York, 1952), pp. 108-110, and Bertrand Russell, *A History of Western Philosophy* (New York, 1945), pp. 495, 500, 512. For the impact of humanism of the Italian brand in Spain, see

Adolfo Bonilla y San Martín, "Erasmo en España (Episodio de la historia del Renacimiento)," *Revue Hispanique*, XVII (1907), 379-548.
[2] Silvio Zavala, "The American Utopia of the Sixteenth Century," *The Huntington Library Quarterly*, X (1947), 339. Zavala quotes Vasco de Quiroga, the oidor and later first bishop of Michoacán, as follows: "for not in vain, but with much cause and reason is this called the New World, not because it is newly found, but because it is in its people and in almost everything as was the first golden age...." For Quiroga, Zumárraga, Alonso de la Vera Cruz, and others, America was truly a *tabula rasa* upon which a new culture could be constructed free from traditional European social, political, and economic patterns.

thinking was the so-called Renaissance Utopia and its attempted application in America. The thought of Campanella, More, and Bacon dominated this movement.[3] The Utopian ideas of the northern humanists found an ally in a reform movement going on within the Spanish Catholic Church whose intellectual mentor in the early years of the sixteenth century was the Dutch humanist, Desiderius Erasmus. Erasmus' philosopy of Christ fitted in very well with the plan to adopt utopian rule in regulating the lives of the natives. Lewis Hanke's thesis of the nature of the conquest of America adequately sums up this thinking: that it was

far more than a remarkable military and political exploit; that it was also one of the greatest attempts the world has seen, to make Christian precepts prevail in the relations between peoples.[4]

The difficulty in implementing the Utopia in Mexico centered on the fact that the conquistador was not imbued with the idealism of the Christian humanist and that furthermore he brought to the American mainland the very culture which the humanist hoped to exclude from the colonization. The conflict between Christian humanism on the one hand and Spanish materialism and greed on the other created grave problems in the framing of colonial policy and generated an amazing amount of intellectual speculation on the nature of the Indian and how he should be treated. Hanke has indicated that the Christian humanist position

became basically a spirited defense of the rights of the Indians, which rested upon two of the most fundamental assumptions a Christian can make: namely, that all men are equal before God; and that a Christian has a responsibility for the welfare of his brothers, no matter how alien or lowly they may be.[5]

Those who would exploit the natives, both conqueror and clergy, denied in fact that the Indian was a human being. Instead he was some kind of animal being, perhaps a dirty dog, and as such fitted into the Aristotelian hierarchy on the lower level. The royal chronicler Oviedo y Valdes gives us the prototype of this argument. He characterized the Indians as

naturally lazy and vicious, melancholic, cowardly, and in general a lying shiftless people. Their marriages are not a sacrament but a sacrilege. They are idolatrous, libidinous, and commit sodomy. Their chief desire is to eat, drink, worship

---

[3] These Utopias were based in large part upon Plato. For the three influential ones, see Agustín Millares Carlo, *Utopías del Renacimiento* (México, 1951). Included are More's *Utopia*, *The City of the Sun* by Campanella, and Bacon's *New Atlantis*.

[4] Lewis Hanke, "The Contribution of Bishop Zumárraga to Mexican Culture," *The Americas*, V (1948), 275. Hanke has characterized this attempt as *The Spanish Struggle for Justice in the Conquest of America* (Philadelphia, 1949).

[5] Hanke, "The Contribution of Bishop Zumárraga to Mexican Culture," *loc. cit.*

heathen idols, and commit bestial obscenities. What could one expect from a people whose skulls are so thick and hard that the Spaniards had to take care in fighting not to strike on the head lest their swords be blunted? [6]

The Dominican Bartolomé de las Casas, as the conscience of the crown and extreme defender of the Indian as the noble savage, employed Aristotle to prove that Indians were human beings:

God created these simple people without evil and without guile. They are most obedient and faithful to their natural lords and to the Christians whom they serve. They are most submissive, patient, peaceful, virtuous. Nor are they quarrelsome, rancorous, querulous or vengeful. Moreover, they are more delicate than princes and die easily from work or illness. They neither possess or desire to possess worldly wealth. Surely these people would be the most blessed in the world if only they worshipped the true God. [7]

The controversy over the rationality of the Indian and his capacity to become civilized and accept and understand the Christian religion consumed the first half of the sixteenth century. In the final analysis the struggle led to a victory of the security of empire and religion over humanism. However, the experiments with utopian ideas and the intellectual speculation behind these ventures provided the philosophical background of the early sixteenth-century Mexican society. In general the Order clergy were divided on the question of rationality,[8] and this issue became inextricably bound up with the question of the ordination of a native Christian priesthood. In general the Franciscans felt that the Indians possessed enough rationality to be converted but lacked the aptitudes necessary for ordination. The eminent ethnologists and antiquarians of the Order, Mendieta and Sahagún, were convinced that the Indians were to be ordered, not to order, and that they were unfit for the priesthood. Many other Franciscans, including Bishop Zumárraga, felt that the Indian was capable of the full cup of salvation, many feeling that the Mexican Church was not adequately constituted because there were no Indian priests.

The Dominican Order, with the exception of Las Casas, and under the intellectual leadership in Mexico of Domingo de Betanzos, was almost unanimous in its opinion that the Indian was a beast not capable of

---

[6] Cited by Hanke, *ibid.*, pp. 276-277, from Oviedo, *Historia general y natural de las Indias* (Sevilla, 1535), primera parte, Lib. 2, cap. 6; Lib. 4, cap. 2; Lib. 5, prohemio, caps. 2-3; Lib. 6, cap. 9. This is a composite statement made by Hanke from Oviedo's remarks.

[7] Bartolomé de las Casas, *Colección de tratados, 1552-1553* (Buenos Aires, 1924), pp. 7-8, translated by Hanke, *op. cit.*, p. 276. Lewis Hanke is the foremost author-

ity on the life and works of Las Casas and all of his books have some bearing on this general theme.

[8] Perhaps the definitive work on the rationality controversy and the administration of the sacraments is Robert Ricard, *La conquista espiritual de México* (México, 1947). This is the Angel Garibay translation of Ricard's French edition published in Paris in 1933.

salvation, but like a child to be the ward of the Church. With this basic premise it followed that there could be no Indian priests because they could not command the respect of the people and they would be liable to error because they were not firmly rooted in the faith. Indeed, many Dominicans felt that the Indians lacked the basic intelligence necessary to understand the things of the faith because of their ignorance of Spanish, and that even if they had a command of the language, they would still be inadequately endowed because mere language could not properly transmit the dogma. Betanzos felt that instruction in Latin must be withheld from the Indian because it would lead him to understand how ignorant the priesthood was.[9] Betanzos was Zumárraga's confessor and the two held divergent views on the Indian. It may have been due to the bishop's influence that Betanzos made a deathbed retraction of his opinion that the natives were beasts.

In many ways the Augustinians were imbued with a deeper humanism in the rationality controversy, as Kubler has pointed out,

. . . insisting more upon the high moral capacity of the Indians than did their Franciscan and Dominican colleagues, and admitting the Indians at communion and extreme unction, sacraments which the Franciscans sometimes refused the Indians. The late-coming Augustinians carried a Christian humanism that in certain respects reached far deeper than their mendicant colleagues, in assuming the spiritual readiness of the Indians and shortening their tutelage.[10]

The rationality controversy seemed to be terminated when Pope Paul III in June of 1537 issued two bulls on the subject: *Veritas ipsa* condemned Indian slavery while *Sublimis deus* proclaimed the aptitude of the Indians for Christianity.[11] The bulls were largely nullified in Mexico when the crown revoked them as interference with the *patronato real*. The controversy continued to rage in Mexico and Spain. Finally, in 1550, a council was convoked at Valladolid to deal with rationality and the treatment of the Indians. Las Casas defended the Indian while Juan Ginés de Sepúlveda upheld the traditional Aristotelian views. The outcome of the Council of Valladolid was indecisive but it generally adopted the Aristotelian view and humanism lost out to Spanish imperial security.[12]

While the rationality controversy was in progress and the Aristotelians were winning out in the decades prior to the Council of Valladolid, another famous Dominican, Francisco de Vitoria, a professor at the

[9] Hanke, "The Contribution of Bishop Zumárraga to Mexican Culture," *The Americas*, V (1948), 277.

[10] George Kubler, *Mexican Architecture of the Sixteenth Century* (2 vols.; New Haven, 1948), I, 14-15.

[11] See Lewis Hanke, "Pope Paul and the American Indians," *The Harvard Theological Review*, XXX (1937), 65-102.

[12] For the Council of Valladolid, see Hanke, *The Spanish Struggle for Justice*, pp. 109-132.

University of Salamanca, was attacking the problem of the Indians from a different point of view. He contended that not only Spain's Indian policy but also its fundamental right to dominion in the New World were based upon untenable premises. Vitoria debunked the right of discovery (*res nullius*) as a just title because the Indians were already the lords of the New World when the Spaniard came. Similarly, the *mare clausum* theory instituted by the bull *Inter caetera* of Alexander VI in 1493 was denied by Vitoria as a basis for Spanish rule because he contended that the pope had no temporal power over Indians as non-Catholics. Consequently, the refusal of the Indians to accept papal dominion could hardly be considered a basis for just war against them or the confiscation of their properties or goods.[18]

Vitoria did concede, however, that the Spaniards had certain rights and responsibilities in America, and were they hindered in the exercise of either, they might wage a just war. In all there were six possible titles to Spanish dominion in the New World. Each was predicated upon a right or a responsibility which, if abridged by the natives, could lead to just war or the assumption of territorial dominium. The first title was derived from the Spaniard's right to travel and to take up residence in America if he did not harm the Indian in doing so. Should the Indian deter him, a just war could be waged. Secondly, the Spaniard had the right to preach and declare the gospel in barbarian lands and if warfare was necessary to do this, it had to be moderate and directed toward the welfare rather than the destruction of the native.

The last four possible titles to dominium were of a more nebulous character. They included the right to intervene and assume power to prevent cannibalism or sacrifice, to deter Indian princes from forcing converted Indians to return to paganism, to establish dominium when the natives truly and voluntarily submitted, and finally, to establish mandates in the natives' interests. The use to which unscrupulous conquisitadores put Vitoria's theories need not detain us. The significance of his work lies in the humanist movement of which he was a part and which dominated the thinking of a large segment of the spiritual conquerors of New Spain.

We have been discussing Renaissance utopianism and Christian humanism in the theoretical sense as it influenced thinking in New Spain.

[18] These views were expressed in two tracts of 1539, *De indis* and *De jure belli*, which are fully analyzed in the definitive work of James Brown Scott, *The Spanish Origin of International Law: Francisco de Vitoria and his Law of Nations* (London, 1934). A good interpretive summary of Vitoria's ideas and his influence is contained in Hanke, *The Spanish Struggle for Justice*, pp. 147-155. See also Justus N. van der Kroef, "Francisco de Vitoria and the Nature of Colonial Policy," *The Catholic Historical Review*, XXXV (1949), 129-162.

A glimpse of these movements in action now becomes essential for our purpose.

Lewis Hanke has summarized the four large questions which confronted the early Mexican humanist in translating his ideas into reality.[14] They were crucial questions, as we shall see: (1) Could the Indians learn to live like Christian Spaniards? (2) Could Spain colonize by peaceful farmers and integrate the Indian into such an agrarian society? (3) Could the faith be preached by peaceful means alone? and finally, (4) Could the encomienda system be abolished?

The attempts to answer these questions became the first social experiments in America. Obviously, the opponents of Las Casas in the rationality controversy were also foes of these experiments. They were carried on before the conquest of the mainland in the Indies, and afterwards in the Venezuelan, Guatemalan, and Mexican areas. Las Casas himself took the lead in the first mainland experiments. He was able to show only moderate success in the Vera Paz venture in Guatemala (1537-1550), and he failed completely earlier at Cumaná on the Venezuelan coast (1521). Despite failure in practical experimentation, Las Casas remained the inveterate foe of the encomienda system, and it was largely due to his efforts that it was eventually tamed.[15]

The only measure of success of the early Christian humanists came in Mexico. While Bishop Zumárraga certainly had some hand in stimulating the utopian experiments in New Spain, it was the first bishop of

[14] See Hanke, *The Spanish Struggle for Justice*, pp. 39-83, and for a fuller treatment, his *The First Social Experiments in America: A Study in the Development of Spanish Indian Policy in the Sixteenth Century* (Cambridge, 1936).

[15] The encomienda was a grant of Indian labor to a conquistador who in return for the Indian's labor was obliged to look out for his well-being and teach him the basic elements of Christianity. Abuses were rampant from the earliest days of the institution in the Indies. In 1512 the Laws of Burgos sanctioned the institution but tried to curb certain abuses. In 1518 the Jeronymite Friars investigated encomienda practices but reached a stalemate. In 1520 Charles V had decided that the Indian was a free agent and could not be a chattel and three years later forbade Cortés to *encomendar*, but due to the necessities of the conquest in 1526 the encomienda was legalized in New Spain with the proviso that no man was to hold over 300 Indians. In 1530 the first audiencia received instructions for the gradual suppression of the institution, while in 1536 the tribute which the encomenderos received from the Indians was regulated, and in the same year it was decreed that encomiendas were to be inherited for only two generations. Las Casas was largely responsible for the New Laws of 1542 because he labored at court two years prior to their promulgation. Article 35 of these laws sought to suppress the encomienda but the Visitor Tello de Sandoval was forced to suspend this article in New Spain because the colony was on the verge of rebellion. On October 20, 1545, Charles V revoked Article 35. The Mexican clergy were nearly unanimous in agreeing that the encomienda had to be kept and even granted in perpetuity because the Church had an economic stake in the controversy and depended upon the encomienda for its livelihood. In 1549 the institution was shorn of much of its power when it was decreed that personal service could not be accepted by the encomendero in lieu of tribute. From this date on the encomienda was essentially a tribute-gathering institution.

Michoacán, Don Vasco de Quiroga, who must be credited with adopting utopian rule in regulating the lives of the Indians.[16]

Vasco de Quiroga had come to New Spain in 1531 with the second audiencia. He became the friend and companion of Zumárraga and was installed as the first bishop of the Tarascan area when it was set up as the diocese of Michoacán in 1538. The major source of his Indian policy was the *Utopia* of Thomas More. Following the latter's writings, he proposed and put into effect a system of Indian *reducciones*, or communities, into which he integrated a rational political system, the Christian faith, and a program for the economic well-being of the natives.[17] The two famous communities were founded at Santa Fe, in the environs of Mexico City and near Pátzcuaro on the shores of Lake Pátzcuaro in Michoacán. His republics were monolithic and theocratic medieval entities geared to deal with both the temporal and spiritual aspects of man but constructed almost entirely from More's outlines.

Quiroga's blueprints as outlined by Zavala give a fascinating picture of the Mexican Utopias:

Once political order and humane relations were established, the roots of all discord, luxury, covetousness, and sloth would be cut out; and peace, justice and equality would reign.[18]

Zavala continues with a summary description of the communities in action:

In his villages of Santa Fe, Quiroga established the common ownership of property; the integration of large families; the systematic alternation between the urban and rural people; work for women; the six-hour working day; the liberal distribution of the fruits of the common labor according to the needs of the

[16] For Mexican humanism in general see: Gabriel Méndez Plancarte, *Humanismo mexicano del siglo XVI* (México, 1946); Víctor Adib, "Del humanismo mexicano," *Historia mexicana*, V (1955), 109-113; Lesley B. Simpson, "Spanish Utopia," *Hispania*, XX (1937), 353-368; Lesley B. Simpson, *The Encomienda in New Spain* (Berkeley, 1950); Hanke, *opera cit.*

The life and works of Vasco de Quiroga have attracted great attention among scholars, although it must be remarked that a balanced study has yet to appear. See Silvio Zavala, *Idearo de Vasco de Quiroga* (México, 1941); Silvio Zavala, *La Utopia de Tomás Moro en la Nueva España y otros estudios* (México, 1937); Silvio Zavala, *New Viewpoints on the Spanish Colonization of America* (Philadelphia, 1943); Hanke, *The First Social Experiments*; Rafael Aguayo Spencer, *Don Vasco de Quiroga: Documentos* (México, 1940); Paul Lietz, "Vasco de Quiroga, Sociologist of New Spain," *Mid-America*, XVIII (1936), 247-259; Paul Lietz, "Vasco de Quiroga: Oidor Made Bishop," *Mid-America*, XXXII (1950), 13-32; Paul Lietz, *Don Vasco de Quiroga and the Second Audiencia of New Spain* (unpublished Ph.D. dissertation, Loyola, 1940); Alfonso Reyes, "Utopías Americanas," *Sur* (Buenos Aires, enero, 1938), 7-16; and Zavala's comment on the latter, "Letras de Utopia: Carta a Don Alfonso Reyes," *Cuadernos Americanos*, II, (1942), 146-152.

[17] In "The American Utopia of the Sixteenth Century," *The Huntington Library Quarterly*, X (1947), 337-347, Zavala summarizes many of his previous studies and gives the best overall account of the subject in English.

[18] *Ibid.*, p. 344.

inhabitants; the foregoing of luxury and of all offices which were not useful; and the election of the judiciary by the families.[19]

Quiroga's hospital-villages, as he called them, set the pattern for general Indian evangelization as the conquest period moved on and the northern frontier was penetrated. The lasting influence of Quiroga on Mexican humanism is best described in the words of Kubler:

The special interest of those communities is that they are the earliest manifestations now known in Mexico, of Humanist and Erasmian ideas of social reform, for Zumárraga's catechisms did not appear until the mid-1540's.[20]

And Kubler continues that Quiroga "stated explicitly in later life that he had patterned his towns upon More's *Utopia*, of which a copy was in the possession of his friend, Zumárraga."[21]

Renaissance ideas among the laymen of early sixteenth-century Mexico were anything but humanistic in the Christian sense. If Quiroga and Zumárraga represented Christian humanism, the conquistador probably represented the extreme materialistic side of humanism. This layman created, initially, a pseudo-Renaissance society in Mexico which was founded on an affected cult of gentlemanliness, an imitation of the Renaissance gentleman by the baser classes in breeding and intellect. The early citizen was usually a soldier-encomendero and had an aversion to manual labor; indeed, as Kubler has suggested, he doubted its ethical value.[22] The exploitation of the Indian was the mudsill upon which he built his society, and he became extremely impatient and malicious with the Christian humanists who sought to undermine the foundations of the new order.

It was in the midst of this struggle that Juan de Zumárraga entered upon the scene of Mexican history, and it was in this struggle that he labored during his twenty years in Mexico.

## II. *The Intellectual Fiber of Juan de Zumárraga*[23]

Fray Juan de Zumárraga, O.F.M., first bishop of Mexico, arrived

[19] *Ibid.*, p. 347. The ordinances for the Quiroga hospital-villages may be consulted in Rafael Aguayo Spencer, *Don Vasco de Quiroga*, pp. 243-267. For related materials on Quiroga's experiments see Nicolás León, *Documentos inéditos referentes al ilustrisimo Señor Don Vasco de Quiroga* (México, 1940).

[20] Kubler, *op. cit.*, I, 12.

[21] *Loc. cit.*

[22] *Ibid.*, p. 15.

[23] The biographers of Zumárraga are numerous but generally lacking in depth and balance. The classic treatment of this life is by Joaquín García Icazbalceta, issued in 1881 but recently reprinted and augmented by Rafael Aguayo Spencer and Antonio Castro Leal, *Don Fray Juan de Zumárraga, primer obispo y arzobispo de México* (4 vols., México, 1947). The best recent biography is by Fidel de J. Chauvet, O.F.M., *Fray Juan de Zumárraga, O.F. M.* (México, 1948). See also: Juan Ruiz de Larrínaga, *Don Fray Juan de Zumárraga, primer obispo y arzobispo de México, Durangués, Franciscano, y servidor de la patria. Al Margen de su Pontificado* (Bilbao, 1948); Daniel J. Mulvihill, "Juan de

at his post December 6, 1528,[24] and he began immediately to assume the
full powers of his office, especially his subsidiary powers as Protector of
the Indians which had been granted him on January 2, 1527, while he
still remained in the Iberian peninsula.[25] Zumárraga's duty, as he saw it,
was to protect the Indian from exploitation, and in his attempt to do this
he came into conflict with not only the soldier-encomendero but also the
Spanish officialdom in New Spain who were either corrupt in office or
derelict in performing their duties.

Zumárraga viewed the Indian as a rational human being who was in
every way capable of salvation, and as Hanke indicated "every one of
his contributions to Mexican culture derived from this belief. . . ."[26] As
Protector of the Indians he was empowered to inform himself of social
and economic conditions among the natives and to protect them in gen-

Zumárraga, First Bishop of Mexico" (unpublished Ph.D. dissertation, University of
Michigan, 1954); Constantino Bayle, *El IV
centenario de Don Fray Juan de Zumárraga* (Madrid, 1948); Alberto María Carreño,
*Don Fray Juan de Zumárraga, teólogo y
editor, humanista e inquisidor* (México,
1950); Estanislao J. de Labayru, *Estudios y
hechos de la vida del illustrisimo y vener-
able Vizcaino Don Fray Juan de Zumárraga,
natural de Durango, primer obispo y arzobispo de México* (Bilbao, 1880), Volume V,
Number 3 of *The Americas* (January,
1949) is dedicated to the memory of Zumárraga. Specific articles will be cited in
the text of this chapter.

[24] Zumárraga was born in Durango, Viz-
caya, in late 1468 or early 1469. We are
largely ignorant of his early years. The
father was a landowner and Juan was
educated by the Bachiller Arrazola in
Durango and later at Valladolid. He joined
the Order at Abrojo and later became
Guardian of the monastery there, and in
1520-1523 was Provincial of the new province of Concepción, in the latter year re-
tiring to Abrojo where he was again
elected as Guardian. In 1527 Charles V
visited Abrojo during Holy Week and
was greatly impressed with its Guardian,
later commissioning him to investigate
witchcraft in Pamplona, and finally pre-
senting him as first bishop of Mexico in
December of 1527. Zumárraga left Sevilla
in late August and arrived in Mexico December 6, 1528. He had left Spain without
the papal bulls of consecration because of
the urgent need for his presence in Mexico.
His lack of consecration provided many
difficulties in the exercise of his functions,

and his appointment as Protector of the
Indians brought him into conflict with the
peninsular population in Mexico. In July
of 1532 the Bishop returned to Spain upon
a summons from the Council of the Indies
to answer charges which the first audiencia
and its president Nuño de Guzmán had
presented against him. He cleared his name
easily and took advantage of the visit to be
consecrated on April 27, 1533, in the
monastery of San Francisco at Valladolid,
and dispatched his legates to Mexico to
take complete charge of the diocese. It
was agreed that the Office of Protector
would be abolished and Zumárraga consented. With the arrival of Mendoza as
the first viceroy of New Spain, on November 14, 1535, the viceregal office assumed the function of looking after the
native population. Zumárraga returned to
Mexico in October, 1534, to exercise his
full episcopal powers. He served as Apostolic Inquisitor from 1536 to 1543 and participated actively in the spiritual conquest. His
appointment as first archbishop of Mexico
reached him just before his death on June
3, 1548.

[25] For the office of Protector and the
controversy in which it involved Zumárraga, see Fidel de J. Chauvet, O.F.M.,
"Fray Juan de Zumárraga, Protector of the
Indians," *The Americas*, V (1949), 283-
295. This study is based partly on Constantino Bayle, *El Protector de Indios*
(Sevilla, 1945). Much of the following
material is taken from the Chauvet article.

[26] Hanke, "The Contribution of Bishop
Zumárraga to Mexican Culture," *The
Americas*, V (1949), 275.

eral, without restriction, against anyone who neglected his duty towards them as an encomendero or maltreated them in any way. Unfortunately, Zumárraga was set up as some kind of supreme judge without prescribed sanctions to enforce his will.

His initial clash with the first audiencia and its president, Nuño de Guzmán, was over the right of the Indian to appeal to the Protector for redress of grievances. In 1529 Zumárraga had made known his jurisdiction throughout the diocese and had invited the Indian to appeal any maltreatment. Flocks of natives took the bishop at his word. When the audiencia forbade Zumárraga to interfere and indicated that Indians who appealed might be hanged and lose their property, Zumárraga denounced the oidores from the pulpit.

The audiencia, in effect, declared war.[27] Vile and infamous charges against the bishop were fabricated; one Franciscan preacher, Father Ortiz, was dragged from his pulpit for preaching against the audiencia, with the result that Zumárraga excommunicated the judges. Nuño de Guzmán countered with a censorship of all of the bishop's mail to Spain, while the oidores filed denunciations against their bishop with the Council of the Indies. Zumárraga had to resort to illicit means to get his side of the story to Spain, namely through certain trusted sailors who carried the letters in secret. Eventually, after a threat on his life and an actual sword pass at his person, Zumárraga placed Mexico City under interdict. Shortly the oidores sought and received absolution, but their letters to the Council netted Zumárraga a censure and an order to report in person to Spain. Zumárraga by his own consent was removed as Protector, mainly as Chauvet has said because ". . . from about the middle of 1529 he came to realize that the Office of Protector of the Indians did not harmonize well with his somewhat severe character, nor with the nature of his office as ecclesiastical superior of Mexico."[28] He felt further that "the conflict stirred up by his office worked to the detriment of the spiritual government of souls."[29]

Zumárraga continued, however, in his capacity as bishop to investigate and make recommendations for the well-being of the natives, particularly in the realm of education and economic betterment. He was convinced that Indians were capable of becoming fine craftsmen and farmers. With these thoughts in mind he urged the importation of flax and hoped to stimulate a native linen industry in Mexico. He was instrumental in seeing that all varieties of seeds planted in Spain were

[27] A recent study of the Zumárraga-Nuño de Guzmán conflict is Fausto Marin-Tamayo, *El primer conflicto colonial civil-eclesiástico (1529)* (Puebla, 1957).

[28] Chauvet, "Fray Juan de Zumárraga, Protector of the Indians," *The Americas*, V (1949), 294.
[29] *Ibid.*

brought to New Spain for experimentation. Silkworms were imported as well as mulberry trees and Moriscoes were allowed to immigrate to teach the natives the techniques of cultivating silk. Zumárraga recognized the practical benefits of the encomienda system and he stoutly contended that the New Laws of 1542 were impractical in Mexico.[30]

In the field of Indian education Zumárraga was the leader. It is true that Peter of Ghent founded the first school for Indian boys at Texcoco in 1523 and that Fray Martín de Valencia had established a similar school in Mexico City two years later, but the real impetus to native education came from Zumárraga, both in the founding of schools personally and the encouragement of other friars and other Orders to found schools of their own. Zumárraga's most famous school was the Colegio de Santa Cruz de Tlatelolco, founded in 1534 for the sons of caciques. In the same year Zumárraga began his educational program for Indian girls, especially expectant mothers. A similar type of school was founded in 1547 for homeless mestizo boys.[31]

The college at Tlatelolco prospered for the first few decades of its existence despite the fact that one of its brightest students, Don Carlos of Texcoco, was burned at the stake for heresy. The Don Carlos episode, coupled with the fact that the Indians were outshining Spaniards in their knowledge of Latin, raised grave doubts as to the value of the school in the minds of some of the clergy. Hanke reports that the college languished and never became the great center that Zumárraga had hoped. The consequences were serious for Mexico for the college had been the obvious training ground for a native priesthood, and with its ineffectiveness the clergy tended to become entirely peninsular or creole. Hanke and Ricard think that the role of the college might have been crucial in Mexican history: "If the Colegio of Tlatelolco had trained only one bishop for the country, the whole history of the Mexican Church would have been far different."[32]

In addition to his contributions to native education, Zumárraga must be credited with four other decisive contributions to Mexican culture. He participated in the movement for the founding of the Royal and Pontifical University of Mexico; he founded great hospitals for the Spaniard and Indian alike; he was instrumental in bringing the first printing press to the colony; and the books which he printed and edited

[30] Carlos Castañeda, "Fray Juan de Zumárraga and Indian Policy in New Spain," *The Americas*, V (1949), 308; Mulvihill, *op. cit.*, p. 179.

[31] For a history of the College at Tlatelolco see Francis B. Steck, O.F.M., *El primer colegio de America: Santa Cruz de Tlatelolco* (México, 1944). By the same author *Education in Spanish North America during the Sixteenth Century* (Washington, D. C., 1943) is also valuable. See also Ricard, *op. cit.*, pp. 375-409.

[32] Hanke cites Ricard, *op. cit.*, p. 419 *et passim*, in "The Contribution of Bishop Zumárraga to Mexican Culture," *The Americas*, V (1949), 280.

for the Indian's religious instruction rounded out as large a contribution to culture as any man could have made in sixteenth-century Mexico.[33]

Beyond a doubt Juan de Zumárraga represented in Mexico the Erasmian brand of Christian humanism with certain modifications.[34] His branch of the Franciscan Order, says Kubler, was "exalted by a spiritual unrest closely akin to that of the Northern Reformation in Europe,"[35] and the climax of their reform movement came in the decade of 1510 under the auspices of Cardinal Ximénez de Cisneros, the great pre-Reformation advocate of the humanist philosophy of Christ in Spain.[36]

The Cisnerian reform was predicated upon a purification of the clergy by revitalizing their preaching mission and reemphasizing the precept of austerity. The result of this movement was the creation of a "spiritual elite of evangelical tendency"[37] who were sympathetic to Erasmus and anticipatory of the Protestant Reformation. These elite, of whom the *Los Doce* of Martín de Valencia were a segment, were members of the observant rather than the conventual branch of the Franciscan Order and followed the reformed *regula* of Juan de Puebla and Juan de Guadalupe, the founders of the *observantias strictissimas* in Renaissance Spain.[38]

[33] For Zumárraga's writings, editings and printings, see Alberto María Carreño, "The Books of Don Fray Juan de Zumárraga," *The Americas*, V (1949), 311-330. This article is a translation with some variations of a section of *Don Fray Juan de Zumárraga: teólogo y editor, humanista e inquisidor. Nuevos documentos* (México, 1950).

[34] The monumental work on Spanish Erasmism is Marcel Bataillon; *Erasmo y España estudios sobre la historia espiritual del siglo XVI* (2 vols.; México, 1950), trans. Antonio Alatorre. Especially valuable for Mexico is the appendix of Volume II, "Erasmo y el Nuevo Mundo," 435-454. By the same author, "Erasme au Mexique," *Société historique algérienne. Deuxième Congrès National des Sciences Historiques, 1930* (Algiers, 1932), is valuable for Mexico, but perhaps the foremost authority on Zumárraga and Erasmus is José Almoina, "El Erasmismo de Zumárraga," *Filosofía y Letras*, XXIX (1948), 93-126. By the same author, *Rumbos heterodoxos en México* (Ciudad Trujillo, 1947) and "Citas Clásicas de Zumárraga," *Historia Mexicana*, VIII (1954), 391-419, are extremely useful.

Other studies of merit are Kubler, *op. cit.*, I, 1-21; José Miranda, "Renovación Cristiana y Erasmismo en México," *Historia Mexicana*, I (1951), 22-47; Alfonso Reyes, *Letras de la Nueva España* (Méx-

ico, 1948); Carreño, "The Books of Fray Juan de Zumárraga," *The Americas*, V (1949), 311-330; Silvio Zavala, "Letras de Utopía: Carta a Don Alfonso Reyes," *Cuadernos Americanos*, II (1942), 146-152, which contains facsímiles de Zumárraga's copies of More, Erasmus, and Gerson with notations in his own hand.

[35] Kubler, *op. cit.*, I, 4.

[36] The soundest and most complete treatment of the pre-Cisneros and Cisnerian reforms in Spain is Herbert Holzapfel, O.F.M., *The History of the Franciscan Order*, Antonine Tibesar, O.F.M. and Gervase Brinkmann, O.F.M. (Teutopolis, Illinois, 1948), pp. 65-117.

[37] Kubler, *op. cit.*, I, 4, has the best summary of this material on Erasmus in Mexico based upon the sources previously mentioned.

[38] See Holzapfel, *op. cit.*, pp. 65-66 for a definition of "conventual," its original meaning and its fifteenth-century significance in all Orders, and especially in the O.F.M.:

One big difference between the Observants and the Conventuals in the Order of Friars Minor lay in their view of the poverty of the Order; the Observants adhered to the abdication of property "in common" and renounced all fixed incomes and landed

Kubler makes the speculation, however, that in 1524 when the Apostolic Twelve came to Mexico

... the Franciscan Missionaries, were not to our knowledge in contact with the political and religious thought of North European Humanism. If the Apostolic Twelve represented Cisnerian Spain, a later group of missionaries under Juan de Zumárraga represented Erasmian thought in Mexico.[39]

Zumárraga was appointed in a Spain whose officialdom were intellectual followers of Erasmus.[40] We are not sure when Zumárraga became an Erasmist, but since he was born some three decades before the turn of the sixteenth century, it is very plausible to think that he had acquaintance with many of the writings of Erasmus of Rotterdam. However, the main documentary evidence that we have of his Erasmism "are the doctrinal books printed in Mexico under his jurisdiction and a copy of More's *Utopia* and Erasmus' *Epigrammata* in his possession."[41]

Bataillon and Almoina[42] have analyzed the *Doctrina breve* (1544) and the *Doctrina christiana* (1545, 1546) of Zumárraga[43] in order to discern his use of Erasmus' ideas. Bataillon correlated parallel passages of the two and came to the conclusion that Zumárraga not only quoted whole blocks of Erasmus' *Epigrammata* and *Paraclesis* as well as the *Enchiridion*, but that he also must have been acquainted with the *Diálogo de doctrina christiana* of Juan de Valdés.[44]

The *Doctrina breve* was issued in 1544 to instruct the priests of the diocese. It contained Erasmus' remedies against vices and used certain sections of the *Paraclesis* as a conclusion. Kubler comments on the Bataillon analysis:

He [Zumárraga] changed Erasmus's *filosofía cristiana* to *doctrina cristiana*, and deleted the name of Erasmus but confirmed the denunciation of scholasticism.

estates. But, in the 15th century especially, the difference consisted not only in the question of poverty, but much more in the general discipline of the Order; this had been relaxed to a great extent among the Conventuals.
...

John of Guadalupe after 1495 introduced the "very strict observance" with the reform of habit:

The Guadalupenses began with a reform of the habit. The capuche was shaped like a pyramid, the mantle was shortened, varicolored pieces were sewn to the habit, and sandals were discarded entirely. The people accordingly called them Discalceati or Capuciati (Fratres de Capucio), also Fratres de sancto evangelio—this latter

either because they wished to live in strict conformity to the gospel, or because they were very active in preaching.

*Ibid.*, p. 113.

[39] Kubler, *op. cit.*, I, 9.
[40] See Longhurst, *Erasmus and the Spanish Inquisition*, pp. 28-34, 70-77.
[41] Kubler, *op. cit.*, I. 10.
[42] Bataillon, "Erasme au Mexique," *Société historique algérienne*, and Almoina, *Rumbos heterodoxos*, p. 169.
[43] For complete titles and publication data, see Carreño, "The Books of Fray Juan de Zumárraga," *The Americas*, V (1949), 314-330.
[44] For a very useful summary of the Valdés *Doctrina*, see Longhurst, *Erasmus and the Spanish Inquisition*, pp. 79-96.

. . . Zumárraga also approved Erasmus's advocacy of the unlimited diffusion of scripture, as in the *Paraclesis*, and kept the doctrine of interior Christianity intact. On the whole, the Pauline formulas of Charity appear as in the *Enchiridion*. The unfavorable remarks about mendicants, were of course suppressed.[45]

The *Doctrina christiana* was prepared as a catechism for Indian use. It was based in great part upon the *Suma de doctrina* of the famous confessor to Charles V, Dr. Constantino Ponce de la Fuente, who was later convicted as the leader of the Sevilla Lutheran movement. It contained "essential Christianity, conceived in the spirit of Erasmus," and insisted upon the primacy of faith over good works. Zumárraga again used parts of the *Paraclesis* as a conclusion to this edition.[46]

When the Montúfar Inquisition examined this work in the late 1550's it did so with the firm conviction that Zumárraga's Erasmism was heretical. It is probably true that the work would have been condemned in Spain in the same year that it was printed in Mexico, 1545. However, modern Zumárraga scholars—and most of them are pro-Zumárraga—contend that although the bishop knew and admired Erasmus, he used only those sections of the noted humanist's works which were orthodox and which he found applicable to the needs confronting him.[47]

Furthermore, Zumárraga's supporters marshal additional evidence to substantiate their claims. It is pointed out that the *Enchiridion* was not condemned in Spain until 1559, nine years after the death of the bishop, and sixteen years after the publication of the *Doctrinas*. Carreño shows Zumárraga's astuteness in editing other books which were to be published under his auspices to make sure that they were completely orthodox.[48] In addition, Carreño takes Almoina's general theme that Zumárraga was laboring to bring about an orthodox reform of Catholicism and supports it, contending that he certainly would not try to do this by unorthodox means, namely heresy and plagiarism.[49] Finally, the classic biographer of the bishop, García Icazbalceta, flatly indicated that "everything about him excludes the idea that by word or writing he ever gave any reason for the slightest suspicion regarding his orthodoxy."[50]

Fernando Benítez, a critic of Zumárraga, marvels that the bishop

[45] Kubler, *op. cit.*, I, 10.
[46] *Ibid.*
[47] Mulvihill, *op. cit.*, p. 32.
[48] When the *Compendio de la manera como se han de hacer las procesiones, compuesto en latín por Dionisio Riguel Cartusiano y romanceado para común utilidad* was published by Cromberger in 1544, Zumárraga inserted an appendix containing his replies to three complaints against the work. "This appendix proves the Bishop's carefulness to provide in doctrinal matters only the most approved teachings, according to his mind and conscience, for the instruction of his spiritual subjects." Carreño, "The Books of Fray Juan de Zumárraga," *The Americas*, V (1949), 324.
[49] *Ibid.*, p. 319.
[50] *Ibid.*, p. 325, citing José T. Medina, *La Imprenta en México* (8 vols.; Santiago de Chile, 1912), I, 38-39.

"dared to launch an Erasmist program of Christianization ten years after Erasmus had died, and when his works were without defenders in Spain, and were the objects of implacable inquisitorial investigations."[51]

Zumárraga's Inquisition has clearly indicated to this author that the bishop was probably orthodox in all things. In 1539, before the publication of the *Doctrinas*, Zumárraga had occasion to try a Castilian, Francisco de Sayavedra, as an Erasmist.[52] This fact must be interpreted to mean that Zumárraga understood the heterodoxies of Erasmus as the Spanish Inquisition had defined them, and that certainly he could not be a party to such errors.

We have some evidence to support the idea that besides an affinity for Erasmian doctrines, Zumárraga had a profound respect for the writings of Sir Thomas More.[53] Kubler has examined Zumárraga's own copy of the *Epigrammata* of Erasmus which was the Froben edition of 1518. This edition also contained More's *Utopia*. Kubler has these comments to make about Zumárraga's marginal notations on the *Utopia*:

For the Mexican humanists, such complexities in the English political situation were irrelevant. The marginal notations to *Utopia* are nearly all in the same rapid hand, and bear an unmistakable resemblance to Zumárraga's known holographs. Zumárraga's notations show him especially sensitive to More's remarks upon the foolish estimation of gold, upon crafts and hospitals, social organization, and religious exercises. They are the notes of a straightforward, simple man of action, revealing a decidedly naive curiosity about the natural and historical identification of *Utopia*, as on page 63 where he glosses More's navigational distances. Zumárraga failed to comment on More's esthetics, or his speculations on health or the pleasures of the mind. Significantly, there is no comment upon the passages treating of war and religious tolerance, but much upon the industry of the Utopians (one marginal note reads "none are idle"), the manner of dying, the laws, the forms of religious community, the size of the *familia* ("30 families eat together"), the status of priests, and the forms of towns, where Zumárraga has underlined the passages describing Utopian architecture with heavy, rapid, agitated strokes.[54]

Zumárraga certainly must have gotten many of his ideas from More, especially on hospitals and Indian crafts. The fact Quiroga used this Froben edition to plan his hospital-villages and write their ordinances made the mere fact that Zumárraga had it in his library of untold significance.

[51] Fernando Benítez, *La vida criolla en el siglo XVI* (México, 1953), p. 85. The author's translation.

[52] The *proceso* is found in AGN, Inquisición, Tomo, II, exp. 8. It is also published in the *Boletín del Archivo General de la Nación*, XVIII (1947), 1-15.

[53] Kubler, *op. cit.*, I, 11.

[54] *Ibid.*

III. *An Evaluation of Zumárraga's Intellectual Background*

I agree with Fernando Benítez who said that Zumárraga, in spite of his affinity for Erasmus, remained in doctrine and practice a medieval friar.[55] One has to conclude that sixteenth-century Mexico did not really belong to the Renaissance but to Dante's *De monarchia*. The main teleology in conquest Mexico was still religion, although the unruly conquistador represented the move toward materialism. There were, to be sure, radical reformers among the clergy, but they simply had not been declared unorthodox until after the Zumárraga period. Humanism was acceptable as long as it fused with St. Thomas, and aspects of humanistic belief which did not fit Thomas were discarded. Tolerance, a supposed humanistic virtue, was lacking in the thought of the friars of Mexico.

Zumárraga was a man of contradiction, a segmented thinker, not untypical of the sixteenth century. Perhaps the greatest contradiction in Zumárraga was his Indian Inquisition. He was convinced that the Inquisition was just and needed in New Spain, but he knew the Indian's frailty and instability in the new religion, and he realized that it was predicated upon inadequate instruction.

One cannot help feeling that perhaps a single ingredient made the Mexican Utopia impossible: the lack of elasticity in the clerical mind to absorb new ideas and integrate them into its thinking. Initially, the clergy tried to compartmentalize their religious orthodoxy on the one hand with a type of philosophical eclecticism on the other. Eventually humanism had to give way to security of the empire and its religion. The Noble Savage, despite his many attributes, had to stay within the boundaries of the new orthodoxy or be punished.

[55] Benítez, *op. cit.*, p. 84.

CHAPTER III

# The Indians and the Inquisition:
## 1536-1543

## (Part One)

### I. *The Religion of the Aztecs*[1]

To generalize about Aztec religion is a difficult and dangerous process. Perhaps the safest general statement came from George C. Vaillant when he said that "Aztec religion was an outgrowth of the recognition and fear of natural forces and the attempt to constrain them."[2] As such it permeated all phases of Indian culture and daily life. Aztec society then was monolithic, and there existed no real distinction between religion, politics, and social life. Consequently it was difficult for the Spaniard to intervene radically in the Aztec's theology without reorienting the entire culture complex.

Aztec mythology taught that the world had progressed through four stages of catastrophic creation and destruction and was embarked

[1] The two definitive primary studies on the Indians of central Mexico are Bernardino de Sahagún, *Historia general de las cosas de Nueva España* (3 vols.; México, 1955), translated from the Náhuatl and annotated by Arthur J. O. Anderson and Charles E. Dibble, *The Florentine Codex: General History of the Things of New Spain* (Vol. I—, Santa Fe, 1950—); and Toribio de Motolinía, *Historia de los Indios de la Nueva España* (Barcelona, 1914), translated and annotated by Francis Borgia Steck, O.F.M., *Motolinía's History of the Indians of New Spain* (Washington, D. C., 1951).
Five modern scholars have distinguished themselves in the archaeology and ethnology of central Mexico: Alfonso Caso, *The Aztecs: People of the Sun*, trans. Lowell Dunham (Norman, 1958); J. Eric Thompson, *Mexico Before Cortez, An Account of the Daily Life, Religion and Ritual of the Aztecs and Kindred Peoples* (New York,

1933); Herbert J. Spinden, *Ancient Civilizations of Mexico and Central America* (New York, 1917); and George C. Vaillant, *The Aztecs of Mexico: Origin, Rise and Fall of the Aztec Nation* (Harmondsworth, Middlesex, 1950). It must be noted that Vaillant's archaeology has been altered by recent Mexican discoveries and by the use of radiocarbon dating. His ethnology, although it is a general composite picture of Aztec culture, remains fairly reliable for my purposes. For added information on Vaillant and modern revisions of his work, see John Paddock, *A Guide to G. C. Vaillant's Aztecs of Mexico* (México, 1956). The most recent and up-to-date work is Frederick Peterson, *Ancient Mexico: An Introduction to the Pre-Hispanic Cultures* (London, 1959).
[2] Vaillant, *op. cit.,* p. 169. The following general characterization of the Aztecs is excellent for our purpose:
The Aztecs and their forebears be-

upon a fifth.[3] The first age was called Four Ocelot and was dominated by the god Tezcatlipoca, "who at the end of the era transformed himself into the sun, while jaguars ate up the men and giants who then populated the earth."[4] The second world was designated as Four Wind and had as its prime mover the god Quetzalcoatl, lord of the wind. When this era terminated the world was destroyed by hurricanes and men were transformed into monkeys. The third world was Four Rain dominated by Tlaloc, the rain god; this world ended in a fiery rain. Four Water, the world preceding our era, was controlled by Chalchihuitlicue (Lady of the Jade Skirts)[5] and it ended with a series of floods while mankind was turned into fishes. Our world was dubbed Four Earthquake and was to be destroyed by the sun god Tonatiuh with great earthquakes.[6]

Vaillant explained that the Aztecs conceived their universe "in a religious rather than a geographic sense . . ."[7] and that they divided it horizontally and vertically. The horizontal universe contained five directions: East, West, North, South and Center. In the Center there was the fire god, and to the East Tlaloc, the rain god, and his companion Mixcoatl, the cloud god. To the South Xipe (The Flayed One)[8] and Macuilxochitl (Five Flower), the gods of spring and flowers, held forth. The North was apparently a place of horror because its god, Mictlantecuhtli, was the lord of the dead. The West was the home of Quetzalcoatl, the god of knowledge, and of Venus, the evening star.[9]

The vertical universe had thirteen heavens and numerous hells, but these were devoid of moral significance except that they were the dwelling places of various gods according to their rank.[10] Tlaloc's heaven, Tlalocan, was reserved for those who were struck by lightning

---

lieved that the forces of nature acted for good or evil very much as does mankind, so that it was logical for them to personalize the elements as gods or goddesses. The process of worship entailed offering presents, uttering prayers, and performing symbolic acts to induce the divine powers to operate for the public benefit. The tribal intellect was mobilized, as it were, to sort out processes of nature, find out how they acted, and devise magical procedures or rituals to win them to be favourable to man. *Ibid.*, p. 168.

Valuable for this basic understanding of Aztec religion is the section on magic and religion in Caso, *op. cit.*, pp. 3-6, 7-8. See also Peterson, *op. cit.*, pp. 125-127.

[3] For the stories of the multiple creations see Caso, *op. cit.*, pp. 14-20; Vaillant, *op. cit.*, pp. 169-170.

[4] Vaillant, *op. cit.*, p. 169.

[5] Caso, *op. cit.*, pp. 15, 41-42, discusses Chalchihuitlicue in the creation myth and as an earth goddess.

[6] It is to be remembered that the Aztecs lived in a great basin which was dominated on the south particularly by giant volcanoes, especially Popocatépetl, Ixtaccíhuatl and Xitle.

[7] Vaillant, *op. cit.*, p. 170.

[8] Anderson and Dibble, *Florentine Codex, Book One—The Gods*, pp. 16-17; Caso, *op. cit.*, pp. 49-51.

[9] Vaillant, *op. cit.*, p. 170.

[10] Caso, *op. cit.*, pp. 58-65, has the most complete discussion of the heavens and hells. See also Peterson, *op. cit.*, pp. 140-141.

or died by drowning or other water accidents.[11] The Eastern heaven was the resting place of warriors who died in battle while the West welcomed women who died in childbirth, "thus sacrificing themselves in the bearing of potential warriors."[12] The remainder of the deceased went to Mictlan, the underworld, where they journeyed through a type of purgatory prior to their final rest.

There were hundreds of gods in the Aztec pantheon, but some were more important than others because they directly affected everyday life, especially the sky gods.[13] In many cases the Aztecs adopted certain gods of the earlier Toltec and Teotihuacano cultures and intergrated them into their theology. One of the most potent Aztec gods was Tezcatlipoca (The Smoking Mirror), special patron of sorcerers.[14] He had a multiphastic existence. In the West he was red and assumed the name of Xipe; in the South he was blue and called Huitzilopochtli; to the North he was black, and to the East white. The white Tezcatlipoca of the East was often Quetzalcoatl, especially in Cholula.[15] He was especially worshipped at Texcoco; Netzahualcóyotl was called the Flute of the Smoking Mirror.[16]

The two chief divinities that the Mexicans of the conquest era borrowed from the Toltecs were Tlaloc and Quetzalcoatl. Tlaloc, the rain god, was as important in the central valley and Tenochtitlán as the Aztec war god, Huitzilopochtli, because of the necessity of rain for survival on the central plateau of Mexico.[17] On the other hand, Quetzalcoatl (The Feathered Serpent) dominated Teotihuacan and shared influence as far south as the Mayan area where he was called Kukulkan in Chichén Itzá.[18] He also led a multiphastic existence. Besides his identity as Kukulkan among the Maya, Quetzalcoatl was also known among the Aztec as Xiuhcoatl and Echecatl. Legend also had it that he was a white god who civilized the Toltecs and left for the east to return again.

In addition to the sky gods many earth gods were closely associated with Mexican daily life. On earth Tlaloc represented fertility while his companion Chalchihuitlicue was the goddess of lakes and rivers. There

[11] Caso, *op. cit.*, p. 60.
[12] Vaillant, *op. cit.*, p. 171.
[13] Peterson, *op. cit.*, p. 127 speculates that "there were two groups of gods. One group—gods of agriculture and fertility, rain, sun, corn and earth—was important to the great agricultural population. The other group—'official gods' of the theologians, with elaborately systematized manifestations, aspects, and functions to suit every occasion—probably meant little to the masses." Peterson (*ibid.*, pp. 131-136) gives a detailed breakdown of gods in the Aztec pantheon.
[14] For a discussion of Tezcatlipoca's attributes see Caso, *op. cit.*, pp. 27-31.
[15] Vaillant, *op. cit.*, p. 173.
[16] See Frances Gillmor, *Flute of the Smoking Mirror* (Albuquerque, 1949).
[17] Caso, *op. cit.*, pp. 41-42 and Peterson, *op. cit.*, pp. 130-131 discuss the importance of Tlaloc as a god of water and vegetation.
[18] Quetzalcoatl is treated in detail in Caso, *op. cit.*, passim.

were many deities connected with corn,[19] and there was even a goddess of maguey, Mayauel, "whose 400 sons were associated with pulque."[20]

Tlaltecuhtli was a powerful god of the earth, as was Coatlicue (Lady of the Serpent Skirts) who was first and foremost a mother: mother of the stellar gods, mother of Huitzilopochtli, and goddess of all earthly mothers. Perhaps she was the same goddess as Tonantzin (Our Mother) who had a shrine at Tepeyac.[21] Caso feels that she was also Tlazolteotl (Eater of Filth): "Since she was the devourer of filth, she consumed the sins of men, thereby cleansing them of their impurities. Hence, the confessional rite that was practiced before the priests of Tlazotéotl."[22] Mictlantecuhtli and Mictlancihuatl (Our Lord and Lady of the Region of Death) rounded out the important earth deities. Most deceased passed to their domain.[23]

The major Aztec deity and the ranking god in Tenochtitlán was Huitzilopochtli (Hummingbird Wizard or Hummingbird of the Left).[24] Legend had it that the Aztecs found the idol Huitzilopochtli in a cave in western Mexico, and that he guided their wanderings and directed the founding of Tenochtitlán in 1325. Huitzilopochtli was a war god and according to the native belief he had an unquenchable thirst for blood. Since he was actually an anthropomorphic god, he needed food and drink. He preferred blood, which the Aztecs called the "divine liquid."

The native population was convinced that a well-fed Huitzilopochtli would direct their lives with kindness and abundance. However, flood, famine, pestilence, or drought were thought to be inevitable if the god were angered by hunger. In preconquest Mexico victims had been recruited voluntarily or through warfare. They were held on the sacrificial altar and their chests were ripped open with obsidian knives. The hearts were plucked from the bodies and collected, along with the blood for the consumption of the god. If the sacrifice were made to Xipe, often the victim was skinned and the human pelt was worn for a period of time by the presiding priest.[25]

The entire Aztec pantheon, of course, was reflected in a ritualistic

[19] Peterson, *op. cit.*, p. 127 describes corn as a sacred plant.
[20] Vaillant, *op. cit.*, p. 175. For an interesting representation of Mayauel consult Caso, *op. cit.*, pp. 47-48, 50.
[21] In speaking of Tonantzin Vaillant (*op. cit.*, p. 177) remarked ". . . and her cult was transferred to the Virgin by the early missionaries, an act exemplifying their intelligent procedure in evangelizing the Aztecs."
[22] Caso, *op. cit.*, p. 56. The Sahagún treatment of Tlazolteotl and her confessional rite may be consulted in Anderson and Dibble, *op. cit.*, pp. 8-11.
[23] Vaillant, *op. cit.*, pp. 177-178. See also Caso, *op. cit.*, p. 56 for the gods of death.
[24] Huitzilopochtli as the tribal god of the Aztecs is discussed in *ibid.*, pp. 12-14, 91-92.
[25] See Anderson and Dibble, *op. cit.*, pp. 15-16 for a description of Xipe and his rite.

system of worship, and in turn the ritual was intricately bound up with the Aztec calendar which was actually the core of the religion.[26]

## II. *The Methods of the Spiritual Conquerors of Mexico*[27]

Given the primitive mentality of the Indians, and their limited capacity for comprehending the spiritual doctrines of Christianity, in the early "rage of conversion" the natives without doubt were often taken into the Church without sufficient preparation or instruction.[28]

This statement by Clarence Haring is an apt characterization of the first two decades of the spiritual conquest of Mexico.

The general theory of the regular clergy was that the Indian was to be baptized very soon after he had been taught some of the basic doctrine of the Church. Given the small number of priests of the three missionary orders in Mexico and the number of Indians evangelized during the years 1520-1540, it is apparent that both pre-baptismal and post-baptismal instruction were very meager indeed. Motolinía left us rudimentary statistics of the mass baptisms which took place in the 1520's and the early 1530's: "I believe that after the land was won, which was in 1521, up to the time I am writing this, which is the year 1536, more than four million souls have been baptized."[29] Later on Motolinía speaks of five million and then nine million baptisms.[30]

The administration of the sacrament of baptism by individual friars in this area cannot be described as anything but a herculean task:

Toribio de Motolinía tells us of some of the early Franciscan friars in New Spain who baptized as many as 1500 Indians, children and adults, in one day. He goes on to say that several of them baptized each over 100,000 during their sojourn there. ...

Peter of Ghent in a letter of June 1529 speaks of 14,000 being baptized in one day.[31]

Motolinía describes the actual administration of the sacrament.[32] First, there was a lineup of all the candidates for baptism with the children in front, and the roll was called. Then the sacrament was administered, "observing in the case of a few the ceremony of the anointing

---

[26] Vaillant, *op. cit.*, p. 186.

[27] The authoritative work on the evangelization of Mexico in the sixteenth century is Robert Ricard, *La Conquista espiritual de México*. See particularly Chapters V and VI of the first book for pre-baptismal instruction and the administration of baptism. Since Toribio de Motolinía wrote his history during the middle of the 1530's, his treatment of the "rage of conversion" and the problems of instruction of the natives is particularly valuable for this

study. See Steck, *op. cit.*, pp. 103-105, 179-204, 245-250. Also valuable is Claudio Ceccherelli, O.F.M., *El bautismo y los franciscanos en México (1524-1539)* (Madrid, 1955).

[28] Haring, *The Spanish Empire*, p. 186.

[29] Steck, *op. cit.*, p. 179.

[30] *Ibid.*, pp. 182, 183.

[31] Haring, *op. cit.*, p. 186, cites Motolinía, *Historia de los Indios de la Nueva España*, Part Two, chapters 2-4.

[32] Steck, *op. cit.*, p. 186.

with the sign of the cross, the breathing, the salt, the saliva and the white cloth."[33] Each child was baptized separately and then each adult. During the ceremony some of the adults were questioned about their instruction. Motolinía said that many of the priests who administered baptism "were often unable to raise the pitcher with which they baptized because their arm was tired."[34]

Early methods of evangelizing and instruction of the Indian were experimental.[35] The prime requisite of any type of religious instruction was to inculcate the concept of monotheism and, in the words of Motolinía, "make them understand who God is."[36] The spiritual conquest had to be first of all destructive of the old religion and then instructive of the new.

Because of the lack of friar personnel and the language difficulty the instruction of necessity had to be elementary and deal only with fundamental tenets of the Christian religion. Besides the belief in one God, three other basic concepts were taught: the nature of the Trinity, the Incarnation, and the Virgin Birth.[37] Some prayers and devotionals and rules of Christian living were given the Indian to round out his instruction. Among these were the Pater Noster, the Ave Maria, the Credo, the Salve, reverence for the Cross, respect for the clergy, punctual attendance at Mass, and the "true character of the sacrament of marriage and the degrees of carnal and spiritual relationship permitted."[38] In some areas a modified type of confession was used.

The major difficulty that the friars faced in evangelizing the Indian was the language barrier.[39] "The missionaries . . . found it indispensable to master the dialects in order to transmit new religious concepts and abstruse theological ideas."[40] However, in the early years of the conquest period the problem was acute because there simply had not been time to absorb the new languages, and the Indian was doubly difficult to reach because he "hated the very name of Christ because the conquerors called themselves Christians."[41]

Consequently nonlingual methods of communication and instruction sometimes had to be adopted. Hieroglyphs were used by the clergy to instruct and by the Indian to reply to the instruction. Frequently,

[33] *Ibid.*, p. 186.
[34] *Ibid.*, p. 254.
[35] Particularly valuable for these methods are Ricard, *op. cit.*; Arthur L. Campa, "The Churchmen and the Indian Languages of New Spain," *Hispanic American Historical Review*, XI (1931), 542-550; France V. Scholes, "The Beginnings of Hispano-Indian Society in Yucatan," *The Scientific Monthly*, XLIV (1937) 530-538; and Steck, *op. cit.*, pp. 103-105, 179-186, 245-246. For the viewpoint of a priest, see Mulvihill, *op.*

*cit.*, pp. 146-153.
[36] Steck, *op. cit.*, p. 103.
[37] See Scholes, "Hispano-Indian Society," p. 536, and Steck, *op. cit.*, pp. 105, 245, 246, for added data on religious instruction.
[38] Scholes, "Hispano-Indian Society," p. 536.
[39] For the best general treatment of the language barrier and the problems of evangelization see Ricard, *op. cit.*, pp. 119-153.
[40] Campa, *op. cit.*, p. 544.
[41] *Ibid.*

illustrated scenes from the Bible were painted and used in the visual program.[42] Widespread use of pantomimes composed by the clergy and acted by the teacher and his Indian students also filled the language gap. Judicious use of chanting and music led to great success in evangelizing, but frequently the Indian came in for conversion and baptism because the music of the friars fascinated him and not because of his love of God.[43]

Very soon the Indians began to cope with the languages of their conquerors, both Spanish and Latin. They proved to be apt students in memorizing sounds and words, although they had no idea of the meanings attached to the new language. Campa gives two prime illustrations of this process.[44] Praying in Latin came to be an easy task for the native for he merely divided the prayer into units and used a pebble to represent each unit. Thus "Our Father" would be equal to one pebble and "which art in Heaven" to a second, and so on. Another technique used by the native was to associate the sounds of Latin with Nahuatl:

A word in Aztec that resembled the Latin was written in the usual hieroglyphical manner: for *Pater* they used *pantli* meaning banner, and painted a banner to represent it. For *Noster* they used *nochtli*, the name of a fruit (tuna) and placed it beside the previous one. With the aid of this mnemonic device the natives were able to memorize entire prayers without knowing what they were saying.[45]

Eventually these makeshift methods passed away as the Mexican churchmen began a systematic study of the native tongues.[46] Until the clergy became proficient they had to rely upon Indian interpreters whose Spanish was as imperfect as the clerical Nahuatl. Usually the priests memorized prayers and sermons which the interpreter had translated into Nahuatl. Campa concludes that the interpreter "must have offered a rather dubious channel for the transmission of abstruse doctrines,"[47] and he indicates that especially in the confessional there must have been many problems with the interpreter system.

Another problem which the spiritual conqueror of Mexico had to face was the fact that the Aztec and Christian religions had many outward similarities. The native affinity for pomp and ceremonialism fitted

---

[42] *Ibid.*, p. 546.
[43] Mulvihill, *op. cit.*, p. 166. In Steck, *op. cit.*, p. 296. Motolinía discusses the use of music in evangelizing.
[44] Campa, *op. cit.*, p. 546.
[45] Gerónimo de Mendieta, *Historia eclesiástica indiana* (México, 1870), Lib. III, cited by Campa, *op. cit.*, p. 546.
[46] There were three stages in dealing with the language problem. From 1519 to 1523 practically no attempt was made; from 1523 to 1530 the first handwritten works, such as the *Artes* and vocabularies, began to appear. This stage was the era of great research into Indian philology. Finally, from 1530 to 1550 the great grammars were being compiled; they were published in succeeding decades. The major Indian languages became a part of the curriculum in the seminaries by 1550. Campa, *op. cit.*, p. 548.
[47] *Ibid.*, p. 547.

in very well with Catholic ritual. Other similarities tended to cause grave problems in the Christianizing process.[48] For instance, the goddess Tonantzin and the Virgin Mary were often confused and, moreover, eventually amalgamated in the mind of the native. Bishop Zumárraga and the Franciscans were able to transfer this allegiance paid to Tonantzin to the Virgin of Guadalupe and to her shrine at Tepeyac which was built on top of the earlier native shrine to Tonantzin.[49] Even with this transfer of allegiance, the Indian thought Mary and God to be the same person and tended to call God and all of the images they saw Santa María.

The Spaniards frequently employed the word *papa* (derived from the Aztec *papatli*) as a general term for the native priests. Consequently the missionary clergy could not use the Latin *papa* (Pope) in religious instruction of the Indians; *Pontífice* (Pontiff) was always used instead.[50] The sacramental system of Christianity also encountered certain outward similarities in the Aztec ritual and tended for this reason to confuse the Indian and to help him remember the old belief.[51]

Despite the zealous conquistadors' destruction of public idols, idolatry and sacrifice continued in private and, for the most part, with the tacit consent of the civil government.[52] After 1524, however, every idol which could be found was confiscated; still the clandestine native practices continued and the calendar cycle with its pagan ceremonies continued to regulate the lives of the Mexicans.

Motolinía informs that in the 1530's the Indians concealed idols in every conceivable place, ". . . at the foot of the crosses or beneath the

[48] It should be noted that the following argument might also be reversed, namely that similarities in the two theologies *aided* the evangelization process. Indeed, missionaries were under general instructions to employ similarities in dogma as a device in evangelizing all over the world. Protestants have used the same techniques since the Reformation in some areas of the world.

[49] Motolinía does not mention Juan Diego, the native to whom the Virgin was reported to have appeared. Steck, *op. cit.*, pp. 103-104 *et passim*, appears to agree with García Icazbalceta on the problem of the *historicity* of the apparition. Neither man, however, was discussing theology. Readers should consult Joaquín García Icazbalceta's *Investigación histórica y documental sobre la aparición de la Virgen de Guadalupe* (México, c1950) for a denial of the historicity; and the official histories of the Virgin by Mariano Cuevas, S.J., *Al-*

*bum histórico guadalupano del IV centenario* (México, 1930), and Fortino Hipólito Vera, *Tesoro Guadalupano. Noticias de los libros, documentos, inscripciones que tratan, mencionan o aluden a la aparición de devoción de Nuestra Señora de Guadalupe* (2 vols.; México, 1887-1889).

[50] Steck, *op. cit.*, p. 99, note 3. The Aztec tern *papatli* referred to "the long and disheveled hair as worn by the ministers of the idols."

[51] The Indians of Mesoamerica had a kind of trinity, a concept of virgin birth, the use of a cross in their ritual, the use of blood in the same manner that Christians used holy water, a hierarchy of saints and martyrs, a kind of communion, a precept of abstinence, a ceremony of baptism, a type of confession, a concept of purgatory, and perhaps an inquisition.

[52] Motolinía indicated that the Spaniards allowed private sacrifice and idolatry from 1521 to 1524. Steck, *op. cit.*, p. 99.

stones of the altar-steps, pretending they were venerating the cross, whereas they were actually adoring the demon."[53] He goes on to describe current idolatry and sacrifice:

The idols, of which the Indians had very many, were set up in many places, in the temples of the demons, in the patios, and in conspicuous places, as in groves or on prominent hills and especially on mountain passes and summits; in short, wherever there was a high spot or place inviting to repose by reason of its loveliness. Those who passed by drew blood from their ears or tongue or offered a little of the incense, called *copalli*, which is found in this land; others offered roses which they gathered on the road; and when they had nothing else they offered a little green weed or some blades of grass.[54]

Shrines continued to be built and rebuilt at springs, large trees, and crossroads. The idols cached there resembled men, lions, jaguars, dogs, snakes, deer, and birds.

Besides the type of sacrifice described above by Motolinía, human sacrifices continued well into the colonial period. Human sacrifices as a general rule had been offered more to the Aztec war god Huitzilopochtli than to any other deity. Especially on an appointed day in the fourteenth month of the Aztec calendar (usually November of the Christian calendar) was the prominence of Huitzilopochtli evident to the Spaniards. It was in this month that the great feast of *Panquetzalistli* was celebrated in honor of the war god.[55] Sacrifices of animals and human blood were made. Despite harsh penalties meted out by Church and state alike to the natives this feast was repeatedly observed by the Mexicans.

Given the methods which the spiritual conquerors used in the era of 1520 to 1550 and the nature of the two religions between which the natives vacillated, it is not surprising that even the baptized Indians were caught in acts of recurrent idolatry and sacrifice. As Catholics, however, they were subject to the discipline of the Church for engaging in such activities.

III. *Zumárraga's Campaign Against Idolatry, Sacrifice, and Superstition: 1536-1540*

A. *The Case of Tacatetl and Tanixtetl, Native Priests
of Tanacopán, 1536*

Zumárraga began to chastise the natives for pagan practices within twenty-three days after he established his Holy Office of the Inquisition

[53] Steck, *op. cit.,* p. 107.
[54] *Ibid.* See pp. 114-115, 116-119 for added data on sacrifice, and pp. 136-140 for actual descriptions of *teocallis*, or temples.

[55] For the feast and sacrifices connected with *Panquetzalistli*, see Anderson and Dibble, *op. cit.*, p. 19.

in Mexico. A Spaniard, Lorenzo de Suárez, made the first denunciation against an Indian in Mexico City on June 28, 1536. Suárez held an encomienda in Tanacopán in the modern state of Hidalgo, and he accused Tacatetl and Tanixtetl of that village for practicing idolatry and offering sacrifices to the rain god, Tlaloc.[56]

Suárez related that he and a companion, Pedro de Borjas, some weeks past had witnessed and broken up pagan ceremonies which Tacatetl and Tanixtetl had initiated. Two youths who had been present had been bled and cut in the legs by Tacatetl, who was training them to be native priests. The boys had taken Borjas to a cave near the ceremonial place in which were found nine large idols and many sacrificial masks. Borjas, who testified along with Suárez, indicated that he had been informed by the natives that Tacatetl was an idolater and sacrificial priest; that he could turn himself into a jaguar; that he had led many of the faithful astray and had killed many without cause; and that he had a daughter by a goddess who collected tribute for him and the other papas.

On August 4, 1536, the Guardian of the Monastery at Tula and the Indians of that area testified to what they knew of Tacatetl and his companion Tanixtetl. They indicated that the two in question were never allowed near the monastery and that away from Tula they always avoided the papas. On August 12 Zumárraga ordered the arrest of the two native priests and brought them to Mexico City. The two native boys were also called in for testimony. The young men were frightened and crying, and they related that they had been intimidated by the accused who threatened to club them to death if they testified. They exhibited the sores on their legs made by the sacrificial knives, and they told Zumárraga that often blood from the ears and other parts of the body was used in the ceremonies. They declared that they were apprenticed to become native priests, that Tacatetl was their instructor, and that they had fasted and had actually seen Tacatetl become a jaguar and a dog with the aid of native potions called *patles*. As a final statement they related that they had seen Tacatetl and Tanixtetl sacrifice ten persons and take their human hearts to the idols for consumption.

With the aid of an Otomí interpreter Zumárraga proceeded to interrogate the two native priests on their life histories and their pagan activities. Tacatetl admitted that he had been baptized Antonio and that he understood Christian dogma and had even been to confession in Tula.

[56] AGN, Inquisición, Tomo 37, exp. 1. This *proceso* and several others cited hereafter have been published in *Procesos de Indios idólatras y hechiceros*, Vol. III of the *Publicaciones del Archivo General de la Nación* (México, 1912). In each case, however, care was taken to consult the original manuscript.

He admitted that he had committed incest with his daughter, had children by her, and was at present having relations with her and his two wives. The sacrifices which he made were directed to Tlaloc, the rain god, in order to alleviate a severe drought among his people. Three other *principales* of the area were implicated by Tacatetl[57] and he also admitted collecting tributes from the natives for the gods.

Tanixtetl testified that he was baptized Alonso in Tepeatepeque and he confirmed his part in the sacrificial ceremonies that Suárez and Borjas had interrupted, but he disclaimed any direct responsibility for leading others astray. He also related that Tacatetl's daughter, María, was adopted. Both defendants testified that all of the chiefs had idols hidden away but they refused to give details. In the end both men refused defense attorneys and pleaded for mercy because they said they had realized their sins.

María, the daughter of Tacatetl, confessed on September 7, 1536. She was not positive that she was his daughter but she gave full details of their conjugal life, and she pleaded ignorance of Christian doctrine on prohibited carnal relationships, indicating that Tacatetl had forced himself upon her.

Zumárraga decided to mete out a reasonably harsh penalty for these two Christians who had relapsed into paganism. They were mounted on burros, bound hand and foot and stripped to the waist, and taken through the streets of Mexico and Tlatelolco with a town crier proclaiming their crime in Spanish and Otomí. They were flogged in the marketplace and along the way. In the market of Tlatelolco they were shorn of their hair and half of their idols were burned publicly. Afterwards the two were returned to the market in Mexico City to witness the destruction of the remainder of the idols. They then were incarcerated in the Inquisition jail. Tacatetl was remanded to the guardian of the monastery at Tula for a three year confinement and his companion Tanixtetl served a year in the same establishment. Both were to do penance and receive instruction in basic dogma. They were furthermore exiled from Tanacopán for an indefinite period with the threat that if they traveled within a five-league radius of the village they would receive a life sentence in jail. They were admonished that the stake awaited them should they again practice idolatry. María, the daughter of Tacatetl, was sent to the Monastery of Santa Clara for instruction. These sentences were carried out between September 25, 1536, and October 23, 1536.

---

[57] Of these three, one Mixcoatl was later brought to trial. See *infra*.

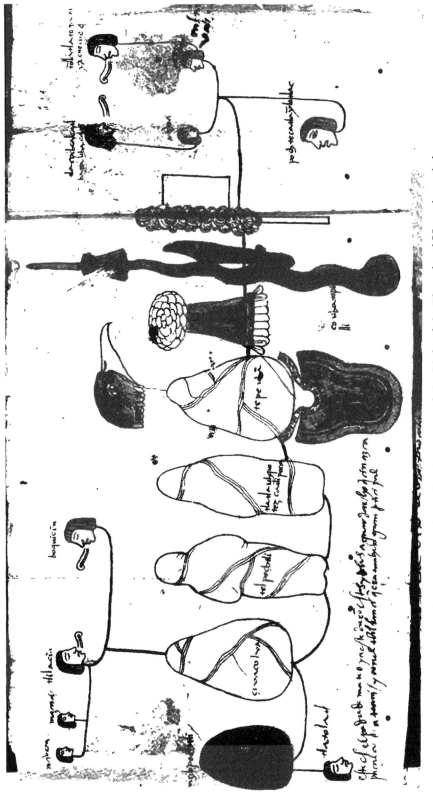

Indian Painting describing the dispersion of the Idols of the Temple of Hutzilopochtli

(Bound in the Proceso against Puxtecatl Tlaylotla in AGN,
Tomo 37, exp. 3  See Chapter III, part III, section E, note 67)

## B. *The Trial of Ocelotl, Mixcoatl, and Papalotl* *for Sorcery*

Within a month after the close of the trial of Tacatetl and Tanixtetl, Zumárraga conducted his first major sorcery trial of an Indian. Indians of the Texcoco area and the states of Hidalgo and Tlaxcala submitted repeated denunciations of a nomadic sorcerer whose name was Ocelotl in Nahuatl and Ucelo in Spanish.[58] Testimony revealed that Ocelotl had performed many sorceries and could foresee the future, and that he was able to transform himself into jaguars, lions, and dogs. He admitted to the natives that he often talked to the devil at night, and he was a dogmatizer, that is, he taught the natives many things contrary to the faith. The friars of the various monastic houses were convinced that Ocelotl had by word and deed impeded the Christianization process.

Ocelotl was greatly respected and feared by the native population because he declared that he was immortal and that the clouds were his brothers and he controlled their rain. He had predicted great famines and droughts and urged the planting of more food for the future. The Indians actually worshipped him as a god because he could prophesy and cure illness; they gave him tribute for his services. He often preached against the teachings of the friars and told the natives of apostles who had come down from heaven and commanded that they return to the old religion.

There was evidence that Ocelotl had incited riot and rebellion and that he encouraged sacrifice and sexual immorality by his own reprehensible conduct. He performed most of his ceremonies in mountain caves. That Ocelotl was a major papa was very obvious from the testimony. It was even ascertained that he was an active warlock before the conquest and that the great Montezuma had imprisoned him for a year and twelve days because, he said, he had predicted the downfall of the Aztec Empire, indeed, the very coming of the Spaniards.

Since Ocelotl was a baptized Catholic and because he had continued his sorceries and had deified himself, the Franciscan friars Pedro de Gante and Antonio de Ciudad Real believed that he was jeopardizing the missionary movement and they recommended that he be banished from New Spain. Ocelotl refused to admit his guilt and tried to vitiate the above testimonies by admitting the circumstances but altering the context of what occurred. The fiscal, Dr. Rafael de Cervanes, demanded the full sanctions of the Holy Office.

Ocelotl was unable to refute the total testimony before Zumárraga,

[58] Ucelo was obviously a corruption of Ocelotl.

and the Apostolic Inquisitor deemed the banishment necessary. On February 10, 1537, Ocelotl was given the usual burro ride through Mexico City with a town crier proclaiming his offense, and later that month he was taken to Veracruz and placed in a ships' brig to be transported to Sevilla, where he was to spend the remainder of his life in jail. His properties, of which there were vast quantities of jewels, were confiscated and sold by the Holy Office on March 27, 1535.[59] Unfortunately, Zumárraga had not heard the last of Ocelotl, because after his banishment reports persisted that he was still performing his rites in the area from Tulancingo to Huauchinango, and the investigation of these tales provided the Holy Office with its next case.

On July 10, 1537, Don Juan, the cacique of Xinantepec, denounced two individuals whom he thought to be the brothers of Ocelotl for idolatry and sorcery; their names were Mixcoatl and Papalotl.[60] Apparently Mixcoatl at times passed himself off as Ocelotl's brother, or as Ocelotl himself. He also claimed to be the brother of Tlaloc who controlled the winds, but who was in his own (Mixcoatl's) power. Papalotl had been the servant of Ocelotl, and at this time (July, 1537) was Mixcoatl's cohort.[61] Both of these men had convinced the natives of the mountainous and coastal regions to the east that because Tlaloc was hungry he sent fire, floods, winds, and snow to destroy their crops. Because of his control over Tlaloc, Mixcoatl acted as intermediary in the sacrificial rites to the rain god.

In some areas Mixcoatl himself was believed to be a god because people knelt before him, sacrificed to him, and endowed him with houses and fertile land in each of their villages.

Mixcoatl was greatly aided in his calling by the very erratic climatic conditions in the area. In the middle of the 1530's rain destroyed the maize and cotton crops and presented him with an ideal situation for becoming a god. His fame was so great that he had bands of disciples who followed him from place to place; indeed, in imitation of Christ he frequently said, "ídos conmigo." Fray Francisco Marmolejo of the monastery of Tulancingo testified that among his people Mixcoatl was regarded as a rain god and was also called Tezcatlipoca, and that the natives sacrificed to him.[62] He made it rain in Metepec and thus saved the corn

[59] For one of the few modern studies of Inquisition materials and a reproduction of the native hieroglyphic inventory of Ocelotl's jewels, See Robert Barlow, "Las Joyas de Martín Ocelotl," *Yan* (1954), pp. 56-59. Barlow relates the story that Ocelotl never reached Spain, having been lost at sea.

[60] AGN, Inquisición, Tomo 38, exp. IA.

[61] At times Papalotl traversed the area proclaiming that Mixcoatl was Ocelotl in disguise and that he now served him. Papalotl shared complicity in the idolatry and sacrifices made by his master.

[62] On August 19, 1537, Father Marmolejo testified, "Muchos pueblos . . . saben como el dicho Andrés, y en nombre de indio Mixcoatl, se hacía dios, y cómo por él llovía, y se hacen todas cosas, y pedía muchas cosas, para quel el sacrificasen."

crop from a severe drought. He told Marmolejo that he could recite incantations which would make it rain or cease to rain and that he could change the direction of clouds. When the natives resisted or displeased him, he made it rain so hard that rivers were formed and whole sections of villages were inundated.

The miracles of Mixcoatl were not limited exclusively to climatic deeds; he was also known far and wide as a doctor and a magician. He cured children and adults with his native remedies for pay, and he was known as far as the coastal plain city of Papantla. He ate weeds that produced visions and aided him in communicating with the occult. The natives were extremely impressed that he could place parts of his body in the fire without being burned. All of these rites were in some way connected with idolatry, and Mixcoatl made use of numerous caves filled with idols where he made sacrifices and the natives sacrificed to him.

Besides participating in superstitious rites, Mixcoatl was also a violent foe of the friars and their mission program. He had preached openly against the Christians in Tulancingo, Huauchinango, and Papantla, criticizing the faith. Mixcoatl urged the natives to resist baptism and to refuse to learn the articles of the faith. He assisted them in making darts which were to be shot at the friars. In a letter to Zumárraga dated September 12, 1537, from Tulancingo, the Franciscan Fray Francisco de Lintone recounted the danger of Mixcoatl and Papalotl to the progress of the faith. Lintone informed Zumárraga that he had arrested the two men and was sending them to Mexico City for trial. Lintone related that the disciples of Mixcoatl were being punished locally.

In September 1537 Mixcoatl testified in his defense before Zumárraga. He indicated that he was a baptized Christian and that he had been instructed in the faith for six or seven days in Texcoco. He admitted dogmatizing against the friars for a period of three years and that he had preached publicly in Tulancingo and other places. The defendant blandly told the Inquisitor that he had been a god to be satiated by idolatry and sacrifice and that he could make it rain. He recounted conversations with the demon and he admitted receiving a regular tribute from the natives.

Mixcoatl contended, however, that human sacrifices had never been a part of his ritual and that he had stopped all of his sorceries because he had realized that they were sinful and that the devil had deceived him. He asked God's mercy, and Zumárraga's, and earnestly confirmed his belief in Christianity and his desire to be a good Christian. The Holy Office immediately embargoed his properties, which included houses in Zacatepec, Metepeque, Thecincoqpeque, Atiztaca, Chiautla, plus certain other arable land scattered throughout the region.

On September 20, 1537, Papalotl testified that he was a Christian, baptized for over a year, and that he had heard instructions in the things of the faith. He had been a servant of Martín Ucelo (Ocelotl) for three years and that the latter had sent him many places on errands, and he, Papalotl, had believed all that Ocelotl taught. He knew that his former master had been banished to Castilla but he had been deceived by Mixcoatl of Tulancingo, who said that Ocelotl was not gone but had merely changed to the form of Mixcoatl.

On December 15 the sentence of the Holy Office of the Inquisition was pronounced upon Mixcoatl and Papalotl. Both were tied on burros and taken through Mexico City while a town crier proclaimed their shame. They were each given one hundred lashes in the market place and then they were transported to the villages in which they had preached to receive added whippings and to publicly abjure their sins and the heresies they had preached. In each town they swore not to return to their pagan practices upon pain of being burned at the stake. Their heads were shorn and they began a year of incarceration in the monastery of Tulancingo, where they were to study and do penance. The Guardian of Tulancingo was given the power to absolve and reconcile them. On December 15, 1537, Mixcoatl's lands and possessions were sold and the funds were diverted into the treasury of the Holy Office. Papalotl's lands were also inventoried and sold on December 15 to Isabel, the wife of the cacique of Tulancingo, for forty *tomines* which the Holy Office collected as a fine from Papalotl.

## C. *The Idolaters of Atzcapozalco*

Prior to the conclusion of the trial of Mixcoatl, Zumárraga had begun the investigation of idolatry in the village of Atzcapozalco, a modern suburb of Mexico City.[63] It was not until November 19, 1538, that formal charges were made. On that day, an Indian alguacil of Atzcapozalco appeared before Zumárraga with certain idols and sacrifical objects which he had uncovered in a house of the village. He brought along several of the residents whom he had arrested for idolatry. Among these were Juan, who had guarded the idols and had sacrificed and fasted for them, and three prominent elders who had ordered the ceremonies and sacrifices to be made.[64]

Juan testified that Tacatecle had ordered a one hundred day fast for a good corn crop and that he had in his home three idols: Huichilobos (Huitzilopochtli), Cialeuque, and Tlalocatecle (Tlaloc). Juan said that the had seen blood on the lips of the idol Huitzilopochtli, and that

[63] AGN, Inquisición, Tomo 37, exp. 2.
[64] These three were Tacuxcalcatl, baptized Martín; Huycanaval, baptized Francisco; and Tacatecle, baptized Pedro.

the idols were inlaid with turquoise and precious stones. Juan mentioned idols concealed in the houses of other *principales* of the village. A search was made for the idols at night and the properties of the three chiefs were confiscated.

Pedro, another Indian of Atzcapozalco, testified about the hundred-day fast. The fast was directed to Tezcatlipoca, and the three defendants made Pedro fast for one hundred days while they ate. Pedro and two others were enclosed in a house where there were no women and they burnt incense once daily and twice nightly with intermittent offerings of copal to the god Tezcatlipoca. Tortillas were also offered and then were eaten by the men after the fast, or were distributed to the boys of the neighborhood as blessed bread.

The three *principales* who possessed the idols and had ordered the fasting and other ceremonies were without any possible defense. One defendant, Martín, testified that he was a Christian, baptized ten years ago, and that he and two others had ordered the fasting. He said that he realized that the devil had been deceiving him for four years and that he had carried on these ceremonies and others without realizing his sin. Now he asked forgiveness, pleaded for mercy, and swore that he would henceforth be a model Christian. The other two gave substantially the same testimonies and the defense attorney threw the defendants on Zumárraga's mercy.

On November 22, 1538, Zumárraga passed sentence. The three convicted were to appear on Sunday, November 24, in church, gagged, with *corozas* on their heads and lighted candles in their hands, and were to stand during the Mass and be the subject of a sermon on their errors; they were then to abjure their sins publicly before the congregation. Since this was a first offense, Zumárraga prescribed that they could be reconciled, but he warned that recurrent idolatry would mean death at the stake. Their property was to be confiscated, and on November 23 they were given one hundred lashes each in the market place of Mexico City and their hair was shorn. On Sunday, November 24, 1538, Zumárraga preached the sermon at Atzcapozalco and the three Indians fulfilled their penance, kneeling and abjuring their sins. The idols and sacrificial paraphernalia were then burned before the assembled populace.

## D. *The Case of Ana, Curandera of Xochimilco*

The only case in which an Indian woman was specially tried by Zumárraga occurred in April of 1538 when Ana of Xochimilco was convicted of being a *curandera*.[65] The denunciation was made by Elvira

[65] "Proceso del Santo Oficio contra una India Curandera," *Boletín del Archivo*

Herrera, wife of Diego Olguín, on April 2, 1538. She accused Ana of
coming to her home to cure a sick woman and of performing sorceries
over the patient and invoking the god of the sorcerers, Tezcatlipoca.[66]
The rites were witnessed by Marta and Catalina, servants of the household.

On April 12, 1538, Ana of Xochimilco was brought before Zumárraga for questioning. She admitted that she was a *curandera* and that she
had performed other such services ("e que ha echado dos veces suertes
con maices para ver si saneba o moría un niño"). Ana confirmed that
she had cured one Isabel in the house of Elvira Herrera, but she indicated
that the illness had not really been caused by Tezcatlipoca. Ana complained that this god had deceived her, that she was truly contrite, and
that she had heard the friars preach against sorcery because she had been
a Christian for eight years.

Zumárraga decided to make an example of Ana of Xochimilco so
that other women would not be inclined to engage in similar rites. She
was made to wear the *coroza* and to stand with a candle in her hand and
hear Mass. At a later time she rode through the streets of Mexico City
and its market with a town crier reading the sentence and she was given
one hundred lashes on her bare back to serve as an example for others.
On April 15, 1538, these sentences were carried out and Zumárraga was
informed of Ana's compliance.

## E. *The Search for Idols and Trials for Idolatry*

As the 1530's came to a close the Holy Office became increasingly
concerned with the problem of hidden idols and the practice of idolatry
and sacrifice in private. Every effort was made to ferret these idols out
from their hiding-places. From composite testimonies of the natives during Inquisition trials of the years 1536 to 1540, it would appear that
many of the idols from the temples of Tenochtitlán were taken from
Mexico City and hidden in various villages of the provinces. Other
testimonies revealed that there were caches of idols still in the city. The
Indians were very devious when they were questioned about the idols,
and even the use of rigorous torture failed to make them divulge the
hiding-places of the Huitzilopochtlis, as they called them. Zumárraga or
his delegates initiated five interesting cases in the two years 1539 and 1540

---

*General de la Nación*, XII (1941), 211-214.
The original is in the *legajos sueltos* of the
AGN.

[66] ... la cual india curantera sahumó a
la enferma y le rució con un poco de agua,
y después pelliscábale el cuerpo y de cada
pellizco le sacaba a la enferma un bocado
de papel tan grueso como el dedo pulgar;
y decía que el diablo Tezcatlepuca había
topado con esta enferma y le había hech-
ado mal y aquellos papeles en el cuerpo,
los cuales eran de aquellos que ella
sacaba ...

in order to find the hidden idols. In 1539 Puxtecatl Tlaylotla (Miguel) of Mexico City; Cristóbal, Catalina, and Hernando of Ocuituco; Tlilanci of Azucar; the cacique of Matlatlan; and Baltasar, cacique of Culoacán were brought to trial. The year 1540 brought a continuation of these cases, but success in finding the idols was negligible.

On June 20, 1539, Mateos, an Indian painter, related to the Holy Office that when Tenochtitlán was captured by the Spaniards the idols of the Temple of Huitzilopochtli were taken to the home of Puxtecatl Tlaylotla of the Barrio of San Juan in Mexico City for safe keeping. Mateos and the Inquisitors believed that the idols should be found and destroyed for the good of the Christianization process. As a consequence of this denunciation Zumárraga began a *proceso* against the denounced Tlaylotla, whose Christian name was Miguel.[67]

Initial testimony revealed that the idols in question were first taken to Atzcapozalco and Tula but that with the passage of time Miguel inherited the post of protector of the idols. The accused denied any knowledge of the disposition of the effects of the Temple Huitzilopochtli. Later he was forced to admit that certain packages had been brought to his house but that he had not known their contents, but that afterwards Indians came to worship the idols and had taken them away from the house. The fiscal of the Holy Office was not at all satisfied with this version of the story and accused Tlaylotla of concealing the idols, adoring and sacrificing to them, and he further alleged that the defendant knew where they were at the time of the trial. Dr. Cervanes then asked extreme penalties for this heretic and idolater.

On August 22, 1539, Vicencio de Riverol, the court-appointed defense attorney for Miguel, answered the fiscal's charges. Riverol contended that the fiscal had no real evidence as to specific facts or dates. Furthermore, Miguel contended that since the events occurred prior to his baptism, he could in no way be considered culpable before the Holy Office of the Inquisition. The defense attorney asked a dismissal of the case on these grounds. When Zumárraga refused to admit Riverol's plea, the defense attorney in the name of his client asked for thirty days to build his defense and secure Indian witnesses. He also requested and received the services of Fray Bernardino de Sahagún as consultant on the case. When the prescribed time had elapsed and the defense was still not ready, Zumárraga not only refused an extension of time for the defense to build the case, but he also proposed to use torture on Tlaylotla to get at the truth.

[67] AGN, Inquisición, Tomo 37, exp. 3. See Donald Robertson, *Mexican Manuscript Painting of the Early Colonial Period: the Metropolitan Schools* (New Haven, 1959), pp. 35-36, for a discussion of some of the native painters involved in the following Inquisition trials.

On January 30, 1540, Tlaylotla filed a deposition to the effect that torture was unjust because of the meager evidence against him, but on March 16, 1540, he consented to the torture and pleaded that it be deferred because he was a sick man. Zumárraga was amenable to postponing the torture but not to dismissing its use. Consequently on May 21, 1540, Tlaylotla was taken to the torture chamber, stripped naked, and tied to the rack. The garrotes were employed three times, but the defendant denied any knowledge of the hidden idols of the Temple of Huitzilopochtli.

Although the sentence of torture was unsuccessful in getting at the truth, Zumárraga was still in grave doubt as to the complete innocence of Miguel Tlaylotla. Consequently he decreed that Miguel should be incarcerated in the monastery of San Francisco under the care of Fray Pedro de Gante for an indefinite time, or until he should remember where the idols were hidden. He was also to be fully instructed in the faith and charged not to leave the monastery without the express permission of Zumárraga. The Inquisition archive bears no additional information on the case of Miguel Tlaylotla.

Zumárraga apparently had information to the effect that some of the idols in question were hidden in the village of Ocuituco, and he sent his special *visitador*, Juan González, to the area to make investigations. González uncovered evidence that the cacique of Ocuituco, whose name in Spanish was Cristóbal, his wife Catalina, and his brother Martín were guilty of concealing idols and other crimes.[68] Servants of the cacique testified that he had married the sister of his first wife without the dispensation of the Church and that he worshipped the stars and sacrificed to them. He frequently burned copal and sacrificed the blood of chickens to Tlaloc and Tezcatlipoca. Francisco Coatl, one of the servants, indicated that Cristóbal had hidden idols and charged him to guard and protect them. Others revealed that Cristóbal imposed excessive tributes on the villagers and that he got intoxicated and performed the ancient rites as a papa with his wife assisting him on occasion. These rites he performed in twenty-day cycles, and he frequently married couples in pagan ceremonies which did not take into account the mandates of the Church.[69]

Cristóbal testified after his arrest that he had married Catalina according to Church requirements and that he was a Christian of ten

[68] AGN, Inquisición, Tomo 30, exp. 9.

[69] González was assisted in gathering the initial information in this trial by Diego Díaz, the parish priest at Ocuituco. Díaz himself fell prey to the Inquisition in the years to come. He was a disreputable character who solicited women in the confessional and bore false witness against the Indians. It was ascertained later that Díaz fabricated some of the testimony in this case. See Chapter VII.

years standing. He admitted marrying his sister-in-law without permission. Although he contended that he knew the Ave, Pater Noster, and the Credo, he did them very poorly. He said that he had been to confession only once because he had been so busy gathering tributes for the Spaniards. He denied the major part of the damaging testimony given by the servants: his post-baptism idolatry, drunken orgies in which he acted as a papa, hiding idols, and sacrificing chicken blood. He admitted that he had performed pagan marriage ceremonies without benefit of the Church. When confronted at the trial with idols that had been hidden in his area, he disclaimed any knowledge of them, but nevertheless he knew their names, Tlaloc and Chicomecoatl. Cristóbal defended this knowledge on the grounds that many people buried and guarded idols and that the entire area in which he lived was rife with sorcery. He named sites and individuals who, he said, had hidden idols.

Catalina, the wife of the cacique, testified that she was a Christian and that she understood that the carnal relationship she enjoyed with Cristóbal was prohibited by the Church. She professed to know the Ave, the Pater Noster, and the Credo, but she was unable to recite them adequately. Catalina indicated that she had been an idolater and sacrificer and that she had given idols to her servant, Tomás Coatl. She implicated her husband when she said he knew of the hidden idols because his father had willed them to him. Catalina denied knowledge of specific idols that she was confronted with at the trial, but she named Miguel of Ocuituco as an idolater. She also admitted having sacrificed to the gods after her husband's arrest in order to abate the anger of the Inquisitors.

The Visitor González sent Cristóbal, Catalina, and Martín and some of their idols, including a gold one, to Mexico City. They appeared before Zumárraga in the first week of September, 1539. Cristóbal and Catalina made no additional pleas, but the brother, Martín, denied any complicity in the idolatry. After rigorous questioning, he retracted his denial and admitted his part in the ceremonies, asking the lenience and pardon of Zumárraga.

On October 11, 1539, Zumárraga pronounced sentence. This sentence is somewhat unique for our period because it involved a forced labor provision, and we are told at the end of the *proceso* how the labor sentence was carried out.

On a feast day to be prescribed by the Holy Office, Cristóbal, Catalina and Martín were to stand barefoot during Mass with candles in their hands, and they were to receive one hundred lashes each in the streets of Mexico City the following day. Cristóbal and Martín were sentenced to three and two years respectively of work with pick and shovel on a chain gang in the mines, and they were exiled for the period of their sentence from Ocuituco. They were required to pay the costs of the trial. On October 12, the sentence was carried out.

The labor services of Cristóbal and Martín were auctioned off in the Zócalo of Mexico City by Juan González, the *pregonero*. It took four days to dispose of their labor services. On November 6, Diego del Castillo offered seven *pesos de oro de minas* for each Indian per year, but on November 8, Andrés de Salinas offered eight pesos. Finally the Indians were rented to Diego González, a merchant, on November 10, 1539, who paid twelve *pesos de oro de minas* a year for each man. It was stipulated that if Cristóbal or Martín escaped or died González was to be reimbursed on a pro rata basis. The money was then deposited with the treasury of the Holy Office of the Inquisición.

On March 16, 1540, the Indian Cristóbal was again brought before Zumárraga because he had left the mines and returned to Catalina in Ocuituco for something to eat. Zumárraga remanded him to the mines to fulfill his sentence and informed him that if he again returned to his village before his three years had elapsed he would be relaxed to the secular arm and his entire properties would be confiscated. Cristóbal was also charged not to return to his pagan practices or to take free Indians to the mines with him to do his work.

Tlilanci, an Indian of the pueblo of Izucar, was the next suspect processed in the search for hidden idols.[70] The evidence was gathered by the vicar of Izucar and comisario of the Holy Office, Fray Hernando de Oviedo. On September 13, 1539, Oviedo had questioned the principal figures of the village, and the composite testimony revealed that Tlilanci's father had been the keeper of the idols in the major temple of Izucar and that upon his death the son had assumed the duty. On that same day Oviedo framed the charges and asked the full penalty for Tlilanci's idolatries and sacrifices. On September 15, 1539, Oviedo interrogated Tlilanci in Izucar and learned that the latter was baptized and that he and his father had been native priests prior to their conversion. Tlilanci admitted that he had sacrificed eight young boys to the gods but said that after his father's death he had left his duties as priest and that he had no knowledge of a cave of idols or the hidden idols of the Izucar temple.

A day later, in order to ascertain the truth of Tlilanci's statement, Father Oviedo prescribed torture. Aften an exhortation to tell the truth, Tlilanci was stripped and tied on a stairway and was submitted to the water torture (*los jarros*). On receiving the third jar of water Tlilanci confessed that the idols were hidden by Don Alonso of Quazalcalco and he mentioned other areas where there were caches of idols, especially in

[70] AGN, Inquisición, Tomo 37, exp. 4 bis.

caves. With this confession Oviedo allowed Tlilanci his freedom until the stories could be verified.

When the idols were sought out, it became obvious to Oviedo that Tlilanci had lied, and he had him arrested again and sent him to Mexico City for trial before Zumárraga. On October 14, 1539, the fiscal made his accusation. The charges were essentially the same that had been made in Izucar: that Tlilanci had performed idolarty and sacrifices; that he had hidden idols and had refused to tell where they were; and that he had been a native priest with full ceremonial powers. The fiscal asked the full penalty for Tlilanci.

On March 16, 1540, Tlilanci's defense attorney, the Licenciate Téllez, concluded a series of demands upon the Holy Office to free his client. Téllez denied that any of the charges against Tlilanci had any validity because they all pertained to the period before the Indian's conversion and baptism. Tlilanci insisted that since his baptism he had remained a good Christian and had committed no crime against the faith. Character witnesses in behalf of the defendant were heard. Téllez insisted that no charge against his client had been substantiated and that the witnesses of the prosecution bore Tlilanci ill will. Zumárraga was again petitioned to set the accused free. On this same day Zumárraga announced his decision. Tlilanci was granted absolution because the fiscal had failed to prove his charges. The case was dismissed.

Fray Andrés de Olmos, a life-long friend of the Apostolic Inquisitor and his cohort in the Pamplona witch trials, was sent to the village of Matlatlán, an encomienda of Francisco de Montejo, the conqueror of Yucatán, to investigate reports of hidden idols.[71] Olmos reported to Zumárraga that the cacique of Matlatlán was an evil man who practiced idolatry and made sacrifices. Olmos, as Zumárraga's delegate, was later empowered to prosecute the cacique on the spot. Servants of the chief and Indians of the village indicated that the cacique had hidden idols of the village and that he saw to their protection. Olmos was able to learn little more of the idols but he carried on the trial of the chief on other more concrete charges.

Testimony revealed that the cacique was a baptized Catholic, married according to the Church, but despite this he had between seventeen and twenty concubines, including some close relatives. He was an inveterate drunkard and he encouraged his subjects to get intoxicated. He seldom went near the church and prevented the baptism of his children. On a recent Sunday he had celebrated the feast of Panquetzalistli in which he sacrificed a chicken in his house while his subjects sacrificed dogs. He had performed sorceries to cure his ill daughter.

[71] AGN, Inquisición, Tomo 40, exp. 8.

The cacique blatantly admitted his crimes when it came time for his testimony. In late November Olmos passed sentence. In view of the incontrovertible evidence and the confession of the defendant, it would appear that Olmos' sentence was very lenient. The entire village had been placed under the ban of excommunication, but Olmos lifted it after a few of the more delinquent did penance. The alguacil was instructed to cut the cacique's hair and to give him one hundred lashes. In addition the cacique was required to attend the school for children in Huetalapa to be taught the Credo and Scripture.

Zumárraga's final effort as Inquisitor to uncover and destroy hidden idols was his investigation of the cacique Don Baltasar of Culoacán in December of 1539.[72] Baltasar indicated that sixteen years previously the Ochilobos (idols of the Temple of Huitzilopochtli) were brought to his village for a period of six days and then they were scattered among caves throughout the provinces. Apparently a son of Montezuma had delivered them and had supervised their dispersal. Baltasar also gave vague data on other caves and sacrificial sites in the Mexican provinces, but no other action of the Holy Office seems to have been taken according to the records of the Zumárraga period.

## F. *Investigations of the Caciques of Tlapanaloa and Iguala*

Two other caciques had altercations with the Holy Office in the period 1538 to 1540, but the records yield only the *informaciones* or *denuncias* of the two cases and we have no way of knowing if the two chieftains were tried or not. On October 19, 1538, Fray Bernardo de Isla at the order of Zumárraga launched an investigation of the crimes of Don Diego, the cacique of Tlapanaloa.[73] Diego was charged mostly with sexual immorality, but the testimonies also revealed that he had dogmatized against the faith. He had been baptized for eight years at the time of the investigation, and he was apparently intelligent enough to grasp the faith, but he did not know the Pater Noster or the Ave Maria.

One witness alleged that Diego had had the body of a woman who had been sacrificed in his home, but Diego indicated that she was dead upon arrival at his home and that he merely certified to her death. It was admitted by the cacique that he had at least six wives and that three of these were sisters. There were innumerable offspring from these relationships. It was further ascertained that Diego had taken his sister as a concubine and she had borne him a child. Although sodomy was implied in the testimony, Diego was cleared of the charge. He was accused of performing an abortion on a slave whom he had gotten pregnant, and when

---

[72] AGN, Inquisición, Tomo, 42, exp. 18.     [73] AGN, Inquisición, Tomo 40, exp. 2.

the abortion was accomplished there were three recognizable fetuses involved! Diego admitted that one of his slaves had aborted, but he denied any part in the proceedings. It was established that Diego was in the habit of taking the wives of other Indians and that he initiated a system of forced swapping of wives in his village. He had put those couples in stocks who refused to submit to the exchange.

Several other charges of a more serious character were levelled against Diego. Because of the outrages with other men's wives and his forced tributary levies on the natives, it was contended that the village was quickly being depopulated. In addition, the cacique by example and deed exhibited a very definite anti-Church policy. He refused to allow his subjects to go to Mass; indeed he often drove them away from the church by force. Diego was deficient in his knowledge of the faith. It was evident that he had pilfered the tithe and used village revenues to build two new wings on his house while the church, which had been under construction for six years, was still unfinished. In view of these rather grave charges it seems strange that Zumárraga did not choose to try the cacique of Tlapanaloa. We have no record past the fact-finding stage that the Holy Office ever prosecuted.

The other cacique who was investigated but not tried was Don Juan of Iguala.[74] His crimes were so atrocious that his wife Doña Ana, and two *principales* of the village made a pilgrimage to Mexico City and denounced Don Juan on July 16, 1540. His maltreatment of the natives of Iguala was common knowledge, and even the former president of the audiencia, Ramírez de Fuenleal, in league with the friars of Cuernavaca, had repeatedly enjoined Don Juan to reform. Despite the fact that Juan had been threatened with the stake, he continued his abusive administration.

Viewing the composite testimony, Don Juan appears to us as a type of sexual athlete apparently without any moral fiber at all. He had actually raped two women in the church at Iguala during Lent, as well as a child of ten years of age sometime thereafter. He had untold concubines, and he took with carnal intent the sister of his legal wife, beating her into submission. Furthermore, he had relations with another sister of his wife who was a natural daughter of his own father—and with her aunt. He kept at least five concubines in his house and insisted that his wife live with the harem, treating her with no more respect than a dog.

Idolatry and sacrifice, accompanied with the usual pagan ceremonies, were practiced publicly in Iguala at Don Juan's command. The people burned copal, gave roses, and offered human blood from the ears, tongue, and other parts of the body. Don Juan customarily burned

[74] AGN, Inquisición, Tomo 40, exp. 7.

copal to the old gods and kept an official sorcerer in his home. When his sister died, Juan had an image of her placed in his house and daily laid offerings of chicken blood at its feet.

Don Juan steadfastly opposed the mission process. He made jokes about the Cross and the natives' crossing of themselves. He refused to let a child of his own house be baptized, and when the child died he buried it under a grain bin, thus, said the record, depriving it of the salvation Christianity offered. He made the *principales* and *vecinos* eat meat on Fridays in defiance of the teachings of the friars.

Doña Ana and her companions testified that all of these scandalous activities had taken place in the last two to three years, and Doña Ana pleaded not to be returned to Iguala as the cacique's wife.

Perhaps because of the factor of distance and perhaps because of lack of personnel, Zumárraga was unusually lax in initiating proceedings against Don Juan. He was merely notified that the Holy Office was taking mercy on him for his crimes but that if in the future he continued his sinful ways, he would be punished according to the law. We have no inkling of the future relations between Don Juan and Zumárraga's Holy Office.

### IV. *A Case of Bigamy*

It was rarely that Zumárraga proceeded against an Indian for bigamy charges alone, but in the case of Martín Xuchimitl of Coyoacán the Inquisitor made an exception.[75] It came to the notice of the Holy Office that Martín had defied the Church and married twice, and that both wives were still alive. On October 11, 1538, Martín was brought before Zumárraga, and he testified that his first wife, Ana, whom he had married seven years previously, had been discarded by him and that he had married María three years ago. He had been kind enough to secure another husband for Ana after he left her. Both wives testified to substantiate Martín's remarks. The defense attorney placed the defendant upon the mercy of the court.

Zumárraga meted out a reasonably harsh punishment to the bigamist from Coyoacán. He was bound hand and foot and taken through the streets while the offense was proclaimed in Spanish and Nahuatl. At the market he was given one hundred lashes. He had to pay the costs of the trial and he forfeited half of his property. Ana was returned to Martín as his legal wife and he was warned not to return to María again upon pain of being relaxed to the secular arm for burning.

[75] AGN, Inquisición, Tomo 23, exp. 1.

# CHAPTER IV

# The Indians and the Inquisition
# 1536-1543

# (Part Two)

### V. *The Dogmatizers Marcos and Francisco of Tlatelolco*

Perhaps the major concern of Zumárraga's Holy Office was with the native dogmatizers, those who preached against the teachings of the missionary friars and urged the Indians to return to paganism. These individuals could not be tolerated by the Mexican Inquisition nor could they be allowed to remain in contact with the native population. The year 1539 was a decisive phase in Zumárraga's campaign against dogmatizers. It ended with the burning of Don Carlos, the cacique of Texcoco.

Preceding the celebrated trial of Don Carlos, two other Indian dogmatizers, Marcos and Francisco of Tlatelolco, were sentenced by Zumárraga.[1] On May 30, 1539, Marcos Hernández Altaucatl was questioned by the Apostolic Inquisitor. Marcos testified that he was a Christian and a native judge for the Tlatelolco district of Mexico City, appointed by Viceroy Mendoza. Marcos admitted that he kept concubines and that the friars had repeatedly urged him to dismiss them. However, he denied the dogmatizing charges: that he had criticized the teachings of the Franciscans and had cast aspersions on their sexual morality. From the testimony it became apparent that both Marcos and Francisco had ridiculed the friars to the native congregations. They had taught that the Franciscans had invented the sacrament of confession, and that it was the friar and not God who wanted to know of the sins of others.

Francisco testified on June 6, 1539, that he had been a baptized

---

[1] AGN, Inquisición, Tomo 42, exp. 17. The Marcos and Francisco *proceso* is fragmentary. It contains only the testimonies of the defendants and the final sentence.

Christian for eighteen years and that he was acquainted with Marcos. He stubbornly denied the dogmatizing charge but he admitted that he heard one Lorenzo of Tlaxcala ridicule the sacrament of confession. He swore that he had not repeated Lorenzo's ideas to anyone.

On June 20, Marcos Hernández was admonished to tell the truth and escape torture. He confessed to being a dogmatizer and expressed his desire to become a true Christian. On the same day Zumárraga passed sentence. Marcos was required to make public abjuration of his statements against the friars and to admit that he had made the statements while temporarily insane or drunk. Both Marcos and Francisco were banished from the Mexico-Tlatelolco area for a period of two years. Marcos was remanded to a distant monastery in Tlaxcala and Francisco was made a servant in the *Hospital de las Bubas* [for syphilitics] in Mexico City. Both men had their heads shorn and received one hundred lashes. Marcos was forbidden to hold any public office in the future without the express consent of the viceroy or the king. An *auto de fe* was held in Tlatelolco on June 22, 1539, and Marcos and Francisco made their abjurations. On the following day they began to serve their sentences.

## VI. *The Trial of Don Carlos of Texcoco for being a Heretical Dogmatizer, 1539*[2]

Don Carlos Chichimecatecuhtli or Ometochtzin was the grandson of the great Netzahualcóyotl[3] and the natural son of Netzahualpilli, both former rulers of Texcoco in the period preceding the conquest. Carlos had been reared in the household of Cortés and had been educated by the Franciscans at the Colegio de Santa Cruz de Tlatelolco. According to his own testimony he was baptized by the Franciscans in Texcoco *circa* 1524. Although he must have had other wives, he was married to Doña María of Guaxutla in 1535. After his famous brother Don Hernando Ixtlilxochitl, the cacique of Texcoco died, probably in the year 1531, Don Carlos succeeded to the caciqueship of Texcoco.[4]

[2] AGN, Inquisición, Tomo 2, exp. 10. This *proceso* has been printed by the Archivo General de la Nación, *Proceso Inquisitorial del Cacique de Tetzcoco*, Vol. I of the *Publicaciones del Archivo General de la Nación* (México, 1910).

[3] Netzahualcóyotl was the poet-king of Texcoco in the late fifteenth century. See Frances Gillmor, *Flute of the Smoking Mirror* (Albuquerque, 1949).

[4] Don Carlos Ahuaxpitzatzin Ometochtzin Yoyontzin Ixtlilxochitl Mendoza is an obscure person in Texcoco history until the Zumárraga trial of 1539. Perhaps because of his many names plus the hereditary title of the Texcocan monarchs, Chichimecatecuhtli, both primary and secondary sources disagree on the events and chronology of Carlos' career. There is evidence that Carlos was Netzahualpilli's choice for his successor in 1516 but that his brothers would not allow him to assume control. There are other stories that he was elected cacique in the immediate post-conquest period but that Cortés vetoed the appointment. Sources even disagree on the date of his

Signature-Rubrics of Zumárraga, Don Carlos, and Sahagún and others
(From the Don Carlos Trial)

In view of his hereditary position as cacique and natural lord of Texcoco, one of the three cities comprising the Aztec Triple Alliance prior to the Spanish conquest, Don Carlos obviously enjoyed considerable prestige and influence among Indians of the Texcocan area. From data recorded in the Inquisition *proceso* we also know that his sister was married to the cacique of the nearby pueblo of Chiconautla, and that Carlos may have been the uncle of the cacique of Tacuba, also one of the cities of the Aztec Triple Alliance. He was related to other native chiefs of the area and to Ferando de Alva Ixtlilxochitl, the sixteenth century Texcocan historian, another grandson of Netzahualcóyotl.

Don Carlos of Texcoco was denounced before the Holy Office of the Inquisition on June 22, 1539, as a dogmatizer against the faith by Francisco, an Indian of the village of Chiconautla. Francisco related that in the first days of June Don Carlos had journeyed to Chiconautla to visit his sister. The Chiconautla area was beset with drought and plague and the Father Provincial had encouraged the Indians to pray for relief as well as to make certain processions as a part of their supplication.

These activities were in progress when Carlos arrived in Chiconautla. He ridiculed the entire procedure and the teachings of the friars who, he said, were deceiving the people. Francisco quoted Don Carlos as saying that Christian doctrine was nothing, that the pronouncements of the friars, viceroy, and bishop were of no consequence, and that the instruction given the *principales* in the *colegios* was of no value.

Carlos pointed out to the natives of Chiconautla that each of the three Orders, the Franciscans, Dominicans and Augustinians, had their own dress and their own way of doing things, and he told Francisco and the others that it was entirely right that the natives should have their own mode of worship and life. Francisco also testified that Carlos had made a speech in which he attacked Spanish rule in Mexico as well as the Spanish Church:

---

final succession to the caciqueship, placing the date anywhere between 1523 and 1531. Francisco López de Gómara, *Historia de la conquista de México* (2 vols.; México, 1943), II, 104, and Francisco Javier Clavijero, *Historia antigua de México* (2 vols.; México, 1917), I 151, 177 place the date early in the decade of the 1520's. The *Annales de Domingo Francisco de San Antón Muñon Chimalpahin Quauhtlehuanitzin. Sixieme et Septieme Relations (1258-1612)* (Paris, 1889), p. 226, establishes the 1531 date, and this chronology is more or less substantiated by the research in other source materials by Rafael García Grana-

dos, *Diccionario biográfico de historia antigua de Méjico* (3 vols.; Méjico, 1952-1953), II, 506 *et passim*. It is obvious that Don Carlos held other positions of responsibility in the native government of Texcoco prior to becoming the cacique. For inconclusive testimony on Carlos and his career prior to the caciqueship, see *Colección de documentos inéditos relativos al descubrimiento, conquista y organización de las antiguas posesiones de América y Oceanía* (42 vols.; Madrid, 1864-1895), XXVII, 389; XXVIII, 66-67, 188; XXIX, 247-263, 295; hereafter cited as DII.

Who are those that undo us and disturb us and live on us and we have them on our backs and they subjugate us? Well here I am, and there is the Lord of México, Yoanize, and there is my nephew Tezapille, Lord of Tacuba, and there is Tlacahuepantli, Lord of Tula, that we are all equal and in agreement and no one shall equal us, that this is our land, and our treasure and our jewel, and our possession, and the Dominion is ours and belongs to us; and who comes here to subjugate us that are not our relatives or of our blood and make themselves our equals, well here we are and no one shall ridicule us. . . .[5]

Clearly Don Carlos was dogmatizing against and attacking Spanish political power in Mexico.

After Zumárraga studied the denunciation he took immediate action. Because of Don Carlos' position and influence the Apostolic Inquisitor regarded the case as very serious. Within a few days he went in person to Chiconautla to review the events recounted by Francisco. On July 4, 1539, he ordered the arrest of Carlos and placed an embargo on his properties. In one of the cacique's houses were found caches of idols including Quetzalcoatl, Xipe, Tlaloc, and Coatlicue.

Between July 4 and July 12, Zumárraga continued the investigation in Chiconautla and Texcoco. He interrogated many witnesses: Carlos' wife and son, his sister Inéz, the governor and several *principales* of Texcoco, the wife of his deceased brother Pedro, the cacique of Chiconautla, and many others.

The testimonies substantiated the charge that Carlos was a heretical dogmatizer. Antonio, the son of Carlos, gave testimony that served to intensify the accusation that Carlos was an enemy of the faith. The boy was eleven or twelve years old, but he had not grown up in the house of God because the father had forbidden him to attend church. He knew nothing of Christian doctrine; he could not *santiguar* or *persinar* nor was he able to recite the Pater Noster, the Credo, and the Ave Maria.

Don Carlos had particularly offended the Church when he preached to the natives on the licentiousness of the friars. He charged them with sexual immorality and concubinage. He alleged that the sacrament of confession was a joke because the friars, and not God, wanted to hear of sin. He asserted that the friars punished the Indian for concubinage and drunkenness while they allowed these privileges to the Spaniard.

Carlos' views on concubinage were especially damaging to Church

---

[5] Quienes son estos que nos deshacen, e perturban, é viven sobre nosotros, é los thenemos á cuestas y nos sojuzgan? Pues aquí estoy yo, y allí está el Señor de México, Yoanize, y allí está mi sobrino Tezapille, Señor de Tacuba, y allí está Tlacahuepantli, Señor de Tula, que todos somos iguales y conformes y no se ha de igualar nadie con nosotros, que esta es nuestra tierra, y nuestra hacienda, y nuestra alhaja, y nuestra posesión, y el Señorío es nuestro y á nos pertenece, y quién viene aquí a sojuzgarnos, que no son nuestros parientes ni de nuestra sangre y se nos igualan, pues aquí estamos y no ha de haber quién haga burla de nosotros . . .

teachings. Carlos taught that concubinage had been a tradition with the Indians and should be continued. He counseled Indian wives to obey their husbands in all things and not to complain when the husbands took other women. He related to others that he slept with his niece Inéz whenever he desired. Inéz admitted that she had been her uncle's concubine. There had been a child from this union which Carlos supported. Other witnesses reported that Inéz was the woman Carlos really favored and that she had control over vast estates while the legitimate wife had only a meager existence and only one slave.

Doña María, the wife of Carlos' deceased brother Pedro, took advantage of the trial to relate some of the demands the cacique had made on her while she was still in mourning. First, she charged that Carlos had pilfered the inheritances left by her husband for his nephews. Then she recounted how Carlos had come to her home to take her as a concubine just after Pedro's funeral. When she refused to receive him, he made a practice of prowling around her house at night making weird noises to frighten her. Carlos admitted his "visits" to Doña María's house but contended that they were merely for conversation and not to "echar con ella." Servants of María's household confirmed her side of the story and condemned Carlos for his improprieties.

There was no clear-cut testimony that Carlos had practiced idolatry. When the cacique's property was embargoed, Zumárraga personally conducted the search of Carlos' houses to uncover hidden idols. In one particular house was found an entire collection of idols: Quetzalcoatl, Xipe, Tlaloc, Coatlicue, and others. The house belonged to Carlos but had been the residence of a deceased uncle. The place had been a pre-conquest shrine and temple. The wife and son of Carlos knew nothing of the idol house and Carlos swore that the dwelling had been closed since his uncle's death. The witnesses offered no evidence that connected the cacique with idolatry or sacrifice.[6]

Zumárraga's discovery of the cache of idols on Carlos' property stimulated an idol hunt throughout the Texcoco area supervised by the governor Don Lorenzo de Luna, an illegitimate brother of Carlos.[7] Much additional knowledge of paganism in the region accrued from this search. The main cult seemed to be worshippers of Tlaloc. In pre-conquest times the idol of Tlaloc had resided in a mountain cave near Texcoco,[8]

[6] Medina, *Inquisición primitiva*, I, 165, comments that it was not unusual to imbed idols in the walls as decorations or as pillars to hold up the structure. Some of the idols uncovered by Zumárraga in Carlos' house were imbedded in the walls.

[7] Lorenzo de Luna as governor of Texcoco had been instructed by Viceroy Mendoza in January of 1538 to search out and destroy idols in the Texcoco jurisdiction. AGN, Civil, Tomo 1271.

[8] For an interesting account of worship of Tlaloc on this mountain in pre-conquest, conquest, and modern times see Fernando

and the Indians had come from Tlaxcala, Cholula, Chalco, and points distant to petition for rain. When the drought of 1539 occurred the natives resumed their propitiation of the rain god. The native officials of Texcoco had noticed smoke issuing from the mountain, and upon investigation found the idolaters, confiscated their idols and masks and other sacrificial instruments. These were brought before Zumárraga during Carlos' trial but had little connection with the case.

Testimony did reveal that Carlos claimed that his father and grandfather were prophets and that they communed with him and gave instructions on how to proceed with the rule of his subjects. He told the natives that Netzahualcóyotl had instructed him to follow the directions of the old sky gods and earth gods of the Aztec religion. Nowhere in the testimonies was Carlos alleged to have made sacrifices.

On July 15, 1539, Zumárraga and his staff moved back to Mexico City to continue the trial, and Don Carlos was brought before the Apostolic Inquisitor for formal interrogation. Fray Bernardino de Sahagún was the chief interpreter. The cacique's testimony on the charges of dogmatizing and heresy was decidedly weak. He insisted that he had encouraged his subjects to become Christians and to remain faithful. He denied dogmatizing and offending God in any way, except for having a concubine. He testified that he had never said that the law of God was a joke, nor had he cast aspersions on the morality of the clergy. He denied slandering Zumárraga and Viceroy Mendoza. Don Carlos refused to admit that he had practiced the old rites, sacrificed, or invoked the aid of the Aztec gods in his government. Finally, Carlos stoutly denied that he had exhorted the natives to return to concubinage or that he had praised the anarchy in morals of the pre-conquest era.

Although he professed loyalty to Church and state, there was no doubt from the testimonies that Carlos had made the treasonous speech reported by Francisco of Chiconautla. This speech was probably the most important factor in the decision of Viceroy Mendoza and the audiencia to support Zumárraga on the relaxation sentence.

The Inquisition fiscal, Cristóbal de Canego, made his accusation against Carlos on August 22, 1539. The charges were really only two: heretical dogmatizing against the faith and morals of the Indian population, and idolatry. When the witnesses ratified their testimonies, Carlos stood convicted for heretical dogmatizing and exonerated of the idolatry charge.

Later in the day of August 22, Carlos, through his defense attorney,

Vicencio de Riverol, answered the accusations of the fiscal. Carlos contended that Canego had no specific evidence as to the time or place of the alleged idolatries and heresies. The cacique repeated that his formative years in the Cortés home and his education at Tlatelolco had made him a model Christian, observing the Sabbath and requiring his subjects to do so. However, even after a thirty-day adjournment to formulate his defense, Carlos was unable to produce witnesses to support his contentions.

As a last resort to save himself, Don Carlos presented a brief in which he charged that he was the victim of a plot by his enemies to secure his post as cacique. He said that they were motivated by hate and vengeance because of certain punishments that he had imposed upon them in his official capacities. Between September 23 and November 4, 1539, Carlos failed in a serious of petitions to secure more time to formulate a defense or to be granted a new trial.

Before Zumárraga pronounced his sentence he sent the entire transcript of the trial to Viceroy Mendoza and the oidores of the audiencia for their views on the matter. This action on November 18 indicated that the Zumárraga was considering relaxing Don Carlos to the secular arm. Apparently the viceroy and the judges registered no objection to Zumárraga's proposed sentence. At least we have no record to the contrary.

The sentence was pronounced on November 28, 1539. It was brief and to the point. Carlos was adjudged to be a *hereje dogmatizador*, and since he had refused to confess or ask for mercy, Zumárraga recommended that he be relaxed to the secular arm. The prescribed civil sentence was burning at the stake. All of Carlos' properties were confiscated. No mention was made of the idolatry and concubinage charges.

On November 29, 1539, a town crier announced to the populace that there was to be an *auto de fe* on the approaching Sunday. All were required to be present upon pain of excommunication if they failed to attend. The *auto* took place on the Zócalo on Sunday, November 30. Don Carlos appeared in the procession wearing the sanbenito and *coroza* with a candle in his hand. He was led to the scaffold on the plaza. Assembled were most of the citizens of Mexico City and Texcoco as well as Viceroy Mendoza, the audiencia and Zumárraga. The bishop preached his sermon and then commanded the Inquisition secretary, Miguel López de Legazpi, to read the sentence. It was translated for the condemned.

At the last moment Carlos became penitent and petitioned Zumárraga to allow him to address the assembled natives in their own language. He urged them to heed his example and to turn from his idolatries and follow the true faith. He was unable to escape the death penalty owing to the lateness of his confession. He was turned over to the civil authorities for the execution of the sentence. We do not know the manner in which Don Carlos died. Don José Toribio Medina speculated that the cacique was first strangled with the garrote and then the cadaver was burned. This was the usual procedure for dealing with eleventh hour confession of obstinate heretics.[9]

The execution of Don Carlos aroused a storm of protest among the officialdom in Spain. Zumárraga was reprimanded for his harsh action.[10] There can be no doubt that the Don Carlos case gave real impetus to the movement for exemption of the Indian from the jurisdiction of the Holy Office of the Inquisition.

The exemption movement, while grounded in the humanistic attitudes discussed in Chapter II, and given force by the Don Carlos case, was slow to come to fruition.[11] The instructions of Tello de Sandoval and Moya de Contreras granted to these Inquisitors jurisdiction without exception.[12] Indians were tried by Tello and the bishops as ordinaries in all New Spain until 1571. Monastic prelates in areas where there was no resident bishop continued their inquisitions under authority of the bull *Omnímoda* until a decree of Philip II of December 30, 1571, which removed Indians from the jurisdiction of all inquisitions and placed them under the direct control of the bishops in matters of the faith and morals.[18]

## VII. *Conclusions on the Inquisition and the Indians: 1536-1543*

Any judgment of Zumárraga's Indian Inquisition would necessarily depend upon one's criteria for evaluation. If one examines this institution as a device to extirpate idolatry and sacrifice and to dissolve paganism, the whole history of Mexico proves Zumárraga to have been a failure. The orthodox churchman would defend Zumárraga's Indian trials as neces-

[9] Medina, *Inquisición primitiva*, I, 173, note 10.

[10] For the reprimand see García Icazbalceta, *Don Fray Juan de Zumárraga*, I, 41, and IV, documents 18 and 19. Ricard, *op. cit.*, pp. 470-473, analyzes the case of Carlos and speculates on the idea of whether Carlos had been the victim of a native plot to secure his position, or perhaps a plot motivated by vengeance. Ricard concludes, and rightly so, that this side of the story must remain in the realm of conjecture. One should bear in mind, however, that damaging testimony was given by Carlos' illegitimate brother Don Lorenzo de Luna. Medina's treatment is found in *Inquisición primitiva*, I, 141-175, and Cuevas' defense of Zumárraga is contained in *Historia de la iglesia*, I, 376-378. As far as we know Tello de Sandoval never reported on the disposition of Carlos' properties or the fate of his son. See Chapter I. Tello's instructions were reproduced in Puga, *op. cit.*, I, 452, 454.

[11] Zumárraga had petitioned the king in 1537 to permit him to castigate as a father the Indians who offended against the faith after having been baptized. Indeed, he proceeded on this philosophy. A cédula of Charles V had exempted the Indian from the Holy Office's jurisdiction and placed him under the direct control of the viceroy. This order was never effectuated. See Genaro García, *El Clero en México durante la dominación española*, pp. 40-44, 76.

[12] See Chapter I.

[18] Lea, *The Inquisition in the Spanish Dependencies*, pp. 210-211.

sary, and he would point out the general leniency of the Apostolic Inquisitor in cases of little significance. He would be quick to contend, however, that firmness and harshness were absolutely necessary in dealing with those natives who would have undermined the spiritual conquest.

Probably the humanist would condemn Zumárraga for his Indian Inquisition. From his viewpoint it would appear to have been harsh, unjust and unnecessary. He would not condone the abandonment of some basic humanist ideas for the security of the empire and religion. The cultural anthropologist would merely contend that the Indian Inquisition was a haphazard device in the process of forced acculturation.

The objective scholar has to vindicate Zumárraga of any guilt in the Don Carlos case. The trial was carried on without legal irregularities and the cacique was convicted upon ample evidence of being a heretical dogmatizer.

# CHAPTER V

# Zumárraga, The Lutherans, and Other Heretics

## I. *Introduction*

Although Protestantism never attained a following among great numbers of the Spanish people, the fear of its doctrines was an obsession with the Spanish Inquisition.[1] Luther was regarded as the great enemy of Spanish society, and the term *luterano* came to be applied to many deviations from orthodoxy that had no connection with Lutheran ideas.[2] If the era 1480 to 1520 was the Judaizante phase of the Spanish Inquisition, the period from 1520 to 1570 must certainly be called its Protestant phase. During this era Spanish society was gripped by the fear of losing its religious orthodoxy, and while the major problem was the fear of heresy rather than heresy itself, the Inquisition set to work to suppress all ideas that were deemed to be unorthodox or on the fringes of orthodoxy.

Spain's imperial emigration policy reflected the unrest at home, and care was taken that persons of unquestioned orthodoxy were the only Spaniards allowed to emigrate or to trade in the New World.[3] Except

---

[1] The most reliable account of Spanish Protestantism remains, Lea, *The Spanish Inquisition*, III, 411-476. Another valuable study is Ernst Schäfer, *Beitrage zur Geschichte des spanischen Protestantismus und der Inquisition* (3 vols.; Gutersloh, 1902).

[2] In Spain the doctrines of Luther, Erasmus, and the *Alumbrados* became confused. In Mexico the term *luterano* was even broader, but usually the *alumbrados* retained their correct identiy. Bataillon, *Erasmo y España* is the best account of Erasmian thought in sixteenth-century Spain. Two monographs of John E. Longhurst should be consulted for valuable information and new viewpoints on Spanish Protestantism: *Erasmus and the Spanish Inquisition: The Case of Juan de Valdés*

(Albuquerque, 1950), especially pp. 7-9, 57-58; and *Luther and the Spanish Inquisition: The Case of Diego de Uceda, 1528-1529* (Albuquerque, 1953) pp. 7-13. Henry C. Lea's, *Chapters from the Religious History of Spain Connected with the Inquisition* (Philadelphia, 1880), pp. 234-245 *et passim*, is valuable for the mystics. Another important study is Bernardino Llorca, S.J., *Die spanische Inquisition und die Alumbrados (1509-1667)* (Berlin-Bonn, 1934). For the Mexican *alumbrados* see Julio Jiménez Rueda, "La secta de los alumbrados en la Nueva España," *Boletín del Archivo General de la Nación*, XVI (1945), 5-32.

[3] The best source for general emigration policy is Clarence Haring, *Trade and*

SELLO OFICIAL DEL TRIBUNAL
DEL SANTO OFICIO DE LA
INQUISICION EN MEXICO

(Authentic Seal of the Mexican Inquisition)

for the period from 1526 to 1549 when Charles V permitted his German and Flemish subjects into the colonies legally, immigration was restricted to peninsular Spaniards.[4] Initially, only Castilians had been allowed because of the nature of the original enterprise, but with the death of Isabella, Ferdinand decreed that all Spanish subjects save heretics or their descendants were to be given access to the New World.

Isabella had launched the policy of exclusion of heretics from the Indies when she required a certificate of *limpieza de sangre* from each person who would emigrate. This policy was continued first by the Suprema and later by the *Casa de Contratación*. The result was a prohibition from embarkation from Sevilla of all Jews or Judaizing Christians, Moors, and all former heretics who had been penanced by the Inquisition. As colonial policy developed, their descendants to the third generation were also barred from sailing.[5]

In 1537, by the bull *Altitudo divini consilii*, Pope Paul III forbade all apostates to go to the Indies and commanded the colonial authorities to expel any who might have come.[6] By 1549 Charles V had to placate native Spaniards by secretly instructing the *Casa* not to issue papers to non-peninsulars for migration or trade in the New World.

Despite the formidable obstacles, foreign and heretic migration continued by devious and illegal means. All over the Americas Inquisition officials set to work to ferret out these people and to compile secret lists of suspects.[7]

An integral part of the attack on heresy in the colonies was the censorship process. Strict Castilian laws were modified for use in the empire and the Holy Office of the Inquisition was granted control over importation of books into the New World, as well as the censorship of books printed there. Possessing, selling, or distributing prohibited books was a serious crime in Mexico and one which the Inquisition investigated with particular zeal.[8]

*Navigation between Spain and the Indies in the Time of the Hapsburgs* (Cambridge, 1918), pp. 96-122.

[4] *Ibid.*, pp. 98-102. In Mexico the Flemings engaged in commerce and silver mining at Zultepeque. Several of them were tried by Zumárraga for blasphemy and heresy in 1540.

[5] In 1501 Ovando was given instructions not to allow among his party to Santo Domingo any Jews, Marranos, Moors, or *reconciliados*. Between 1508 and 1517 Ferdinand issued a series of decrees prohibiting the migration of the descendants of the above to the third generation. See Medina, *Inquisición primitiva*, I, 25-30.

[6] Lea, *The Inquisition in the Dependencies*, p. 194.

[7] Prince Philip, on August 14, 1543, had ordered all colonial officials to investigate Moorish slaves of free-men, recently converted, or sons of Jews who were resident in the New World, and to banish them to Spain. This order prompted Juan Muñoz de Parrales, an Inquisition clerk, to present Tello de Sandoval a "Memoria de hijos de quemados y reconciliados que hay en esta Ciudad," dated May 13, 1544. This document is found in AGN, Inquisición, Tomo IA, exp. 25.

[8] For the censorship process in the Indies see Lea, *Chapters*, pp. 20-24, 56-68; Irving

Prior to 1536 heresy had occupied the efforts of the Mexican Inquisition very little. Besides Santa María's burning of Morales and Alonso and his trial of Ocaña in 1528, all for being Judaizantes, only one case of major heresy was tried, that of Andrés of Rhodes for being a Greek schismatic.[9] It was Zumárraga who really launched the anti-heresy phase of the Mexican Inquisition.

## II. *Luther in Mexico: The Trial of Andrés Alemán 1536-1540*

Zumárraga's first Lutheran trial proved to be the most important of his Inquisitorial ministry. On August 14, 1536, Alonso de Paz, a scribe denounced Andrés Alemán, a Moravian jeweler for Lutheranism.[10] Within a week Alemán was arrested and the testimonies were gathered.

The Inquisition *proceso* yields a fair amount of biographical data on the accused. He had been born in the province of Brunn in Moravia and had grown up as an apprentice to an Austrian noble. Apparently he was of Slavic background. At the age of fourteen Alemán had spent a year and a half in Bohemia learning German and other central European dialects. He became familiar with the Bohemian religion and the sacraments used in their worship services. In his own testimony Alemán described the sacraments of infant baptism and the Bohemian practice of deathbed confession. He did not mention the name of John Huss.

It was evident from his testimonies that Alemán's travels in central and western Europe had been very broadening from the standpoint of religion. He had ranged throughout Hungary and the Low Countries, engaged in his profession as lapidary, and had fought in the wars in Flanders. In each country he had observed and studied religious customs. The *proceso* does not inform us of the year of Alemán's arrival in Mexico. His testimonies proved him to be an intelligent and well-read person, and his adjustment to the procedures of the Holy Office showed a remarkable ability to make the best of his unfortunate situation.

Apparently Alemán traveled great distances in the pursuit of his jewelry trade in Mexico. Alonso de Paz' denunciation and other testimonies placed him in Colima and Jalisco where he had contended that confession need only be mental and be directed to God and not to men.

Leonard, *Books of the Brave* (Cambridge, 1949); José Torre Revello, *El Libro, la imprenta, y el periodismo en America durante la dominación española* (Buenos Aires, 1940); and Diego de Encinas, *Cedulario indiano* (4 vols.; Madrid, 1945), I, 228-229. Particularly valuable for Mexico after the Zumárraga period is Francisco Fernández del Castillo, *Libros y libreros en el siglo XVI*, Vol. VI of *Publicaciones del Archivo General de la Nación* (México, 1914).

[9] AGN, Inquisición, Tomo I, exp. 14. The year was 1528.

[10] AGN, Inquisición, Tomo 2, exp. 1. Medina, *Inquisición primitiva*, I, 135-137, lists the accusations of the fiscal in this case, but it is evident from his commentaries that he has not seen the actual *proceso*.

On these business trips Alemán carried with him certain books in foreign languages which the witnesses believed were prohibited by the Holy Office.

Alemán repeated many other unorthodox views on religion in the northwest Mexican provinces which led Zumárraga to believe that the jeweler was proselytizing for Lutheranism. In addition to possessing suspect books and defending the doctrine of mental confession, Alemán spread other ideas that were Lutheran in orientation: he said that veneration of images took honor from the Son of God and bestowed it upon Mary and the saints; and he contended that papal bulls were worthless and that papal indulgences and pardons were a fraud. Alemán's views on the clergy convinced Zumárraga that the jeweler was a Lutheran because he had stated his firm belief that priests should be married and that they ought not receive rents and other monetary rewards.

Other testimonies charged Alemán with heresies of a more nebulous nature. Leonor de Casteñeda and Margarita Alemán (who was no relation to Andrés), women to whom the defendant had talked in Mexico City, tried to link his ideas with the teachings of Erasmus of Rotterdam. Although the name of Erasmus appears several times in the *proceso*, specific ideas are not mentioned, indicating the confusion in both lay and clerical minds on the nature of the Lutheran and Erasmian heterodoxies, and the common stereotype adopted in which all heresies were labeled as Lutheran or Erasmist. Pedro de Celaya, a scribe in Colima, testified that Alemán had supported the *Lutheran* doctrine of communal wives while he was in that area. This was evidently a confusion on Alemán's part of Lutheranism with certain radical ideas of the left wing of the Reformation, perhaps Anabaptism, which when carried to extremes led to sexual promiscuity. It is not at all unlikely that the idea of communal wives was the product of Alemán's imagination.

After two sessions with the Inquisitor between August 26 and September 7, Alemán confessed to the above allegations and more. It was ascertained that the books which he carried were prohibited versions of the Psalms of David, the Epistles of Paul, and other fragments of the New Testament. Zumárraga was particularly interested in Alemán's views on the writings of the Sacred Doctors of the Church. He maintained with Luther that commentaries were of no value and that the individual could consult the Scripture and interpret it.[11]

The accusation of the fiscal of the Holy Office, Dr. Rafael de Cervanes, was made on September 7, 1536. The charges made against Andrés Alemán were the following:

11 ". . . que decia el dicho Alemán que el Lutero decia que los Evangelios y Sagrada escritura no se habia de entender sino al pie de la letra . . ."

1) That Alemán had proselytized Lutheran doctrines and had tried to undermine the sacrament of confession.

2) That he had contended that excommunication was offensive to God and was unchristian.

3) That he held Lutheran ideas on images.

4) That he contended that priests should marry.

5) That he criticized the monies that the Church accumulated.

6) That he contended that papal bulls, indulgences, and pardons were of no value.

7) That he doubted the truth and authority of the pope.

8) That he favored individual interpretation of Scripture.

On September 8, 1536, Andrés Alemán answered the charges of the fiscal. He denied that he was a dogmatizer but he admitted the Lutheran errors and other heretical propositions of which he was accused. He tried to convince Zumárraga that he was truly sorry that he had offended God and the Church. He lamented his indiscreet conversations. Alemán asked absolution from his sins and a suitable penance.

On September 26, 1536, Andrés Alemán renounced the usual thirty-day period allowed for framing the defense and announced that he would enter no plea. He reaffirmed his faith in God and the Roman Catholic Church, and he indicated that he detested his previous errors.

Of his own free will, on Sunday, October 15, 1536, Alemán appeared in the cathedral of Mexico, and while kneeling with a candle in his hands, abjured his heresies one by one before the assembled congregation. After this ceremony, he took the *juramento de la fe* in front of Zumárraga, Viceroy Mendoza, and the oidores of the audiencia of Mexico. He reiterated his Christian beliefs, his renunciation of all heretical tenets, and he promised to fulfill the penance prescribed by the Holy Office. After the oath Zumárraga granted him absolution and he was reconciled with the Church. The Apostolic Inquisitor then pronounced sentence.

The sentence was simple and surprisingly lenient in view of the clear testimony against Alemán coupled with his own confession. He was to wear the sanbenito for an unspecified time. He was banished perpetually from New Spain and the Indies and all of his property was confiscated. He was to embark on the first boat to Sevilla and there he was to be under the immediate supervision of Inquisitor General Manrique and the Suprema. This sentence was pronounced and signed by Zumárraga on October 15, 1536, the same day as the abjuration ceremony.

By the fall of 1538 Andrés Alemán had become a well-established jeweler in the city of Sevilla and seemed to be suffering from none of the censures usually associated with reconciled heretics.[12] On October 29, 1538, he began a two-year campaign aimed at the restoration of his properties. He also petitioned for more freedom in practicing his profession. On this day he admitted his errors again to the Sevilla Inquisition and petitioned to be allowed to live among Christians in Spain. Because he had been able to convince the Inquisitors of his remorse, on November 28, 1538, Alemán was given freedom of mobility in the Iberian Peninsula but was charged not to leave Spain without express authorization.

On February 12, 1539, Alemán petitioned the Inquisition to be allowed to follow the court of Charles V outside of Spain in the exercise of his profession. His request was granted. Fortified with these documents and with ideas of forgery in mind, on December 12, 1539, he tried to recover part of his properties because he had returned to the Catholic fold, and because "ahora no han hallado culpa en mi de lo que me acusaban por luterano." He had hoped with the aid of a Sevillan *escribano* to modify the documents and send these credentials to Mexico City to be used in a suit for the restoration of his properties.[13] Although his plan was discovered and the scribe reported him to the authorities, we have no record that he got his just deserts. Indeed, just eight months later, on August 16, 1540, he began his campaign anew. This time his line of attack was slightly different. He had hoped to build up the illusion in Zumárraga's mind that the Suprema had absolved him of his previous crimes and that it was behind him in his suit for restoration of his property. His letter to Zumárraga related his sentence for Lutheranism and his banishment from Mexico. He indicated that he had worn the sanbenito and that it had been hung, as was the custom, in the cathedral of Mexico City. He said that upon his arrival in Spain that the Suprema had reopened his case and had revoked that part of Zumárraga's sentence which had required him to wear penitential garb. He therefore requested that it be taken down from the Cathedral and destroyed.

Zumárraga was suspicious of the Alemán request. He indicated that his intention had been for Alemán to wear the sanbenito perpetually and that he was confused on exactly how it came to be hung in the cathedral in the first place. In any event, he demanded more clear and official documents from the Suprema on the matter before he would act. Later, for some inexplicable reason, Zumárraga ordered the sanbenito taken down.

[12] Alemán's Spanish career can be followed in certain correspondence from the Sevilla Inquisitors to Zumárraga. The letters and Zumárraga's comments on them are scattered throughout the *proceso*. It was therefore necessary to rearrange them in chronological order to calculate their significance.

[13] In 1537 his wife Catalina de Caxas was able to recover part of the property which she proved had been part of her dowry. AGN, Inquisición, Tomo 42, exp. 11.

The last record of Andrés Alemán that we have showed him dili-
gently pressing his case and with moderate success, for on September 15,
1540, he was able to liquidate certain debts he owed in Mexico from the
confiscated properties which the treasurer of the Holy Office had in
escrow. This action was surely taken with the approval of Apostolic
Inquisitor Zumárraga. Whether Alemán was able to complete his ruse
must remain, for the present, a mystery.

### III. *The Dissemination of Lutheran Ideas: 1536-1540*

Although the Lutheran heresy was slow to spread in New Spain,
four additional trials occupied Zumárraga's Inquisition prior to his re-
tirement as Apostolic Inquisitor in 1543. The case of Juan Nizardo was
initiated in 1536 and spanned the next three years, owing to some pe-
culiar circumsances.[14]

We know from the interrogatory framed in 1539 that Nizardo had
been convicted on at least one count of Lutheranism in 1536. He had
been proven guilty of destroying a papal bull and other acts indicative
of a disrespect for the Church and its pope. He was sentenced on July 1,
1536, to perpetual banishment from New Spain to Castilla, and tied and
gagged he was taken through the streets of Mexico City on a mule while
a town crier proclaimed his crime. He was then given one hundred lashes.
Zumárraga ordered that he leave Mexico by July 7, 1536. Nizardo
was admonished that should he break the terms of his banishment and
return to New Spain, he would be relaxed to the secular arm and burned
at the stake.

Three years later it was determined that Juan Nizardo was still in
Mexico. He had apparently moved frequently to escape detection and
apprehension. After living for a period in Pánuco, he felt it advisable to
move to Mestitlán, where he was eventually arrested again by the Holy
Office.

Testimony taken between February 4 and February 28, 1539, led
to Juan's downfall.[15] He was arrested and jailed on the latter date. Without exception the witnesses knew of Nizardo's previous record. Why he
was not denounced earlier is curious. In both Pánuco and Mestitlán he
had consistently refused to go to Mass and when prompted by the laymen and priests to attend, he became abusive, uttering such blasphemies

[14] Fragments of the Nizardo case are contained in AGN, Inquisición, Tomo 30, exp. 1. Unfortunately the full details of the original trial are lacking, but the Interrogatory of February 4 to February 28, 1539, is still extant. The final disposition of the case must remain unknown because the records have been lost or destroyed.

[15] García Alonso and María de Allón from Pánuco testified, as did Guillermo Flamenco and Juan Rubio, *calpisque*, from Mestitlán.

as "Mal a Dios," "Pese a Dios,"[16] "Que cosa la Misa," "Pese a tal que con la Misa," and "Let me live according to my own law." He also said on frequent occasions that the abbot of Mestitlán was a hunchback. It was discovered that he had fled from Pánuco when the authorities there had sought to force him to attend church.

Nizardo was questioned in the week following his arrest. He admitted that he had been tried for Lutheranism and had been banished from Mexico by the Holy Office in 1536. He said that he did not embark at Veracruz because the Holy Office had not arranged passage for him. He could not afford to pay his own fare, and after begging the ship captains to give him free passage and having been refused, he went to Pánuco to live. He admitted refusing to go to Mass and blaspheming when his neighbors urged him to attend. He expressed true contrition for his sins and promised to do better in the future. Of his ultimate fate we have no evidence because the document is incomplete.

An elderly teacher, Maestro Pedro of Sevilla, was brought before Zumárraga in October of 1537 on charges of Lutheranism.[17] This gentleman of over seventy years of age had been rash enough to contend on shipboard from Sevilla to Pánuco that priests ought to marry. He was also reported to have said that he had been tried by the Sevilla Inquisitors for these views, as had his brother, and that he had been sentenced to wear the sanbenito prior to fleeing to Portugal. When Zumárraga interrogated him on this point, he admitted saying that *it would be better for* priests to marry than to sleep illicitly with concubines. He asserted that he had seen married priests and monks in parts of the Indies. He never elucidated on this statement. It was true that his brother had been reconciled by the Spanish Inquisition but Pedro denied that he was a fugitive *reo*. He ended his testimony with a denial of the worth of Luther's teachings and an affirmation of deep faith in Catholicism.

On October 8, 1537, Dr. Cervanes, the fiscal, made the accusation that Pedro was a Lutheran. On the following day, Maestro Pedro answered the charges. He contended that his words had been twisted out of context, and he denied that he ever had any intention of offending God or the Church. He asked mercy and penance.

Pedro and his lawyer spent the next three weeks establishing evidence of his good and Christian character. Even his priest indicated that he was a good Christian and a solid citizen. The fiscal repeatedly de-

[16] "Pese a Dios" is difficult to translate. An approximation colloquially might have been "God damn," "To Hell with God," or "God gives me a pain." For details see Chapter VII, "The Problem of Blasphemy and the Enforcement of Morality."
[17] AGN, Inquisición, Tomo 30, exp. 3.

manded sanctions against Pedro. The old man constantly referred to his advanced age and his failing health. He was allowed to have his home as a jail.

On October 12, 1537, testimonies were taken from Pedro's traveling companions on the ship from Sevilla. One receives the impression that Master Pedro was a cantankerous old man who insisted upon giving everyone his advice. The Lutheran allegations were more or less substantiated. Pedro charged that these people were malicious and bore him ill will. He later modified his plea and said that he did not remember making heretical statements and that if he had done so, it was during a temporary mental lapse. He again called attention to his age and infirmities.

Zumárraga was reasonably lenient when he pronounced sentence on October 30, 1537. Master Pedro was ordered to refrain from contending that clergymen should be married, and to be on the safe side, to abjure the teachings of Martin Luther in the cathedral of Mexico, kneeling and with a candle in his hand, on November 1, 1537. Furthermore, he was fined fifty *pesos de oro de minas* for his impetuous statements.

The trial of Alonso Delgado for Lutheranism need hardly be mentioned.[18] On April 26, 1537, Zumárraga questioned this humble and ignorant man. Alonso Delgado admitted that he had said that it was better for priests to marry than to live in mortal sin with concubines, and upon this point he agreed with Luther. If this was heresy, he said that he was sorry, and asked penance because he had not intended to offend God. Zumárraga perceived that Delgado was contrite and ignorant of the fact that he had erred, and he ordered him to make a pilgrimage to San Miguel and to recite along the way a short devotional entitled "La Corona de Nuestra Señora."

## IV. *The Trial of the Fleming Juan Banberniguen, 1540*

Juan Banberniguen was a native of Amberes in the Brabant country. He was one of the Welser miners that Charles V allowed into the colonies in 1526, and he and other Welser employees exploited the mines of Zultepeque near Taxco in Mexico.

Banberniguen was denounced to the Holy Office on April 2, 1540, by Peti Juan, a tailor, who resided in Mexico City but who traveled in the Taxco area making clothes.[19] The denunciation and subsequent testimony revealed that Banberniguen was guilty of heresy on two counts: his denial of the existence of purgatory, which was Lutheran, and his denial of the real presence in the sacrament of the Holy Eucharist. This later heresy was not Lutheran, because Banberniguen's views would have also denied the Lutheran doctrine of consubstantiation. His actual state-

[18] AGN, Inquisición, Tomo 125, exp. 6.     [19] AGN, Inquisición, Tomo 2, exp. 11.

Despues delos dos dias viernes veynte y siete dias del
mes de abril del dicho año susodicho hizo parecer ante el
dicho señor [...] y parecido mando [...] del juramento
en forma de derecho el qual le hizo las preguntas siguientes
preguntado como se llama / dixo que alonso delgado [...]
preguntado de donde es natural de los reynos de castilla / dixo que es
natural del lugar de ambres baxas [...] en la [...] de portugal
y que se ha criado en la cibdad de xerez de la frontera [...]
preguntado [...] estando hablando con ciertas personas [...] dixo [...] bien [...]
dixo [...] que si sean casados / y que [...] que no [...]
estuviesen seys y siete años amancebados y que el luto lo ayudava
[...] y [...] que se lo con que supo [...] los que estavan presente [...]
[...] dixo que [...] si que [...] a cierta el luto
de que los dichos [...] casados [...] que a cierto dize quinientos
[...] dixo y [...] lo que [...] dixo que estando hablando
con ciertas personas sobre que [...] los dichos [...] bien [...] que sean casados
[...] dixo este declarante [...] que bivia mas [...] en [...]
[...] estuviese casado [...] que es pecado mortal el que
en esto [...] el luto tenia [...] color y que en lo [...] que dira
[...] y que esto no dixo este declarante con [...] juntas [...]
y [...] si en ello [...] y pide misericordia a nuestro señor y [...] y que [...]
palabra otra dixo segun que se acuerda y pide [...] / e [...]
[...] el juramento [...] hizo y no lo firmo porque no lo sabia [...]

Two-page trial record of Alonso Delgado written in Zumárraga's hand.
*(Continued on verso of sheet)*

q[ue]e si aquello q[ue] dize el test[igo] lo aprueba p[o]r b[ue]no · oy lo y dicho me[...]
lo q[ue] manda y tiene · dijo q[ue] todo lo del test[igo] tiene p[o]r malo y q[ue] [...]
~ que lo que tiene y manda la s[an]ta madre ygl[esi]a p[o]r b[ue]no y acep[...]
to q[ue] y manda la s[an]ta madre ygl[esi]a y q[ue] esto es la verdad p[ar]a el juram[en]to [...]
otro s[i] &c

Yten[?] Juan Gonç[ale]z ynst[...] en confession [...] e que es p[er]sona y nom[...] y
[...]tos en conp[...] dijo q[ue] la manda na y mando al [...] Valens[?]
del q[ua]do q[ue] baya a S[an]t m[igu]el en penit[encia] de lo que dize · y q[ue]
eze de aq[u]i alla la anima de N[uest]ra Señora &c

ment was the following: ". . . que paresme a mi que nosotros no somos dignos que Dios viniese en nuestras manos pecadoras."

The tailor Peti Juan had urged Banberniguen to see a priest about these doubts that he had concerning the Eucharist. When Banberniguen came to Mexico City, he conferred with Fray Domingo de la Cruz in the Dominican monastery there, but he later confided to Peti Juan that he left the friar more confused than when he had come to him. Juan's own testimony later revealed that he had discussed purgatory with Fray Domingo but not the Eucharist.

Banberniguen's ideas on purgatory had come directly from the Low Countries. When Jacob de Cayzer and two other Flemings had come to Zultepeque they related to Banberniguen the progress of Lutheranism in his homeland and explained to him certain of Luther's teachings, including the negation of purgatory. This same Cayzer was later tried by Zumárraga for heretical blasphemy.[20] Cayzer testified that as far as he knew, Banberniguen had not fallen into heresy but that he did possess certain books dealing with religion, and that among these were sections of the New Testament and a treatise of Erasmus, the title of which he could not recall. He remembered, however, that the Erasmus book had the seal of examination of the Inquisition.

Juan Banberniguen's testimony resulted in a straight-forward confession. He waived his right to a defense attorney and threw himself on Zumárraga's mercy, promising to do penance and be a model Christian in the future.

On May 23, 1540, Juan Banberniguen was sentenced. He was forced to stand in church, barefoot and with a candle in his hand, during the entire sermon, after which he was required to abjure his heresies before the congregation. He was fined one hundred and fifty *pesos de oro de minas* and admonished to lead a life of scrupulous orthodoxy in the future.

The Banberniguen trial was the last trial for heresy that Juan de Zumárraga conducted. While Lutheranism was slow to penetrate New Spain, the cases of Alemán, Nizardo, Pedro de Sevilla, and Banberniguen indicate that when the penetration came it was a thorough one.

## V. *The Trial of Francisco de Sayavedra for Erasmism, 1539*[21]

Sayavedra's trial is of some interest because it represented the only early sixteenth-century case of Erasmism in Mexico. To be sure, it is a

[20] AGN, Inquisición, Tomo 14, exp. 36.
[21] AGN, Inquisición, Tomo 2, exp. 8. Julio Jiménez Rueda has published this *proceso* in the *Boletín del Archivo General de la Nación*, XVIII (1947), 1-15. The original *proceso* does not charge Sayavedra with Erasmism. It merely indicates that he was guilty of heretical propositions. For a brief commentary on the case, see Bataillon, *Erasmo y España*, II, 438-440.

very weak statement of Erasmus' teachings, but it shows his influence in Mexico, and perhaps more important, proves that Zumárraga could not be considered a follower of Erasmus.

Sayavedra exhibited a disrespect for the formal ceremonies of the Church. Indeed, his trial record implied that he considered the ceremonies not as necessary as faith. If he had more important things to do, he forewent Mass, and he worked on Sundays and required his household to work on feast days. On March 4, 1539, Sayavedra was called before Zumárraga to testify. He indicated that he was a native of Medellín in Castilla, that he could read and write, although he did not understand Latin very well. The Erasmian ideas which led to his conviction were the following: he contended that men ought not to pray to images or saints but directly to God;[22] he admitted that he had ridiculed a book owned by Pedro de Zalaya which promised that one could gain merits by reading the book and reciting its prayers. Sayavedra charged that the authors of the book had inserted the promise to sell more copies. He admitted that he had not attended Mass for six months because he had been ill. Later he testified that he had been ignorant that a day was a feast day when he ordered his servants to work, but upon learning that it was the feast of the Ascension of Our Lord, he ordered the work to cease.

Sayavedra affirmed his belief in each article of the faith before the Inquisitor and promised to go to Mass and confession in the future. He was allowed to remain under house arrest until sentence was passed, but Zumárraga demanded one thousand pesos bail. Sayavedra was ordered to deliver an arroba (approximately twenty-five pounds) of oil to the monastery of San Francisco of Cuernavaca and to tell the fathers there to say Mass for him and ask God to pardon his sins. In addition he had to recite the rosary of Our Lady three times and pay a fine of one hundred *pesos de oro de minas*.

## VI. *Zumárraga and the Other Heretics*

Cases of minor heresy were frequent before the Mexican Inquisition from its earliest days. Only a few of the more interesting trials will be mentioned here. As a general rule the minor heresy cases were connected with blasphemy and the accused were of a low character: mule drivers, gamblers, or sheepherders. Perhaps the most interesting minor offender was Juan de Toledo, who was the son of a *reconciliado* and a native of Almagro in Spain. At the time of his denunciation on June 6, 1536, he was the

---

[22] He contended that he had gotten this idea and others from a book by Erasmus which said ". . . que mas querían los santos que les imitasen en las obras que no que les rezasen diez Pater Nosters." Bataillon, *op. cit.*, II, 439, and Almoina, *op. cit.*, p. 189, agree that this must have been the *Enchiridion*.

alcalde mayor of Tehuantepec.[23] Besides being the son of a reconciled heretic, he was denounced for saying the following: "... que los angeles se abian de comer asados y los Cherubines fritos y que las cruces que se ponen en las calles ... no se abian de poner." We have no record of the proceedings in this trial.

On July 1, 1536, Hernando Núñez was denounced and tried on three counts of heresy.[24] In the heat of a card game he had said that if Moorish territories were nearby, he would leave Christianity and become a Mohammedan because that way of life was better. He also gave his opinion that the Passion of Jesus Christ was a fable and that he did not believe in the dogma of the Virgin Birth. After several interrogations before Zumárraga and the fiscal, Núñez confessed his errors and begged for mercy. Apparently he was able to convince Zumárraga of his earnest repentance, because he merely had to hear Mass barefoot with a candle in his hand. He was fined thirty *pesos de oro de minas*, but seeing his contrition, Zumárraga commuted the money payment to additional spiritual penance.

Two cases of heretical blasphemy occurred in October and December of 1537 which were prototypes of the usual trials Zumárraga judged. Luis Heredero was denounced on October 26, for saying "Pese a Dios," "No creo en Dios," "Mal grado haya Dios," and "Mal grado hayas tu Dios y tu hijo y tu madre."[25] He received the usual spiritual penances and the comparatively stiff fine of eighty *pesos de oro de minas*. On December 11 of the same year, Gonzalo Herradura was tried for similar heretical blasphemies.[26] He had shouted that he did not believe in the Mother of God nor her Son and ended his expletive with "Pese a Dios." Afterwards he repented, confessed, and waived any defense, throwing himself on Zumárraga's mercy. The Inquisitor was not as merciful as he might have been. Herradura had to attend church barefoot, with a candle in his hand and a gag in his mouth. Later he recited the Pater Noster and the Ave Maria thirty times each while kneeling before the saints.

Gaspar de Plaza was a habitual blasphemer and appeared before the Holy Office three times in ten years. In 1536 he was tried for saying that it was not a mortal sin to have relations with an Indian woman.[27] He again appeared before Zumárraga for having written a heretical letter in which he had likened the Cross to a crossbow.[28] Countless trials for minor heresy centered around the problem of sexual morality. The trial of the brothers Alonso and Rosino Valiente in 1538 exemplified the usual

[23] AGN, Inquisición, Tomo I, exp. 12.
[24] AGN, Inquisición, Tomo 30, exp. 2.
[25] AGN, Inquisición, Tomo 30, exp. 4.
[26] AGN, Inquisición, Tomo 2, exp. 7.
[27] AGN, Inquisición, Tomo 2, exp. 6.
[28] AGN, Inquisición, Tomo 1, exp. 10a.

heretical statement: [29] that simple fornication, that is relations between two unmarried people, was not a mortal sin. The Church was diligent in trying anybody who made this statement openly. The usual punishment was one hundred lashes.

Frequently people who had committed minor heresy or blasphemy denounced themselves to the Inquisition, as in the case of the simple shepherd, Cristóbal de la Hoz, who had denied the existence of the Mother Mary. [30] These folk were ordinarily devout and moved by a deep sense of grief for offending God. Their crimes were usually brought on by anger or other emotional disturbances. Zumárraga was kind to them but nevertheless firm. Cristóbal de la Hoz was required to recite seventy Ave Marias and Pater Nosters and pay a fine of one-half of a *tomín*.

In addition to the Lutherans and minor heretics, one other large area of heresy occupied Zumárraga's efforts in the era 1536 to 1540: the converted Jews who were discovered practicing their old rites. They are the subject of the next chapter.

[29] AGN, Inquisición, Tomo 2, exp. 4.          [30] AGN, Inquisición, Tomo 30, exp. 6.

# CHAPTER VI

# Zumárraga and the Judaizantes: 1536-1540

## I. *The Jews in Mexico, 1519-1536*

During the reign of Ferdinand emigration restrictions on the Jews and Judaizantes broke down.[1] Ferdinand and his successor, Charles V, attempted to restrict the migration of Judaizantes and other apostates to the third generation,[2] but their policy was a failure because, in the words of Haring, "the *conversos* or New Christians comprised the very class most apt to possess the capital required to develop the colonial trade."[3]

Illegal migration was the general rule during the first three decades of the sixteenth century. Traffic in forged passports became a lucrative business. Many Jews and others boarded the ships in the Canary Islands and with the use of generous bribes obtained passage to Mexico or the Isthmus. They usually changed their names or hispanicized them. The result of these developments was in influx of *conversos* and others almost immediately after the conquest of Mexico. Jews came with Cortés and Pánfilo de Narváez and with subsequent colonizers in the 1520's. There was a sizeable Jewish community in Mexico by 1536 and despite the Inquisition the colony continued to grow and prosper throughout the sixteenth century.

The first activity of the Mexican Inquisition against Jews and Judaizantes came in 1523 with the ordinance against heretics and Jews.[4] Anticipatory of the Santa María Judaizante trials of 1528 was an edict of the cabildo of Mexico embodying the crown's orders on the exclusion of Judaizantes and their relatives. This municipal pronouncement of May 17, 1527 prescribed the following: ". . . que en esta Nueva España no haya ningun judio hijo nieto ni viznieto de quemado ni de reconciliado

---

[1] In 1509 the king allowed these groups to come to the New World for a limited time to engage in trade but only after payment of twenty thousand ducats into the royal treasury. Lea, *The Inquisition in the Dependencies*, p. 194; Medina, *Inquisición primitiva*, I, 29-30.

[2] See Chapter V.

[3] Haring, *Trade and Navigation*, p. 104.

[4] This was the lost ordinance mentioned in Chapter I.

dentro del cuatro grado. . . ."[5] If such individuals happened to be in New Spain they were to depart on the first ship, and if they failed to do so, they would be deported and their property confiscated. The proceeds from the sale of the property were to be divided equally between the royal treasury, the judge, and the person who framed the denunciation.

Although there is some evidence that the friar-inquisitors of the 1520's imposed capital punishment on the natives, we find that the converted Jews were the first to receive the formal sentence of burning at the stake. The burnings have been shrouded in mystery and the only concrete accounts of them come from testimony taken some forty years later.[6] The sentences were executed on October 17, 1528, during the inquisitorial ministry of Fray Vicente de Santa María.[7] Three Judaizantes, Hernando Alonso, Gonzalo de Morales, and Diego de Ocaña, were tried, and two of them were burned on this date. The third was reconciled and escaped punishment because he had influence in high places.

Hernando Alonso,[8] one of the *relajados*, was a native of the Condado de Niebla in Spain. He had come to Mexico from Cuba with Pánfilo de Narváez in 1520 and had joined Cortés after his contest with Narváez. He was around sixty years old at the time and was married to Beatriz de Ordaz, who may have been the sister of the conquisitador Diego de Ordaz. He remarried twice.

Alonso was an iron-smith and carpenter by trade and he proved a useful companion to Cortés, whom he had known in Cuba since 1516. He was with Cortés during *la Noche Triste* and he helped Martín López build the brigantines on Lake Texcoco which the conqueror used in the reconquest of Tenochtitlán.[9] After the subjugation of the Aztecs, Alonso was rewarded with grants of land and encomiendas in Actopan.[10] He

[5] *Primer libro de las actas de cabildo*, p. 132.

[6] These documents, which I shall call the "Testimonies on Sanbenitos," were published by Alfonso Toro in *Los Judíos en la Nueva España* (México, 1932), pp. 20-32. In 1574 one of the senior inquisitors on the Tribunal launched an investigation because certain of the old *procesos* had disappeared and the sanbenitos of the *relajados* and *reconciliados* had not been placed in the cathedral. The witnesses were all seventy or eighty years of age, but their recollections of the burnings of 1528 were consistent.

[7] The actual date was established by a document in the notary archives which mentioned the burnings. Agustín Millares Carlo and J. I. Mantecón, *Indice y extractos de los protocolos del Archivo de Notarías de México, D.F.* (2 vols., México, 1945), I, 353.

[8] The only research on the *auto* of 1528 was done by G. R. G. Conway, "Hernando Alonso, a Jewish Conquistador with Cortés in Mexico," *Publications of the American Jewish Historical Society*, XXI (1928), 9-31. Much of the following material is gleaned from Conway.

[9] For this enterprise see C. Harvey Gardiner, *Naval Power in the Conquest of Mexico* (Austin, 1956), especially pp. 121-128.

[10] For Alonso's land grants, encomiendas, and business enterprises see *Primer libro de actas de cabildo*, pp. 62, 129, 131, *passim*; Millares Carlo and Mantecón, *Protocolos del Archivo de Notarías*, p. 407, *passim*.

became an important personage in Mexican affairs of the 1520's. His military career was distinguished by his part in the final siege of Mexico City and his campaigns against Garay in Pánuco with Gonzalo de Sandoval. He participated in the turbulent events of 1525 and 1526 in Mexico and was present when Luis Ponce de León arrived to take the Cortés *residencia*. He remained a moderate supporter of Cortés but always felt that he had not received his fair share of the conquest spoils.[11]

Hernando Alonso's name occurs frequently in the *Libros de cabildo* of Mexico City in the interim of March 1524 and March 1528, and he was a prominent *vecino* and meat merchant.[12] Apparently he raised beef and mutton in Actopan and sold it to the viceregal capital in line with procedures outlined by the cabildo.[13] He was said to have been a close friend of Alonso de Estrada, the acting governor of New Spain (1527-1528). In the six months between April and October of 1528, he fell from favor and was tried before the Holy Office then under the control of Fray Vicente de Santa María.

The "Testimony on Sanbenitos" revealed that both Hernando Alonso and Gonzalo de Morales were relaxed to the secular arm for being guilty of Jewish practices that were, to say the least, scandalous. According to testimony of Fray Vicente de las Casas, they were forced to march in penitential garb to Tlatelolco, where they were burned in the presence of Cortés' representatives, Licenciado Altimirano and Governor Estrada.

Alonso had initially been accused of performing a Jewish ceremony in which a child was rebaptised. At first he pleaded ignorance of the rebaptism but later, under threat of torture, he confessed that this act had been done in mockery of the sacrament of baptism. Alonso, one Palma, and others had taken an infant two years of age in Port Royal, Santo Domingo, and had placed it in a basin and poured wine over its head, and the wine that ran down the body of the child and what dripped from its penis was gathered into a cup and drunk. While this was taking place they sang certain Jewish songs.[14] Similarly, according to the law of Moses, Alonso forbade his wife, Isabel de Aguilar, to attend church dur-

---

[11] Alonso and Diego de Ocaña had testified in a suit between Juan Tirado and Cortés that lasted from 1526 to 1529. According to Conway, *op. cit.*, p. 12, the full evidence given by Alonso is contained in an unpublished fragment of a manuscript in the archive of the Hospital of Jesus.

[12] *Primer libro de actas de cabildo, passim*; Conway, *op. cit.*, p. 14.

[13] For the meat trade see *Primer libro de actas de cabildo*, p. 161, where Alonso and Bartolomé de Morales contracted to supply the city for a year. For the procedure see William H. Dusenberry, "The Regulation of Meat Supply in Sixteenth-Century Mexico City," *Hispanic American Historical Review*, XXVIII (1948), 38-52.

[14] Medina, *Inquisición primitiva*, I, 122, mentions this case. There is a confusion as to whether the fluid was water, wine, or something else.

ing her menstrual period. There was testimony that Alonso had rebaptized other children in conformity with the Mosaic Law.

The charges against Gonzalo de Morales were also serious.[15] Witnesses in 1574 testified that Gonzalo de Morales had been tried after Bishop Manso of Puerto Rico had written a letter to the Dominican monastery in Mexico City stating that Morales' sister had been burned at the stake in Santo Domingo as a Judaizante, and that she had inculpated Gonzalo. The sister related that the two of them had flogged a crucifix placed on a door latch. Morales also kept concubines.

During the course of the trial, Morales was proven guilty of another crucifix incident, this time with Palma, the same man who had mocked the sacrament of baptism with Hernando Alonso. They had urinated on the crucifix and then Morales flogged it, after which Palma ". . . le ponía los pies arriba y la cabeza baja y el dicho Morales decía como merece." It was ascertained that Morales had a brother in Guatemala who had been reconciled by the Mexican Inquisition for saying, among other things, "que Dios tenía hijo."[16] Gonzalo de Morales had confessed when taken to the torture chamber and ordered to disrobe.

It appeared from the testimonies in 1574 that both Alonso and Morales had confessed and asked for mercy. Subsequent officials, including President Sebastián Ramírez de Fuenleal, had remarked upon the harshness of the sentence and inquired the reason for not granting mercy. He was told, as was Licenciado Bonilla in 1574, that the confessions had come too late for the heretics to be reconciled. There remains some doubt as to whether Alonso and Morales received due process of law in these convictions.[17] Perhaps these burnings led to the dismissal of Santa María as Commissary of the Holy Office in Mexico.

The third Judaizante was Diego de Ocaña, a scribe and a resident of Sevilla. Ocaña had arrived in Mexico from Santo Domingo in June of 1525 and was licensed by the cabildo to become a notary on June 20, 1525.[18] By November 13, 1525, he bore the title of *escribano público y de gobernación*.[19] Ocaña was a bitter critic of Cortés. He wrote a series

[15] Conway, "Hernando Alonso," p. 20. See also Millares Carlo and Mantecón, *Protocolos del Archivo de Notarías*, p. 445, *passim*.

[16] Diego de Morales, the brother, was a merchant and miner who worked in and out of Mexico City. The Inquisition *proceso* is still extant (AGN, Inquisición, Tomo I, exp. 11) and it indicates that Diego was reconciled in the same *auto* that ended in the burning of his brother, October 17, 1528. Millares Carlo and Mantecón, *Protocolos del Archivo de*

*Notarías*, I, 445, give corroborative evidence.

[17] One cannot control the impulse to speculate whether these burnings had political overtones. The Dominicans and Cortés were at odds over the death (or murder) of the judge of *residencia*, Luis Ponce. It seems strange that the two pro-Cortés men were burned while the violent foe of Cortés, Diego de Ocaña, was reconciled.

[18] *Primer libro de actas de cabildo*, p. 44.

[19] AGI, Patronato, Leg. 54, núm. 2.

of letters to the Casa de Contratación in Sevilla in which he denounced the conqueror's greed and dishonesty in the administration of New Spain.[20]

Ocaña's crimes against the faith are not given in detail in the "Testimonies on Sanbenitos." We are informed that he killed chickens "por el espinazo," that he ate meat on Fridays, "y los demás días tiburón y otros pescados, al modo judaico." Other than his eating habits, we are merely told that he performed Jewish ceremonies and followed the Law of Moses. Ocaña was in the cell next to Gonzalo de Morales but he was allowed to communicate with no one. Morales confessed that Ocaña either talked to himself or the wall and said: "a ti digo, pared, que no confieses, porque los testigos son muertos," words which Morales heard perfectly.

That there were other charges more serious against Diego de Ocaña is evident. We learn that he was able to escape the death penalty only upon the intervention of the secretary of Gonzalo de Salazar, the treasury official, and that even then he lost his properties, was banished from Mexico, and had to wear the sanbenito for six months, along with the *coroza*. Ocaña was married and had a son, Hernán Xuárez, who, seeing the father in penitential garb, declared that he was not Ocaña's son, but a servant in the household. Ocaña later disinherited Xuárez for this denial. Bernal Díaz del Castillo informs us that Ocaña was able to secure a license to return to New Spain and that he married a woman from Castilla.[21] Medina indicates that he returned to Mexico and lived many years.[22]

## II. *Zumárraga and the Judaizantes: Gonzalo Gómez, 1536*

Apostolic Inquisitor Zumárraga set out to deal with the Judaizantes immediately after he organized his tribunal. On September 19, 1536, Cristóbal de Valderrama of Mexico City denounced Gonzalo Gómez of Michoacán as a *reconciliado* from Spain who persisted in observing the Jewish Sabbath and working on Sundays and saints' days.[23] He was also accused of baptizing a dying Indian and laughing while he did it.[24]

Zumárraga's trial of Gonzalo Gómez gives us a clear expression of Jewish practices in Mexico. After the testimonies had been taken, the fiscal made his accusations. He indicted Gómez on thirteen counts of heresy:

[20] Conway cited these letters in DII, XIII, 348-356 and 393-406.

[21] Bernal Díaz del Castillo, *Historia verdadera de la conquista de la Nueva España* (2 vols.; México, 1904), II, 353, 397.

[22] Medina, *Inquisición primitiva*, I, 124n. The Ocaña will, dated 1533, is published in *La Vida colonial*, Vol. VII of the *Publica-* *ciones del Archivo General de la Nación* (México, 1923), 1-8.

[23] AGN, Inquisición, Tomo 2, exp. 2.

[24] Valderrama said that the Christian witnesses to the baptism were horrified when Gómez proceeded to say "Yo te bautizo en el nombre del Padre y del Hijo y del Espíritu Santo."

1) That he and other Spaniards had baptized a dying Indian, saying that the sacrament meant nothing, and that it was a joke.

2) That he had said while examining various religious paintings of judgment day, hell, and purgatory that such things were wishful thinking.

3) That he had said that he would not go to Mass, nor did he care to see God during all his life.

4) That he had taken down a Cross from the patio of a farm that he owned, placed it on the roof of a straw hut, and had hung strings of chili peppers on the Cross to dry.

5) That on Good Friday he had broken the arms from three Crosses on the same farm.

6) That when a pilgrim asked for directions, he told him to go in the same direction that a stick that used to be a Cross was pointing—this he said as a joke.

7) That he had a building on his ranch which the clergy had used for Mass, but at times when the priests were not around, Gómez allowed it to be used by the Indians and Spaniards as a rendezvous for fornication. He encouraged friends to bring their concubines there, and the place was very dirty and infested with fleas.

8) That when discussing images with a friend, he said that he must hurry home to burn a crucifix which he had broken.

9) That en route to Mexico City on horseback, he had raised his eyes to Heaven and renounced his belief in God.

10) That he had persistently made his Indians and other servants work on the Sabbath and holy days.

11) That it was his habit to observe the Jewish Sabbath. When he traveled he secured lodgings on Fridays, rested on Saturdays, and resumed his journey on Sundays.

12) That he refused to go to confession, blasphemed, and tried to pervert the beliefs of others.

13) That he was a *converso* whose parents and relatives had been *reconciliados* in Spain, and as such he had come to New Spain illegally.

The fiscal demanded the full sanctions for Gonzalo Gómez as a Judaizante.

The Mexican Judaizante of whom Gómez was a prototype was seldom convicted solely for practicing Jewish rites. He was ordinarily a person who showed great disrespect and contempt for Christianity by word, deed, and example, especially in sexual morality. He frequently tried to undermine the faith of others and of the native population. For these reasons he was considered to be more dangerous than other heretics.

Although Gómez contended to the last that the above charges had been fabricated by his enemies, Zumárraga could not be swayed to leniency. He commanded Gonzalo to present himself at the cathedral of Mexico, barefoot and with a candle in his hand. On his knees Gómez had to recite ". . . cinco Ave Marías consuelo por Nuestra Señora a las plagas que Nuestro Redentor recibio en el arbol de la Cruz por salvar el humano linage" and also the rosary five times so that God would pardon his sins. Zumárraga also sentenced him to an indefinite reclusion in a monastery to meditate upon his sins and fined him the stringent sum of four hundred *pesos de oro de minas*. He was admonished not to continue his observance of Saturdays or his blasphemies upon pain of relaxation to the secular arm.

### III. *Zumárraga's Campaign against the Jews, 1539*

Zumárraga's most celebrated Judaizante case proved to be that of Francisco Millán, a Mexico City saloon-keeper. The denunciation came on December 3, 1538, when Juan Garzón of Mexico City indicated that María, a Moorish slave of Millán, had told him of an incident that convinced him that Francisco had reverted to Judaism.[25] María had discovered her master flogging an image of the Virgin Mary and demanding that it give him money. When questioned, María could describe no other Jewish ceremonies that her master performed. It was fairly clear that although Millán might be a Judaizante, María was motivated by a slave's hate of the master, especially since it was learned that he had forced himself upon her with carnal intent.

Throughout December of 1538 and January of 1539 the accused desperately tried to conceal the fact that he was the son of *conversos* who had been tried and penanced by the Spanish Inquisition. His first testimony revealed that he was an orphan and that he had no recollections of his parents. He indicated that he had traveled throughout Spain and Portugal as a merchant but that he had never fled to Lisbon to escape the jurisdiction of the Inquisition, as had been charged. He feigned ignorance of the term *"relajado."* He was not even sure that he was a baptized Catholic, but he indicated that if this were not the case, he would welcome the sacrament at the first opportunity. He denied flogging an image of the Virgin and demanding that it provide him with money. He testified that his wife and three sons lived in Xerez de la Frontera in Spain and that they were practicing Catholics. Zumárraga was not convinced of the sincerity of the defendant, and he ordered the embargo of Millán's properties until the truth could be determined.

On December 27, 1539, Francisco Millán came before Zumárraga

[25] AGN, Inquisición, Tomo 30, exp. 8.

to indicate that he had been deceived by the devil into giving false testimony and that he wished to rectify the matter. He admitted, by stages, his parentage, using the information given him by a mythical friend in Lisbon who ostensibly had known his father and mother. He confirmed their Jewish faith and the fact that they had been tried as Judaizantes. He admitted flogging the image and two crucifixes in his home because he had been deceived by the devil. For the same reason he had eaten meat on Fridays.

In order to draw the attention of Zumárraga and his staff away from himself, he resorted to the time-honored device of incriminating others and named a dozen or more *conversos* who, he said, were living in the viceregal capital and practicing the old religion. Among these were people who had given evidence against him: Juan Garzón, Francisca de Herrera, and others.

After prompting from the fiscal and the nuncio of the Holy Office, Millán confessed that he considered himself to be a Jew and that he had lived according to the Law of Moses in Portugal. He expressed genuine contriteness about his past, asking Zumárraga's mercy. He told the Inquisitor that he would publicly abjure all his heresies and that he would give the names of many Jews from Xerez de la Frontera in Mexico City.

Among the denounced were the entire family of the tailor Alvaro Mateos; an Antón Carmona who had been penanced in Sevilla; a Francisco Martín who was a fugitive from the Sevilla tribunal; Alvar Pérez, a *converso* from Xeres; a wine merchant, Francisco Serrano; a silversmith, Juan Ruiz; a certain teacher called Redondo; a *reconciliado* by the name of García de Morón; and countless others. While there may have been many Judaizantes among these people, it was obvious that Millán was letting his imagination run rampant.[26]

In order to ascertain the truth, and because Millán had certainly showed himself to be a person who trifled with the truth, Zumárraga determined on February 26, 1539, to subject the accused to torture. Juan Rebollo, Zumárraga's provisor, was ordered to supervise the torture, and he recommended to Millán that he avoid the anguish by giving a complete and true confession. Francisco was stripped and placed upon the rack. With successive tightening of the cords he refused to alter the testimony concerning himself and the Jewish colony in Mexico City.

On February 28, 1539, Zumárraga signed the petition that Millán receive the sacrament of baptism because he had demonstrated his sincere desire to turn from his life of Judaism. Zumárraga maintained, however, that this conversion did not exempt the accused from punishment for his crimes against the faith. Sentence was passed on this same day.

[26] For investigations of many of these individuals and others, see below, pp. 97, f.

On March 2, 1539, Millán was conducted from the Inquisition jail
to the cathedral with a candle in his hands, and on his knees he publicly
abjured, detested, and retracted all of his errors and his Jewish past. He
was condemned to wear the sanbenito and *coroza* until the Inquisitors
of the Sevilla Tribunal should allow him to do away with these garments.
He was banished perpetually from New Spain and the Indies and was
charged to leave on the next sailing from Veracruz. All of his properties
in Mexico were confiscated by the Holy Office. He was to remain in
confinement in his home until passage to Sevilla could be arranged.

Millán's penance was observed by the most illustrious personages in
Mexico City. Viceroy Mendoza, the Marqués del Valle de Oaxaca,
Hernando Cortés, the bishops of Oaxaca and Michoacán, and the oidores
of the Audiencia of Mexico witnessed the abjurations. Although Millán
possessed moderate wealth, the Holy Office netted little from the estate
in the long run, for the next two years were filled with lawsuits by Millán's creditors to recover their just debts.

Francisco Millán, like the Lutheran Nizardo, did not leave Mexico.
In July of 1539 he was reported to have visited the mines of Taxco as a
beggar. He wore the sanbenito, but under his other clothes and not over
them as canon law prescribed. He then moved on to the Zultepeque area
to visit old friends and to beg from them. As late as August 1539 he was
seen in Toluca begging at the mines nearby and on the city streets. The
*proceso* does not inform us that Millán ever fulfilled the sentence of exile.

Immediately after Millán accused them of being Judaizantes, the
tailor Alvaro Mateos and his wife Beatrice Gómez were brought before
Zumárraga for trial.[27] On the whole the evidence against these two was
nebulous. They were accused of being Jews, but the accusation was
never proven. Millán claimed that he had known the tailor's mother in
Xerez and that Alvaro's father had exhorted him to be a good Jew.

Apparently Mateos and Beatriz never went to church although
they professed to be practicing Catholics. They always went out of their
way to avoid passing church buildings. Their method of preparing food
and their dietary habits smacked of Judaism. One witness testified that
he had visited the couple at home and that they were in the fruit arbor
preparing certain meats according to Jewish practice.[28] There was also
scattered evidence that Mateos had engaged in the traditional Jewish disrespect and ridicule of Christianity, and that on one occasion he had con-

[27] AGN, Inquisición, Tomo 30, exp. 9
and 9b.

[28] ". . . y su muger estaba despelizcando
cierta carne en un lebrillo que le parecio a
este que declara que le estaba espulgando e
quitando las landrecillas de la dicha Carne
e que se afirma que es verdad que le estaba
quitando las landrecillas a forma de Judio.
. . ."

tended that Zumárraga did not understand what he was saying in the sermons he preached.

In view of the questionable denunciation of Mateos and Beatriz by Millán and the lack of clear-cut testimony and evidence, Zumárraga finally decided that the fiscal, Canego, had been unable to offer sufficient proof that this couple were Judaizantes. He therefore absolved them of any crime against the faith, although they were admonished to lead more exemplary Christian lives in the future.

The Millán trial and his denunciations of other alleged Judaizantes in Mexico City prompted the Holy Office to launch an extensive investigation. Zumárraga framed a general interrogatory and testimonies were taken from some dozen people. The witness was required to state his name and birthplace. He was asked his marital status and how long he had been in Mexico. Then the interrogatory moved to the business at hand: Was he a New Christian of the son of a New Christian? Was he of a *converso* family? Had either he or his parents been reconciled or relaxed? Was he a fugitive from the Spanish Inquisition? Did he know anyone in Mexico who fitted the above descriptions?

Testimonies of seven of the individuals mentioned by Millán are extant. García de Morón,[29] Anton Cercado,[30] Francisco Serrano,[31] García Hernández,[32] Beatriz Hernández,[33] Juan Ruiz, *platero*,[34] and Rodrigo de Soria,[35] all testified and convinced the Holy Office of their *limpieza de sangre*. In the course of the investigation eight other persons were denounced: Juan de Salamanca,[36] Antón de Heredia,[37] Manuel Borallo, Juan Rodríquez and Diego Machuca,[38] one Alonso de Avila who was accused of having a crucifix under his desk and resting his feet upon it,[39] and Juan de Baeza.[40] Only Baeza was tried. Juan de Baeza exhibited the usual Jewish loathing for Catholicism but combined it with proselytizing. His most scandalous crime was the circumcision of Indian children with his fingernails. On May 14, 1540, Zumárraga fined him twenty *pesos de oro de minas* and the costs of the trial, an extremely lenient sentence in view of his nefarious activities.

In the case of the Judaizantes as well as the Indian idolaters and

[29] AGN, Inquisición, Tomo 40, exp. 3 bis. F.

[30] AGN, Inquisición, Tomo 40, exp. 3 bis. D.

[31] AGN, Inquisición, Tomo Ia, exp. 21.

[32] AGN, Inquisición, Tomo I, exp. 18.

[33] AGN, Inquisición, Tomo I, exp. 19.

[34] AGN, Inquisición, Tomo Ia, exp. 22.

[35] AGN, Inquisición, Tomo Ia, exp. 20.

[36] AGN, Inquisición, Tomo 125, exp. 1.

[37] AGN, Inquisición, Tomo 40, exp. 3 bis. E.

[38] AGN, Inquisición, Tomo 22, exp. 9.

[39] AGN, Inquisición, Tomo Ia, exp. 23 bis. This is an *averiguación*. No other mention was made of this charge.

[40] AGN, Inquisición, Tomo 125, exp. 5 and 7. In this and the above bibliographical references, I have given the Tomo and expediente as they are defined in the Catálogo. In many of these cases the numbers do not conform to the actual documents, although the documents cited may be found in the general area cited.

sorcerers, Zumárraga's Inquisition failed. The Jewish community continued to grow in Mexico City, Pachuca, and the Nuevo León area, and the *conversos* discreetly practiced the old rites in private. It was not until the last two decades of the sixteenth century that the tribunal of the Holy Office made a concerted effort to eradicate the Judaizantes.[41] Again the effort failed, perhaps because the converted Jew had evolved a hardiness and cunning with which the Holy Office could not cope.

[41] This campaign centered around the Carvajal family of Nuevo León. Its ramifications were much wider in that the tribunal hoped to use the example of the Carvajal burnings to restrain the other Mexican Judaizantes. Not all of the Carvajal trials have been published. See Alfonso Toro, *Los Judíos en la Nueva España*, pp. 209-372; his two volumes on *La Familia Carvajal* (México, 1944) are the most recent study. See also *Procesos de Luis de Carvajal (El Mozo)*, Volume XXVIII of the *Publicaciones del Archivo General de la Nación* (México, 1935) and Pablo Martínez del Río, *Alumbrado* (México, 1937), but his classification of Luis Carvajal as an illuminist is open to argument.

# CHAPTER VII

# The Problem of Blasphemy and the Enforcement of Morality

## I. *The Nature of Blasphemy*

Henry C. Lea has defined blasphemy as "an imprecation derogatory or insulting to the Divinity."[1] The Levitical Codes prescribed death for the offense, but canon law and civil law by the end of the fifteenth century had mitigated the punishment to scourging and cutting out the tongue. Neither ecclesiastical nor civil authorities ever developed a clear rule on what constituted simple blasphemy as opposed to heretical blasphemy. The Spanish Renaissance Inquisitor Nicolas Eymeric had made this uneasy distinction. To Eymeric blasphemy was non-heretical when the imprecation reviled God or the Virgin or expressed ingratitude to them, but this he contended was of no concern to the Inquisition. On the other hand, heretical blasphemy entailed some denial of the articles of the faith.[2]

In the Spanish Inquisition words uttered in anger while emotionally distraught were generally considered to be blasphemy and not heresy. Apparently only the worst cases were tried, and frequently denunciation was not required if the blasphemer had not denied an article of the faith. Lea contended that blasphemy was a trait of the Spanish character:

The Spaniard was choleric, and not especially nice in his choice of words when moved by wrath; gambling was an almost universal passion and, in all lands and ages, nothing has been more provocative of ejaculations and expletives than the vicissitudes of cards and dice.[3]

Lea indicated that although these expletives might have been irreverent and indecent, they were not necessarily heretical:

[1] Lea, *The Spanish Inquisition*, IV, 328. Lea's chapter on blasphemy is found on pages 328-335. Very valuable is John W. Melody, "Blasphemy," *The Catholic En-cyclopedia* (New York, 1910), II, 595-596.

[2] Lea, *The Spanish Inquisition*, IV, 328; Eymericus, *op. cit.*, n.p.

[3] Lea, *The Spanish Inquisition*, IV, 330.

There was a class of these, which seem to have been in the mouth of everyone, ineradicable by the most severe legislation, such as "Mal grado aya Dios" (May it spite God), "Pese a Dios" (May God regret), "Reniego a Dios" (I renounce God), "Descreo de Dios" (I disbelieve in God) etc., for which Ferdinand and Isabella in their laws of 1492 and 1502 provided penalties ranging from a month's imprisonment for a first offense to piercing the tongue for a third. . . .[4]

In Spain the Inquisition concerned itself less and less with blasphemy as the sixteenth century advanced, perhaps because of a growing popular reverence, but most likely from a growing disinclination to denounce those guilty. In Mexico this was not the case. To be sure, only grave offenders were tried but there were hundreds of denunciations. In addition there was no clear distinction between heresy and blasphemy.

## II. *Blasphemy among the Mexican Conquistadores: 1520-1528*

We know that both civil and religious authorities were greatly concerned with the problem of blasphemy in Mexico from the earliest days of the conquest. Cortés had issued ordinances against the crime in 1520.[5] The second edict issued by the obscure inquisitors of 1523 had been directed against all persons who by word or deed did things that seemed sinful.[6]

Upon his appointment as Commissary of the Holy Office in 1526, the Dominican Fray Domingo de Betanzos devoted his entire inquisitorial efforts against blasphemy among the colonists. There were nineteen trials conducted by Betanzos in 1527.[7] For the most part simple spiritual

[4] *Ibid.*, p. 331. While Lea's translation of "Pese a Dios" as "May God Regret" or "May God Repent" may have been academically correct, colloquially it had a stronger meaning, such as "To Hell with God" or "God Damn" or "God gives me a pain."

[5] These were published in *Escritos sueltos de Hernán Cortás* (México, 1871), pp. 16-17. The original ordinances are found in AGN, Hospital de Jesús, Leg. 271, exp. 11: "Item: por cuanto de los reniegos é blasfemias Dios Nuestro Señor es mucho deservido, y es la mayor ofensa que á su Santísimo Nombre se puede hacer, y por eso permite en las gentes recios y duros castigos; y no basta que seamos tan malos que por los inmensos beneficios que cada dia dél recibimos no le demos gracias, mas decimos mal y blasfemamos de su Santo Nombre; y por evitar tan aborrecible uso y pecado, mando que ninguna persona, de cualquiera condicion que sea, no sea osado de decir no creo en Dios, ni pese, ni reniego, ni del Cielo, ni no ha poder en Dios; y que lo mismo se en-

tienda de Nuestra Señora y de todos los otros santos, sopena que demas de ser ejecutadas las penas establecidas por las leyes del reino contra los blasfemos, la persona que en lo susodicho incurriere, pague quince castellanos de oro, la tercera parte para le primera cofradía de Nuestra Señora que en esas partes se hiciere, y la otra tercera parte para el fisco de su magestad, y la otra tercera parte para el juez que sentenciare."

[6] AGN, Inquisición, Tomo I, exp. 3. I have previously related that this edict disappeared from the Mexican Archive.

[7] The blasphemers were as follows:
Diego Núñez, AGN, Inquisición, Tomo I, exp. 7.
Juan Bello, exp. 8.
Gil González Benavides, exp. 9.
Juan Rodríguez de Villafuerte, exp. 9a.
Cristóbal Díaz, exp. 9c.
B. Quemado, exp. 9d.
Alonso de Espinosa, exp. 9e.
Rodrigo Rengel, exp. 10.
Francisco González, exp. 10b.
Francisco Núñez, exp. 10d.

penances were meted out as punishment along with reasonably stiff fines. The most serious case was that of Rodrigo Rengel, a conquistador more than eighty years of age, who was convicted of being a horrifying blasphemer.

After extensive testimonies the fiscal indicted Rengel on twenty-nine counts of blasphemy and scandalous language. Most of these statements were uttered in anger or in time of ill health. He had repeated the usual blasphemies: "No creo en Dios," "Descreo en Dios," "Reniego de Dios," "Mal grado haya Dios," "Pese a Dios," "No tiene poder Dios," and other *maldichos*.

Other statements blasphemous and indecent horrified the Inquisitors. When ill, the old man had said that God did not have power to cure individuals or cleanse their sins. Frequently from his bed he spat upon certain images because God had not given him relief from pain. When well he was an inveterate gambler. The gambling caused his expletives to flow like the wine he drank. He often announced that the devil was his master and helped him with the cards and dice because God could not help him to win. He often sang songs into which he incorporated his blasphemies and obscenities, spitting towards Heaven and threatening God. He was abusive to those who tried to restrain him. He did disgusting things with crucifixes.

In addition there were statements which would have been deemed heresy had it not been for his age and ill health and general cantankerousness. He had opined that the Indians should be allowed to practice their idolatries because he saw little harm in them. He had blasphemed against the Holy Mother and Saint Anne, the grandmother of Christ. He doubted the virginity of the Virgin and referred to her as a *puta* (whore). He was sure that Joseph had taken carnal access to Mary and was therefore Christ's father. He had often expressed his own doubts about the sacrament of marriage. There were evidences of cruelties, if not sexual perversion, in Rengel's treatment of his slaves and others.[8]

Sebastián de Arriaga, the fiscal, demanded that Rengel be punished to the full extent of the law and added that he felt that the old reprobate

Diego García, exp. 10c.
Gregorio de Monjarás, exp. 10e.
Alonso de Carrión, exp. 10f.
Bernaldo de Luna, AGN, Inquisición, Tomo IA, exp. 14.
Juan de Cuevas, exp. 15.
Alonso de Coriallana, exp. 16.
Lucas Gallego, exp. 17.
Hernando García Sarmiento, AGN, Inquisición, Tomo 14, exp. 2a.
[8] "Yten: Digo que el dicho Rengel es hombre cruel y sin piedad y se deleita en hacer crueldades sin causa y razon por que muchas vezes por su deleite y pasatiempo haze desnudar a los muchachos y muchachas Judios Esclavos y esclavas y los haze muy cruelmente e azotar y pingar en su presencia teniendo esto por pasatiempo ... como hombre enemigo de la naturaleza humana y de las criaturas criadas a imagen y semejanza de Dios."

should be burned. The defendant's reply to Arriaga was that of a humble man. He indicated that he had never been able to control his temper and that he was spasmodically ill with headaches and the like.[9] He confessed and asked for mercy, but not until he had recapitulated the story of his services in the conquest as Cortés' campmaster and he had affirmed his *limpieza* of the lineage of *cristianos viejos*.[10]

Motolinía, who acted as Commissary in Betanzos' absence, imposed a fairly harsh sentence especially from the financial standpoint. His attendance was required at Mass where he had to stand with a candle in his hand and then he was remanded to a monastery for a five-month incarceration during which he was to meditate upon his sins and do penance and pious works. He was ordered to provide food for five poor people for an indeterminate time and he was fined five hundred *pesos de oro de minas* to be used for the following pious works: a *marco de oro* (eight ounces) was to be given to the monastery of Santo Domingo in Mexico City to purchase a silver chalice and to carry on pious works; the church at Veracruz was to receive ten *marcos de oro* and a silver chalice; ten pesos each were to be given to the *Cofradías de Nuestra Señora de los Angeles* and *Nuestra Señora de la Cruz*; the remainder of the five hundred pesos was to go to the monastery of Santa Clara for the use of the poor and the orphans. Finally, Rengel was ordered to use his Indians to complete a hermitage under construction near Tacuba and to give to the Franciscan monastery in Mexico City three dozen tables to be used in its various activities.

The Rengel sentence was signed by Motolinía, September 3, 1527. Only one blasphemer, Diego de Morales was tried in 1528 by Fray Vicente de Santa María, who assumed the office of Commissary that year.[11] Morales was the last blasphemer tried before the Holy Office until 1536 and the Zumárraga campaign against blasphemy.

### III. *Zumárraga and the Blasphemers: 1536-1540*

The Apostolic Inquisitor was a diligent foe of the blasphemer and particularly second and third offenders. The Zumárraga period yielded some fifty-six cases of blasphemy, by far the most prevalent crime.[12] Approximately one third of these were self-denunciations.

---

[9] The tone of the *proceso* indicated that Rengel was suffering from the ravages of syphilis, although the specific word is not employed.

[10] Rodrigo Rengel was an important person in the Mexican society of the 1520's. Besides having been Cortés' campmaster, he was also an alcalde ordinario of Mexico City and later a regidor on the cabildo.

He was also a man of considerable wealth.

[11] AGN, Inquisición, Tomo 1, exp. 11. Diego de Morales was the brother of the Judaizante Gonzalo de Morales who was relaxed to the secular arm in 1528. Diego did his penace and migrated to Guatemala.

[12] The majority of these trials are found in AGN, Inquisición, Tomo 14. The remainder are scattered throughout the *ramo*.

In point of chronology, the first case was that of Juan Franco, the "Limper," whose trial began in February and ended in November of 1536. Franco denounced himself as a gambler who often, in the heat of the game, uttered such oaths as "Por vida de Dios" and "Pese a los Santos" and "Voto a Dios" (Confound God). His contrition moved Zumárraga to lenience, but nevertheless he was fined thirty *pesos de oro de minas* after doing spiritual penance. He was required to recite the penitential psalms if he could read and the rosary of Our Lady if he could not read. This sentence was passed on November 9, 1536.[13]

September 22, 1536, saw the initiation of a blasphemy trial involving Marín Cortés[14] who had by *auto-denuncia* testified that he habitually said "Peze a Dios e no creo en Dios y descreo de Dios y como Dios es verdad e como Dios es Trino ... y por la Virginidad de Nuestra Señora." He swore his contrition and threw himself upon Zumárraga's mercy. After a cursory reading of the *denuncia* which said that the accused had traveled and lived in Guatemala and Honduras, Don Alfonso Toro concluded that the defendant was Martín Cortés, son of the conqueror.[15] A careful reading of the testimonies revealed that Marín was the son of Jorge Cortés and Leonor Marín of Murcia in Spain. In this testimony Cortés admitted having been jailed in Campeche by the adelantado Montejo for alleged blasphemies but denied the veracity of the charge, contending that Montejo had a personal animosity for him. Gagged and barefoot with the traditional candle in his hand, Marín Cortés did penance in the cathedral of Mexico City. Since he was a person of little means there was no fine.

The gambler Alonso de Carrión was denounced to Zumárraga by Cristóbal de Buenaventura as a habitual blasphemer and one who had declared publicly "No creo en Dios si me puedes hacer mas mal," and had raised his eyes saying "Descreo en ti y de quien te pario."[16] It developed in Carrión's testimony that he had been tried in 1527 by Betanzos for the same crime.[17] As a second offender he had no other choice but to plead for mercy. He was lucky to have convinced the Inquisitor of his contrition. The sentence was pronounced on October 14, 1536: Carrión was to appear at Mass barefoot and hatless, gagged and with a candle in his hand, and was to remain standing during the ceremonies. After he had consumed the sacrament of the Eucharist he was to recite Pater Nosters and Ave Marías until the people dispersed.

A Negro by name of Alonso Garavito was sentenced in late 1536

[13] AGN, Inquisición, Tomo 38, exp. I bis.

[14] AGN, Inquisición, Tomo 14, exp. 16.

[15] Toro, *Los Judíos en la Nueva España*, prólogo. The son of Cortés to whom Toro refers could have been no more than a child in 1536. See also Ibáñez, *op. cit.*, p. 70.

[16] AGN, Inquisición, Tomo 14, exp. 3.

[17] AGN, Inquisición, Tomo 1, exp. 16.

because of certain blasphemies uttered during ball games, usually in ex-hortation of his teammates or by shouting "Por vida de Dios."[18] His initial reply to the charges was a denial, but upon being informed of the penalties for perjury, he confessed and was fined ten *pesos de oro de minas.*

Juan Fernández del Castillo, a scribe, was a nefarious person. He had been tried by Betanzos in 1527 for encouraging the natives to practice idolatry,[19] and on September 12, 1536, he was denounced as a blas-phemer.[20] The usual "peses" and "reniegos" brought Fernández a fine of twenty *pesos de oro de minas* and public humiliations in church. It is odd that the sentence was not stiffer.

Women, but usually lower class ones, were frequently tried for blas-phemy. A short but somewhat unusual case was that of María de Es-pinosa, who in a moment of anger was reported to have renounced the chrism.[21] Her sentence was to stand without a shawl or shoes, gagged, during Mass and to take the Holy Eucharist, kneeling, after which she was required to recite various devotionals.

Zumárraga tried eight blasphemers in 1537 but none of these cases was unique. The confusion between blasphemy and heresy was never alleviated in the decades of the 1530's and the 1540's.[22] The year 1538 brought thirteen of these cases, but again the charges were routine. In March of the next year, García González, a mule driver, was sentenced for saying "pese a Dios y descreo de Dios y de sus Santos y . . . reniego del Cielo y de la tierra y de cuantos en el Cielo. . . ."[23] He was fined some twenty *pesos de oro de minas* and made to perform the customary spirit-ual penances.

The tailor, Juan de Villate, appeared before Zumárraga's court on May 2, 1539, as a blasphemer and a heretic.[24] The final disposition of the case was blasphemy. Villate had severely chastized his wife for pray-ing to an image of the Virgin Mary. In a fit of rage he had beaten the woman and instructed her not to pray to God but to the devil. The tailor was sentenced on May 22. A fine of ten *pesos de oro de minas* was made payable to the treasurer of the Holy Office, but an additional one *peso de oro común* was required to be given as alms to the Hospital de las Bubas in Mexico City. Villate was ordered to present the receipt

[18] AGN, Inquisición, Tomo 14, exp. 12 bis.

[19] AGN, Inquisición, Tomo 40, exp. 3 bis. A.

[20] AGN, Inquisición, Tomo 14, exp. 14.

[21] AGN, Inquisición, Tomo 14, exp. 17. bis. Chrism is consecrated oil used in the sacraments of baptism, confirmation, and ordination.

[22] In Chapter V I have included certain of the heretical blasphemers who seemed to be definite heretics. It is admitted that the distinction is often nebulous.

[23] AGN, Inquisición, Tomo 2, exp. 5.

[24] AGN, Inquisición, Tomo 2, exp. 9.

for the gift to the Holy Office and to recite the rosary of Our Lady five times as penance.

December of 1540 produced a case of some interest because the blasphemy involved a member of Viceroy Antonio de Mendoza's household, his female baker.[25] While fighting with Manuel Fernández both the woman and Fernández said "Voto a Dios" and insulted the person of Bishop Zumárraga. The woman escaped punishment, but Fernández was required to recite the Ave María and the Pater Noster five times each and to make a pilgrimage barefoot to the church at Tlatelolco in penance, and at the same time to pay the costs of the trial.

The Fleming from Zultepeque, Jacob de Cayzer, who had testified against Juan Banberniguen, was processed for blasphemy in April of 1540.[26] To be on the safe side, the Apostolic Inquisitor made sure that Cayzer held none of the views of his compatriot. The case ended with a simple blasphemy charge. Cayzer was prone to say "Juro a Dios" and he had used abusive language when Pedro de Medinilla, the alguacil of the Holy Office, took him into custody. Since his offense was slight, the sentence was merely spiritual penance.

Zumárraga tried his last two blasphemers in January of 1541. Both Juan de Avila[27] and Alonso Bueno[28] had denounced themselves for the usual expletives such as "Por vida de Dios" and "Pese." Only light fines were levied against the defendants.

Zumárraga's campaign against blasphemy was moderately successful during his ministry as Apostolic Inquisitor. The more serious trials probably resulted in some restraint on the part of those who would blaspheme. To assume, however, that blasphemy was eradicated by the Zumárraga Inquisition would be a mistake, for the records show a voluminous amount of prosecutions in succeeding years. It is interesting to note that Indians very rarely blasphemed. The sixteenth century recorded only one Indian blasphemer, Melchor of Santiago de Guatemala.[29]

## IV. *The Problem of Bigamy and Sexual Morality*

Care was taken in the early days of the conquest to send to Mexico only clergymen and laymen of unquestioned moral standards and purpose. The major concern of the crown and the Church was to present

[25] AGN, Inquisición, Tomo 14, exp. 37.
[26] AGN, Inquisición, Tomo 14, exp. 36.
[27] AGN, Inquisición, Tomo 14, exp. 39. See Suárez de Peralta, *op. cit.*, p. xii for Federico Gómez de Orozco's prologue in which he relates that Martín de Campos, secretary of Zumárraga's Holy Office, kept some of the *procesos* which were inherited by his son. The son sold part of the Avila *proceso* to Avila's son, Juan Suárez de Avila, for twenty pesos and a white horse. Apparently Campos' son had other *procesos*, relates Gomez de Orozco, ". . . y pensando que sería buen negocio adquirirlos para venderlos a los herederos de los allí procesados, los compraron todos."

[28] AGN, Inquisición, Tomo 14, exp. 40.
[29] AGN, Inquisición, Tomo 16, exp. 11.

good examples of Christians to the Indians. Despite this idealistic policy, many reprobates entered the kingdom of New Spain. The Holy Office was reasonably diligent in ferreting them out and punishing them as bad examples of Christianity. Especially in the area of carnal relations did serious problems arise.

The conquest enterprise was a military venture and as such excluded family colonization in the early years. As the decade of the 1520's came to a close, the crown began to place added emphasis on family colonization in Mexico. In theory miscegenation was discouraged, but since the wives were left in Spain, a mestizo population, arising out of illicit relations for the most part, resulted. In order to correct this deplorable situation and to prevent the sins of bigamy and concubinage among the colonists, Charles V decreed in 1530 that married men could not emigrate to the New World without their wives. Encomenderos to retain their rights had to bring their wives to Mexico within a specified time limit. Merchants could spend three years in the New World but had to return to Spain for their spouses at the end of that time or face deportation penalties.[30]

The gap between the law and actual practice was enormous. Bigamy, concubinage, and prostitution were inevitable. Bigamy and concubinage were both civil and religious crimes, but due to the Church's monopoly in administering the sacrament of marriage, the Holy Office of the Inquisition assumed jurisdiction overe these and related crimes. The friar-inquisitors, and later Zumárraga, experienced real difficulty in inculcating the precept of monogamy among the Aztecs. Polygamy had been one of the bases of social organization in the pre-conquest period and was a specific privilege of the Aztec nobility. Wives were regarded as wealth and even used as a medium of exchange. The example of licentious conquistadores and clergymen did much to vitiate the teachings of the friars:

The absurdity, however, of trying to suppress concubinage among the Indians in view of the growing multitude of half-breed children running about must have impressed the Council, and it instructed Bishop Zumárraga, who had charge of the moral policing of the colony, to refrain from fining the Indians a mark (eight ounces) of silver for keeping mistresses. He must, of course, continue in his efforts to reform them, but *poco a poco*.[31]

Trials for bigamy among the colonists of Mexico occupied a large part of the time of the Mexican Holy Office. Between 1536 and 1541

[30] See the *Recopilación*, Book IX, title 26, laws 28 and 29 for these and other laws on emigration designed to protect the institution of holy matrimony.
[31] Lesley B. Simpson, *The Encomienda in New Spain*, p. 116. This is a citation based upon a letter from the queen to Zumárraga of June 26, 1536, reproduced in Puga, *op. cit.*, I, 384-385.

Apostolic Inquisitor Zumárraga tried some twenty individuals of all walks of life for being married two or three times or more.[32] The trials were all more or less on the same pattern. As a rule the punishments were exceedingly stringent and designed to warn others of the penalties prescribed for breaking the marriage vows.

Both men and women were processed by Zumárraga for bigamy and no distinction was made in the sentences meted out. Usually as stiff a fine as the culprit could afford was levied, along with one hundred lashes or a prison term, or both. Without exception the bigamist was required to return to the legitimate spouse. It was a costly and time-consuming thing to prove that one's wife had died in Spain and that the second marriage was therefore legal. This was one of the devices used with frequency by the guilty to stall for time or to divert suspicion from their culpability.

Sexual perversion of all kinds was under the jurisdiction of the Mexican Holy Office, although civil authorities could take cognizance of the crime also.[33] Homosexuality, and particularly sodomy, was a prime concern to the Inquisition, and the *procesos* leave no detail of the crime to the reader's imagination.[34]

Incest was peculiarly prevalent among the native populations because in pre-conquest times it had been a perfectly acceptable practice. Caciques continued to demand their privileges among their subjects after the Spaniards came. Incestual relations within the families of conquistadores were very unusual. However, carnal relations between Spaniards and mother and daughter of other families was a fairly common occurrence.[35]

## V. *Special Problems in the Enforcement of Morality*

The high moral standards which Church and state prescribed for the spiritual conquerors often broke down. These deviant priests were a debilitating force in the Christianization process:

However, there were religious as well as military adventurers who flocked to the New World, men who looked on an ecclesiastical career in America merely as

---

[32] Many of these cases are found in AGN, Inquisición, Tomos 22 and 23.

[33] Lea's chapter *The Spanish Inquisition*, IV, 361-370 on unnatural crimes is valuable for background materials. The civil jurisdiction over homosexuality in Mexico of the first half of the sixteenth century can best be examined in France V. Scholes and Eleanor B. Adams, *Proceso contra Tzintzicha Tangaxoan 'el Caltzontzin formado por Nuño de Guzmán, año de 1530* (México, 1952).

[34] Of these trials the most interesting concerned two sailors who were brothers, Cebrian and Antonio Lipares. AGN, Inquisición, Tomo 212, exp. 11.

[35] AGN, Inquisición, Tomo 212, exp. 2 relates the most important of these cases: Diego Díaz por tener aceso carnal con madre y hija. AGN, Inquisición, Tomo 36, exp. 6 contains the trial of Martín Xuchimítl, an Indian accused of having four sisters as concubines. The denunciation is in hieroglyphics.

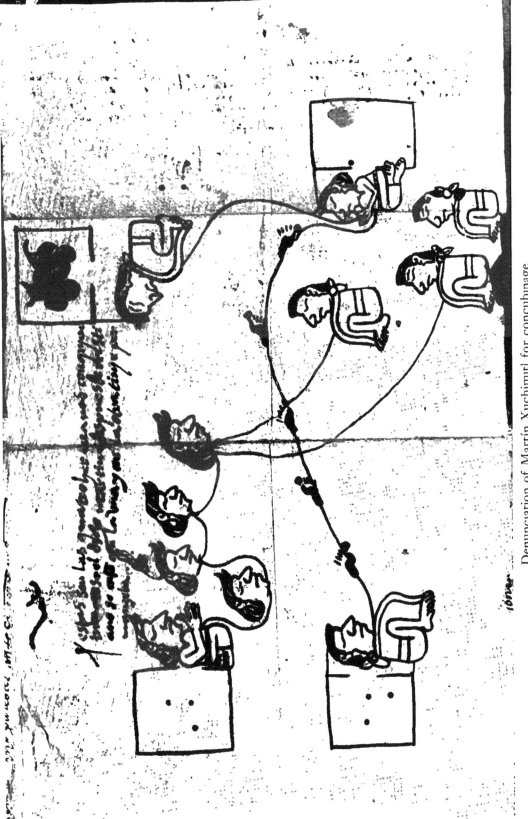

Denunciation of Martín Xuchimtl for concubinage
(From AGN, Tomo 36, exp. 6. See Chapter VII, note 35.)

an opportunity to gratify the desire for a life of ease and self-indulgence. Priests and friars, men of mediocre lights who had little prospect of success or distinction in the old country, came out to the colonies to seek their fortune.[36]

With this type of psychology described by Haring, it is not surprising that we have accounts of priests leaving their habits and living in sin. Some of the clergy had concubines, gambled, and threw riotous parties. Others became thieves and developed licentious habits. To correct this situation Charles V issued a cedula in 1530 which empowered the Casa de Contratación to license all clerics going to the Indies.[37]

The licensing process was not entirely adequate in controlling the emigration of questionable clerics to Mexico. On May 1, 1543, the crown found it necessary to issue another cedula prescribing the procedure to be followed in dealing with Mexican priests who had left their habits for the world.[38] The most notorius cleric tried by Zumárraga was Father Diego Díaz, the one-time parish priest at Ocuituco. Díaz had come to Mexico with Cortés in 1530 and launched a career that was scandalous. He appeared three times before the Inquisition and his crimes shocked the entire hierarchy of the Mexican Church.[39]

Father Díaz was first tried by Zumárraga in 1540 because it was proven that he had recruited two witnesses to denounce the cacique of Ocuituco for idolatry.[40] It had been his intention to allow the cacique to bribe him to withdraw the witnesses. After this plan failed for reasons which we do not know, Father Díaz was tried for perjury when the plot became known to Zumárraga. Although we do not have a record of Díaz' sentence in 1540, we know that he went to jail until 1542. While incarcerated he was sued in 1542 by his wine merchant, Juan Ruiz, because he would not pay his bill. From the testimonies we must conclude that Díaz also drank heavily, as the bill was extremely large.

Although it seems inconceivable, Díaz again presided as parish priest in Ocuituco from 1542 to 1548. It was learned that for six years he had been making immoral proposals to women in the confessional, and he was tried in 1548 as a *solicitante*.[41] Since the evidence was conclusive, we must assume that he was convicted, but we have no record of the sentence. Beyond a doubt there were many clerics as reprehensible

[36] Haring, *The Spanish Empire*, p. 206.

[37] Medina, *Inquisición, primitiva*, I, 40.

[38] This cedula was reproduced by Genaro García in *El clero de México durante la dominación Española*, pp. 94-95.

[39] For some mysterious reason all three of the Díaz *procesos* are fragmentary. They are found in AGN, Inquisición, Tomo 37, exp. 3 bis. (1540); AGN, Inquisición, Tomo 42, exp. 21 (1542); AGN, Inquisición, Tomo 68, exp. I (1542-1548). They are published by the Archivo General de la Nación in *Procesos de Indios*, pp. 221-258.

[40] For a discussion of this trial see Chapter III.

[41] Lea, *The Spanish Inquisition*, IV, 95-134, gives full treatment to the *solicitantes*.

as Díaz, but their biographies are not to be found in the Inquisition archives of this era.[42]

On the whole, Haring's vindication of the colonial Mexican clergy must be accepted:

If we wish to judge the clergy fairly we cannot separate it from its environment. Given the men with whom it had to deal, it perhaps did its best to prevent them from being worse and did all that could possibly be demanded of it.[43]

[42] In 1537 Father Sebastian Fragoso was tried for leaving his habit and living with a concubine saying that she was his wife. AGN, Inquisición, Tomo 34, exp. 2. In 1540 Father Alonso Ruiz de Arévalo was investigated in Pánuco for living with a married woman. AGN, Inquisición, Tomo 34, exp. 5.

[43] Haring, *The Spanish Empire*, p. 208.

# CHAPTER VIII

# Sorcery and Superstition in Mexico
# 1536-1543[1]

## I. *Introduction*

Sorcery and the occult arts had been a concern of the Spanish inquisitors from medieval times. No clear-cut policy against these offenses emerged until the Renaissance period; however, there was a general feeling of toleration of these activities unless the law was broken. Eymeric and his followers taking the lead of the theologians at the University of Paris, altered the viewpoint on sorcery at the turn of the fifteenth century. It was then assumed that soothsayers, curers, and practitioners of black magic (*nigromante*) had accrued their powers by entering into a pact with the devil. Such an act was inferential heresy and the Inquisition assumed jurisdiction over the problem.[2]

Witchcraft was regarded as a crime different from sorcery. Lea tells us that the Inquisitors were convinced that the "witch has abandoned Christianity, has renounced her baptism, has worshipped Satan as her God, has surrendered herself to him, body and soul, and exists only to be his instrument in working the evil to her fellow-creatures, which he cannot accomplish without a human agent."[3] The witch-madness of the fifteenth to eighteenth centuries was predicated upon this belief.

In sixteenth century Mexico, sorcery and superstition must be dealt with in a dual manner, Indian and Spanish. Native superstition and wizardry had a different purpose, namely the pacification of the gods and the direction of the forces of nature for man's benefit.[4] The Spanish

---

[1] Sorcery and superstition in Mexico may be studied from Julio Jiménez Rueda, *Herejías y supersticiones en la Nueva España* (México, 1946). An extremely useful, and rare source on the occult in early sixteenth century Spain is Pedro Ciruelo, *Reprobación de las supersticiones y hechicerías* (Salamanca, 1541).

[2] For the general nature of sorcery and

witchcraft, see Lea, *The Spanish Inquisition*, IV, 179-225.

[3] Lea, *The Spanish Inquisition*, IV, 206.

[4] Besides Caso, Motolinía and Sahagún, an extremely valuable encyclopedic reference on Indian sorceries and superstition is Jacinto de la Serna, *et al., Tratado de las idolatrías, supersticiones, dioses, ritos, hechicerías y otras costumbres gentílicas*

sorcerer and magician was essentially a nefarious person who capitalized on the ignorance and credulousness of his subjects, and his actions were surreptitious. The Mexican Inquisition proceeded against both of these groups with equal fervor. Sentences were harsh, but as a rule torture was not prescribed to elicit the confession.

## II. *Zumárraga and Sorcery and Superstition among the Colonists*

Since Indian superstition has been discussed in a previous chapter, I shall limit this section to trials of Europeans by Zumárraga's Holy Office for the crimes of sorcery and related offenses. Zumárraga had been particularly interested in combating the occult since his 1527 commission from Charles V to investigate witchcraft in the Pamplona region. We are told of this task by Mendieta[5] but the most recent biographer of Zumárraga concludes that the bishop-to-be could not have done more than initiate the proceedings in Biscay before he was called away to his post in Mexico.[6]

The Mexican Inquisition Archive records only one denunciation for sorcery prior to the Zumárraga period,[7] but when the Apostolic Inquisitor assumed his office, a large part of his effort was directed against sorcery and superstition. Of the twenty cases tried between 1536 and 1543, fifteen of the defendants were women. It would seem that midwifery and other pseudo-medical functions performed by women lent themselves to the occult.

We do not have the complete record of Zumárraga's first sorcery trial, that of Elvira Jiménez, a female cowherder.[8] Elvira had performed acts of divination in Puerto Rico in which she cut off the wings and legs of five chickens and used the limbs and blood in her incantations. She had been tried in San Juan and suffered public humiliations, including a burro ride through the streets while wearing penitential garb. In Mexico she had instructed Brígida García, a widow, in certain sorceries to be used in procuring another husband. Brígida was to light a small candle between one and two o'clock in the morning and recite a prayer given her by Elvira. After doing several *vueltas* around the candle, she was instructed to wait for it to fall from its holder, and according to the direction in which it fell and into which hand it fell, Brígida was to receive her desired spouse. The *vaquera* admitted her reputation as a sor-

*de las razas aborígenes de México* (México, c.1954). These treatises were written in the sixteenth and seventeenth centuries and often deal with the fusion of European and Mexican superstitions on some levels.
[5] Geronimo de Mendieta, *Historia eclesiástica indiana*, pp. 629, 636, 644, as cited by Lea, *The Spanish Inquisition*, IV, 215.
[6] Ruiz de Larrínaga, *op. cit.*, pp. 63-66.
[7] 1528, Denuncia de una hechicera por Benito de Bejel. AGN, Inquisición, Tomo I, exp. 12.
[8] AGN, Inquisición, Tomo 40, exp. 1.

cerer to Zumárraga and confirmed the instructions given to the widow García. The close of the *proceso* of the cowgirl-sorceress is missing.

On August 9, 1536, Zumárraga initiated a very interesting trial against Juan Franco, a jeweler, for participating in occult rites with his Indians in order to foretell the events of the future.[9] Franco's wife testified that she had seen the lapidary talking to the devil, who appeared at times the color of blue and at other times gray and black. Franco's medium was an Indian slave named Beatriz in whose powers he fervently believed, and who was also his concubine. Franco was accused of being a Jew because of his dietary habits and the fact that he was circumcised.[10] Almost a year of investigations took place before the fiscal Cervanes made his accusations on August 3, 1537. Juan Franco was indicted on twelve counts, not all of them for sorcery, the crime for which he was convicted. The charges were as follows:

1) Franco and Beatriz had performed sorceries to ascertain whether the turquoise mines of Xauhtepec would yield great profits and whether the recently arrived Viceroy Mendoza would make grants of land to the citizens. The entrails of chickens had been used in this ceremony. When away from home exercising his profession, Franco performed similar rites to determine what his wife was doing.

2) Through Beatriz, Franco was able to tell his companions what was transpiring in their homes even though they were far away. The process took some four hours.

3) Franco had been associated with Jews in Spain and in the Indies and had adopted their religious observances.

4) Franco was outspoken in his contention that Hernando Alonso, the Jew whom Santa María had burnt in 1528, had been unjustly condemned. Franco insisted, perhaps rightly, that Alonso should have been reconciled.

5) It was charged that the defendant had given the Indians some chickens to sacrifice to the devil in order to find out the true worth of the turquoise mine mentioned above.

6) Franco had publicly defended another relaxed Jew, one Montero, saying that if he were burned, Franco himself merited burning since they both believed the same things.

7) Franco was charged with using potions to make the devil appear as described in his wife's testimony.

8) It was alleged that the lapidary ordered his food prepared according to the Mosaic Law, although he contended that he prepared the food in that manner merely because he liked it.

[9] AGN, Inquisición, Tomo 38, exp. 1.
[10] Franco contended that the operation was performed by a barber in Española to alleviate the effects of venereal disease

9) Franco was accused of selling idols and charms to the Indians. He claimed that these were only dolls.

10) He was charged with long-standing concubinage with Beatriz, although each year keepers of concubines were excommunicated.

11) He had frequently taken the glands of animals from the butcher shop to be used in Jewish ceremonies.[11]

12) Many times Franco had asked his sister-in-law to perform sorceries, apparently to check on the veracity of his other mediums.

Cervanes demanded that Juan Franco be punished as a sorcerer and purveyor of superstition to the Indians and Spaniards alike, and that he was doubly guilty of being a new Christian and a *circumcidado*. Although the defendant claimed that the witnesses against him were motivated by hate, Apostolic Inquisitor Zumárraga was convinced of the lapidary's guilt. Sentence was passed on November 9, 1537, and was surprisingly lenient. The convicted was required to make the usual humiliating appearance at Mass and to recite the Penitential Psalms, consume the Eucharist while kneeling, and pay a fine of twenty *pesos de oro de minas*. Beatriz was to appear with Franco and was required to wear the *coroza* and recite Ave Marias so that God would pardon her sins.

In the first week of September, 1536, Zumárraga moved against five lower class Negro women of Mexico City for sorcery and superstitious practices.[12] The first defendant was Marta, a slave of Pedro Pérez, who had performed sorceries in the home of the treasurer Juan Alfonso de Sosa by using the ears of rabbits and the claws of chickens. Marta also dispensed potions and composed incantations for those who would procure a husband.[13] In the course of her testimony, Marta inculpated four other women who belonged to her social circle and who also performed sorceries. They all relied upon the potions and aphrodisiacs of Antón, an Indian from the environs of Mexico City. These medicines were reputed to promote love and marriage, to induce masters to set female slaves free, or to bestow upon them precious gifts. The midwife of the group, Isabel Morales, chanted incantations while delivering children, and to further insure successful delivery, called upon God and the Virgin in the same orations.[14] Isabel also performed illegal surgeries on the recently delivered mothers.

---

which he contracted from an Indian woman there.

[11] ". . . que ha sacado muchas veces la landrecilla del Carnero por ceremonia judaica."

[12] AGN, Inquisición, Tomo 38, exp. 2. This is a composite *proceso* of the five

trials and is extremely difficult to analyze because the pages are bound out of order.

[13] One of these husband-seekers was later tried separately by Zumárraga. The case of María Bárcena is found in AGN, Inquisición, Tomo 38, exp. 5.

[14] ". . . dize las palabras siguientes: En

The slave Marta was severely punished by Zumárraga. After spiritual penance in the cathedral, she was taken, bound and gagged, through the streets of Mexico City, wearing the *coroza* and stripped to the waist, and was given two hundred lashes in the old San Juan market. A town crier proclaimed her crime to set an example for other superstitious people. The slave Margarita Pérez, inculpated by Marta, was convicted of using Antón's aphrodisiacs in her master's food and sprinkling them in the bed where they had carnal relations. Because she was able to convince the Inquisitor of her ignorance and complete repentance, Margarita was absolved by Zumárraga after doing spiritual penance. María, the slave of the merchant Diego, had also used Antón's potions on her master in order to secure better treatment and, if possible, her freedom. María received the same sentence as Margarita Pérez.

María de Espinosa, the slave of the merchant Andrés de Espinosa, proved to be the ringleader of this group of sorcerers. She had introduced the use of the potions and had used them on her master to insure that he treated her well and slept with no other woman. It was alleged that she had practiced alchemy of a sort in that she had created jewels and had given them to the other women in return for their help in soliciting additional clients. After an extensive interrogatory of many witnesses, on June 28, 1537, Zumárraga prescribed that after she had performed spiritual penance in the cathedral of Mexico, María de Espinosa should be taken to Veracruz and exiled perpetually from New Spain and the Indies.

Isabel Morales, the *partera*, was convicted of performing illegal surgeries on her patients and eliciting the aid of the devil with her incantations. She was incarcerated in a monastery for an indefinite period and charged never again to return to her occult practices. The Indian, Antón, who had provided the powders for these women, was taken through the streets of the viceregal capital and given two hundred lashes in the marketplace. Viceroy Mendoza and the oidores of the audiencia witnessed the flogging of Antón.

The sorceress María de Armenta was tried before Zumárraga's Holy Office in October of 1536, and because of recurrent superstitious practices was processed again the following year.[15] María availed herself of the services of an aged Indian *curandera* to enhance her powers of love-making. The surgery was successful, so much so that María got denounced to the Holy Office for having carnal relations with the two

---

el Nombre del Padre y del Hijo y del Espíritu Santo Santa María parió un hijo no mas este vivió y vivirá para siempre jamas asi como esto es verdaderamente y

verdad así le quite toda fatiga y todo mal ..."
[15] AGN, Inquisición, Tomo 38, exp. 3.

Ríos brothers. María confessed her errors to Zumárraga and waived all defense. She was forced to wear the *coroza* during Mass and served a prison term that was to be shortened according to her penitence and good behavior. Having earned her freedom a year later, María was unable to adjust to monogamy or simple recourse to prayer to solve her problems, with the result that she again appeared before the Inquisition and was banished perpetually from New Spain. The Armenta case ended Zumárraga's activities against the sorcerers for the year 1536.

It was not until July of 1537 that Zumárraga resumed his campaign against sorcery. María de Bárcena, the wife of the tailor Medina, was brought to trial because she had participated in occult rites to restore her ruptured husband's potency and then additional sorceries to assure that Medina would confine his carnal relations to herself, his wife.[16] Zumárraga showed understanding in this case, for he prescribed spiritual penance and a light fine of twenty *pesos de oro de minas*.

When María de Bárcena's trial was completed, the Apostolic Inquisitor initiated proceedings against three other women who had performed sorceries connected with the bewitching of the men of their choice. María Marroquina, Leonor de Saravia, and Francisca, the Negro slave of Luis Marín, had methods in common in practicing their art.[17] They used mixtures of their menstrual blood in preparing stews for their lovers and also used blood-wine mixtures as a beverage. Frequently locks of hair were used in the bewitching ceremonies. It was ascertained by Zumárraga that the evidence against Marroquina was hearsay, and she was absolved. We do not know the fate of Leonor de Saravia, but we do have the sentence of the Negro slave: spiritual penance, public humiliation, and one hundred lashes.

Zumárraga's last case against a woman sorcerer was that of Esperanza Valenciana, initiated in May of 1539.[18] This woman had been a resident of the island of Tenerife after coming to the New World from her native Valencia. In Tenerife she had learned certain incantations which she used to invoke the aid of the devil in bringing men, including clergymen, to her bed, and in foretelling the future. She possessed esoteric scrawlings on pieces of paper which contained the invocations. She used her powers to aid other women in having affairs with men of their liking or in securing husbands. It was said that those who availed themselves of her services would have good luck in business and in love.

After the fiscal proved his accusations, Zumárraga passed sentence on October 8, 1539. Esperanza Valenciana abjured her sorceries in the

[16] AGN, Inquisición, Tomo 38, exp. 5.     [18] AGN, Inquisición, Tomo 40, exp. 4.
[17] AGN, Inquisición, Tomo 38, exp. 6.

cathedral and was confined in a private inn for thirty days. Each day she did penance for her sins and recited rosaries and Ave Marias. She was warned upon her release that recurrent sorceries would mean burning at the stake.

Besides Juan Franco and the Indian Antón, two other men, both of them illustrious, were tried for sorcery and superstition by Zumárraga. Dr. Cristóbal Méndez was tried for quackery in 1538 and the cleric Pedro Ruiz Calderón was processed as a practitioner of black magic in 1540. These two cases are of unusual interest and merit special treatment.

### III. *The Attack on Quackery: The Trial of Cristóbal Méndez, 1538*[19]

Cristóbal Méndez was a medical doctor who was denounced on November 15, 1538, for sorcery. He had encouraged his patients to have silver and gold medallions made and to wear them when the sun entered certain phases of its orbit. These medallions when worn around the neck were reputed to have great curative powers, especially in curing the sickness of the kidneys. Apparently many of the principal figures of Mexico City were patients of Dr. Méndez.

The testimony of Méndez revealed that he was learned in astrology and used this knowledge in prescribing the medals which he said not only promoted good health but good fortune as well. He attributed this wisdom to the writings of Dr. Arnaldo de Villanueva, whose books he had read in the library of the cathedral of Mexico.

Testimonies of Dr. Méndez' clients revealed that they gave him pure and refined gold to use in making the medallions. The implication was that Méndez and the *platero*, Francisco de Toledo, pocketed much of the gold and used baser metals in the manufacture of the charms. Méndez was reported to have told close friends that this whole matter of the medallions was a fraud and a joke. His contention that the laws of astrology, and not of God, were the forces that shaped man's destiny got him into trouble with Zumárraga's Inquisition. Méndez insisted that he had not intended to offend God or the Church by his activities, and he asked the mercy of the Holy Office in dealing with his offense. It is unfortunate that the conclusion of the *proceso* is no longer extant. Dr. Méndez' fate must remain a mystery.

### IV. *The Trial of Pedro Ruiz Calderón for Black Magic, 1540*[20]

This trial for necromancy was by far the most important sorcery case tried by Zumárraga and in the total picture ranked with the Alemán Lutheran trial and the Don Carlos case.

Bachiller Pedro Ruiz Calderón was a *sacerdote de misa* who had

[19] AGN, Inquisición, Tomo 40, exp. 3.     [20] AGN, Inquisición, Tomo 40, exp. 5.

recently arrived from Spain. He had, by word and deed, publicly announced that he had a command of black magic and that with his powers
he was able to ascertain the location of pre-conquest buried treasure.
Many prominent conquerors, including Gil González de Benavides, and
perhaps Cortés himself, had discussed the problem with Ruiz Calderón,
and some of them had contracted his services. In some cases he had been
able to deliver the goods, and rumor had it that his powers were truly
phenomenal.

Ruiz Calderón practiced other occult arts. It was thought that he
could make himself invisible when he desired, and that he could trans-
port himself or others through time and space, to Spain or Santo Domingo, and return them home within a few hours. During a luncheon it
was reported that he had dispatched one person some four hundred miles
to gather fresh fruits.

Ruiz was supposedly adept in the science of alchemy for he could
change baser substances into gold and silver and vice versa. In Spain
and France he had practiced the art of casting out devils from the insane
or otherwise infirm. He was a student of astrology, gave readings to his
companions, and contended that the stars and the devil guided man's
destiny. He had the ability to hypnotize women and forever keep them
in his power. He had taken women freely and lived with them for
periods of time in Europe. He was a blasphemer and used the popular
"Pese a Dios."

This *sacerdote de misa* had an extensive library collected in Europe
from which he drew his incantations and spells. In one book he claimed
to have the signature of the prince of devils, which he had secured in Italy
at the time that he had made a descent into hell! This signature endowed
him with great supernatural powers. In order to escape the sanctions of
the law and the Church, this priest impersonated a teacher of science,
licensed by the pope. Frequently he claimed to be a papal legate or an
inquisitor.

Zumárraga's Inquisition had rather full details on Ruiz Calderón
when the trial was initiated in January of 1540. His own testimony
coupled with Zumárraga's investigations presents a fascinating picture
of the priest's biography and travels. He was a native of Guadalcanal in
Castilla and came from a family of *cristianos viejos*. He had received the
degree of Bachiller of Theology at the University of Alcalá and had
become a *sacerdote de misa*.[21]

[21] His own testimony gives the details of
his clerical career:

Preguntado quien le ordeno y donde
y que tanto tiempo ha Dijo que de

primera Corona le ordeno Don Juan
de Tapia de Lisas con . . . del Arzobispo de Toledo y examinado y apro-
bado quien era de linaje de este que
declara y que por el titulo pareciera

The Inquisition trial record gives details on Ruiz Calderón's alleged education in the science of black magic. In the Levant he had studied, he said, among the wizards, learning his lessons in Chaldean, Hebrew, and Greek. In addition, he learned another esoteric language, a tongue used only by the cult of black magicians. Ruiz Calderón possessed books written in this secret cipher.

A very important phase of his education, according to what he told others, took place in Italy. There he had assisted the viceroy of Naples in uncovering hidden treasures by the use of necromancy, and he had been handsomely rewarded. It was after his Naples service that he had received a papal license to take four other men and explore a cave which extended three thousand leagues below the surface of the earth. Ruiz Calderón related that he had remained in this cave for three years after his companions had perished. Then he told of his descent into hell to learn the secrets of the science of alchemy. He said that he brought back certain books with him from the underworld, including the signature of the prince of devils. In Germany he had continued his apprenticeship as a magician and had learned more about alchemy. Among the books which he had acquired in central Europe was a notebook of Arnaldo de Villanueva, the same authority that Dr. Méndez had used in his medallion experiments.

In Paris a master magician had taught him supernatural medicine and the methods of casting out devils from the sick and insane. He had used this knowledge in Sevilla to cure one Reinaldo Villafranca and to cast out eight hundred thousand devils from a maiden there. He had also learned to make himself invisible, a trick he found useful when caught *in flagrante delicto* with other men's wives.

Apparently Bachiller Pedro had spread these tales with unabashed modesty. When the suspicious or devout indicated that he was committing crimes against the faith, Ruiz Calderón indicated that he had a papal license to exercise his art and that Zumárraga had given approval to his practices.

When it came time for the interrogation of the defendant, his manner became meek. He had to deny that he was a practitioner of black magic and that he had a papal license. He altered the story of his devil-casting career. Now he asserted that he was merely a spectator while another bachiller actually performed the rites.

Ruiz Calderón was forced to reveal the location of his library and

---

el tiempo que hace que de grados se ordeno en Roma y de Epistola y Evangelio le ordeno el Arzobispo de Mecina en Cicilia y de sacerdote le

ordeno Cesar de Monteleon Teniente del Arzobispo de Melite en la Ciudad de Calabria que estas ordenes Sacras recibio literas Dimisorias del Papa.

Zumárraga ordered the books confiscated. The books were inventoried by the Inquisition and included some interesting items. There were the usual doctrines, breviaries, and the like. The library included an archive of letters written in a mysterious cipher. Books of Albertus Magnus, Dominican sermons, manuals of chanting, the lamentations of Jeremiah, and various philosophical treatises rounded out the collection.

The most interesting part of the Ruiz library were the books on sorcery. There was a book of Dr. Arnaldo de Villanueva on methods to be used in finding buried treasures. There were several treatises on healing, and one which prescribed the method of casting out devils from the sick and insane. The inquisitors were most disappointed that the book containing the signature of the prince of devils was not found in the bachiller's library.

Since his case was ridiculously weak, Pedro Ruiz Calderón decided to confess and throw himself upon Zumárraga's mercy. He pleaded deception by the devil in his past career as a necromancer. Since his incarceration and owing to the dampness of his cell, he had apparently developed some type of pulmonary ailment, and his ulcer was causing him great discomfort. He asked that he be given a healthful penance in Castilla.

It would appear that Apostolic Inquisitor Zumárraga was unusually lenient with this sorcerer in light of the stiffer sentences meted out to Andrés Aleman and Don Carlos of Texcoco. On April 4, 1540, the Bachiller was forced to be present in the cathedral and hear his errors read publicly, after which he abjured them individually. The oidores of the audiencia were witnesses to the abjuration ceremony. Later that same day Zumárraga pronounced sentence.

Ruiz Calderón was prohibited from saying Mass for a period of two years and was sentenced to banishment in Castilla where the archbishop of Toledo was to reexamine his case and provide suitable penance. The confiscated books were sent to the archbishop for his scrutiny. Apparently Ruiz was taken immediately to the hospital after the sentencing, because the next day, April 5, 1540, he was visited there by the Inquisition notary, Miguel López de Legazpi, and others.

From the events related in the closing paragraphs of the *proceso* we learn that Pedro Ruiz Calderón was still recounting his exploits as a practitioner of black magic from his hospital bed. He told of other books of great value which he possessed and which contained incantations and other devices that could be utilized in the recovery of buried treasure. His parting tale was about an incident in Sevilla when the devil appeared to him in the confessional and he actually confessed Satan! It is a pity that we have no record of the career of the *sacerdote de misa* after he fulfilled his exile in Spain.

## V. *Conclusions on Zumárraga and the Sorcerers*

Although Fray Juan de Zumárraga moved with great zeal against sorcery and superstition in New Spain during his ministry as Apostolic Inquisitor, it is to be doubted that common superstitions were eradicated. In fact, the occult probably became more secretive and its practitioners more careful of those who would denounce them. Perhaps some progress in curtailing major sorceries of the type described in the Méndez and Ruiz Calderón trials was made, but the female sorceresses continued to cast their spells, as they still do in modern Mexico.

# CHAPTER IX

# Zumárraga's Special Jurisdictions
## as Inquisitor

Besides prosecuting persons who deviated from orthodoxy, Zumárraga's Holy Office of the Inquisition carried on certain trials of an administrative nature. It also made investigations of and administered the properties of those who came under its censure. It is the purpose of this chapter to investigate these special areas of activity of the early Mexican Inquisition.

## I. *Investigatory Functions*

The Zumárraga period, as known through the documents, showed a great interest in the affairs of the area to the north and east of the bishopric, especially the district of Pánuco. Zumárraga ordered frequent investigations of the orthodoxy of the inhabitants of Pánuco in the decade of the 1530's. The Inquisitor's concern with Pánuco perhaps might be explained by his enmity for Nuño de Guzmán, who was governor of the area, although he served in the dual capacity of president of the first audiencia from 1528 to 1530.

The Holy Office in Mexico City showed less of an interest in the area to the west than it did in Pánuco. While Zumárraga did dispatch visitors to Matlatlán and other Indian villages, the far west had little or no supervision in matters of faith. The crimes of the cacique of Iguala indicated this situation.[1] On the other hand, Taxco and its environs were closely scrutinized at intervals to insure that the foreign colony there was keeping within the bounds of orthodoxy.

The Pánuco investigations of 1539 and 1540 yield heresy and blasphemy cases of the usual character. In 1539 Zumárraga's inquiry concerned the heretical blasphemies of Alonso de Paz, an *escribano*, who used expletives concerning the Virgin and sacraments when he conducted auctions or when he bargained with clients over the fees he was

---

[1] This case has been fully examined in Chapter III.

to charge for writing letters and other legal documents.[2] Paz was imprisoned but he escaped jail and fled to the northwest country where the Holy Office lost track of him.

The following year Zumárraga found it necessary to send his archdeacon, Juan Infante de Barrios, to Pánuco as his delegate to deal with several causes of faith which had been reported to Mexico City. Barrios actually conducted trials and passed sentences in San Esteban. He concerned himself primarily with the activities of one Gonzalo Bernal who had been denounced to Zumárraga as a heretic, a sorcerer, and a blasphemer. We do not have the record of the sentence.

Juan Infante de Barrios was instructed to investigate other deviations from orthodoxy which had been reported to the Mexico City Holy Office. The parish priest at San Esteban, Alonso Ruiz de Arévalo, had been accused of having concubines and illegitimate children. Arévalo was also suspect for certain irregularities in the sale of the bull of the *Cruzada* and pocketing the proceeds from this lucrative enterprise.[3]

Besides his interest in Arévalo's conduct, Zumárraga wished an investigation of a Carmelite friar whose sexual practices had been brought to his attention. It was also part of Barrios' instructions to investigate the prevalence of idolatry and superstition among the Totonac Indians and other tribes of the coastal area. It is unfortunate that the Barrios visitation of Pánuco and his activities as Zumárraga's Commissary of the Holy Office are not treated in more detail in the Inquisition archives.

In addition to investigatory functions like those described in Pánuco, Zumárraga's Holy Office performed many other investigatory services of a more perfunctory type. Several of these are preserved in the documents. *Limpiezas de sangre* of important officials or of those who fell under his jurisdiction were compiled by Zumárraga. Very frequently he had to ascertain whether spouses still lived in Spain when he tried alleged bigamists. These investigations and many more were part of the Holy Office's daily functions.

## II. *Cases of an Administrative Nature*

Several trials occurred during the Zumárraga era which had a direct connection with the actual functioning of the Holy Office. Perhaps the most interesting of these concerned two trumpeters, Antón Moreno and Cristóbal de Barrera, who were tried because they refused to play for the opening of Zumárraga's tribunal and for the procession which it made from the Hospital of Jesus to the Palacio de la Inquisición.[4] The trial was begun on June 8, 1536, just three days after the Apostolic In-

---

[2] AGN, Inquisición, Tomo 30, exp. 9 bis.     [4] AGN, Inquisición, Tomo 42, exp. 3.
[3] AGN, Inquisición, Tomo 34, exp. 5.

quisitor assumed his post. The two defendants had refused to play because Zumárraga would not pay them in advance. They were arrested but allowed to go free after posting fifty *pesos de oro de minas* as bail.

During the course of the trial it became apparent that the trumpeters's fears that they would not be paid were fairly well grounded. Zumárraga felt that they should have donated their services. They replied that they could not eat air! The bishop of Oaxaca, Don Juan López de Zárate, who acted as fiscal in this case, informed Zumárraga on June 12 that Cristóbal de Barrera had threatened to reveal certain information about Zumárraga that would cause him great harm. Indeed, Barrera threatened to take the story to Viceroy Mendoza, along with a charge that Zumárraga had exceeded his powers in trying to force the musicians to perform free. Barrera indicated that he was a person of some intelligence when he contended that Zumárraga had no jurisdiction over his person in the first place, because he was a subject of the bishopric of Tlaxcala and Zumárraga's commission empowered him to try only residents of his own bishopric. Barrera promised to carry the matter to the king if Mendoza failed to act.

The intriguing reference to harmful evidence which Bearrera had against Zumárraga created quite a stir during the trial, but when Viceroy Mendoza interrogated him, it became clear that the trumpeter was resorting to bravado. Both musicians asked the mercy of the Holy Office in the end. Each did a suitable penance and paid a fine. Thus the dignity of the Holy Office was protected. The fine was six pounds of white wax to be delivered by each offender to the cathedral of Mexico City, but in addition, because he had insulted Zumárraga, Barrera forfeited his fifty pesos bail. Barrera complained bitterly of the injustice done him, but Mendoza upheld Zumárraga's sentence.

An interesting but confusing jurisdictional dispute between Zumárraga's Holy Office in the bishopric of Mexico and the inquisitorial powers of Don Julián Garcés, Bishop of Tlaxcala, arose in July and August of 1536.[5] The canon and vicar general of the church of Puebla de los Angeles, Francisco de Leyva, precipitated the misunderstanding. On July 17, 1536, five of the regidores of the cabildo of Puebla addressed a curious letter to Zumárraga in Mexico City. They related that Francisco de Leyva had read a letter in church the day before which said that Zumárraga had assumed the office of Inquisitor General of all New Spain. All persons who knew of any deviations from orthodoxy were ordered to report them to Leyva. Leyva said that these instructions had come from Mexico City.

[5] AGN, Inquisición, Tomo 40, exp. 5-III.

The regidores had requested Leyva to show them the letter after the services, and he had refused. They had therefore communicated with the Holy Office in Mexico City to learn the details of Zumárraga's instructions and to inform him that they wished that he would appoint some other delegate in Puebla because they considered Leyva a poor choice for the job.[6]

Even though he had no authority in Puebla, Zumárraga determined to investigate this situation in order to ascertain if Leyva were usurping his powers or was merely ignorant of the fact that his authority extended only throughout the bishopric of Mexico. The *proceso* leaves some doubt that there was such a letter from Zumárraga dispatched to Leyva.

When questioned Leyva was sincere in contending that he was ignorant of that fact that Zumárraga was merely inquisitor of the bishopric of Mexico and not of the entire viceroyalty. He insisted that such a letter had been received and had been filed in the care of the sacristan of the Puebla Church. He convinced Zumárraga that his only motive in reading the letter to his flock was promoting purity of the faith. Zumárraga determined to let the matter rest. Leyva was instructed that all causes of faith were to be referred to Bishop Garcés, who was empowered to deal with them as ecclesiastical judge ordinary. Because the *proceso* is fragmentary, we have no record of Garcés' views on this interesting case.

Zumárraga presided at another administrative trial in October of 1543. Nicolás Salinas, the lieutenant of the alguacil of the Holy Office, was tried for violation of the right of sanctuary after he had dragged Francisco Ramírez out of the cathedral of Mexico by force.[7] Ramírez had pleaded with Salinas to respect his right of sanctuary, but Salinas had said before the assembled congregation that he would take Jesus Christ out of the church if he were paid for it. Several witnesses verified this story. Again we must be content to speculate upon Nicolás Salinas' fate because we do not have the conclusion of the *proceso*.

As we saw so clearly in a previous chapter, friars and inquisitors were forced to rely upon the services of Indian interpreters. The interpreter system was looked upon as a sacred trust by the Holy Office. Especially in Indian trials were competent and honest interpreters a necessity. The trial of Diego, an interpreter for Zumárraga's Holy Office, for dereliction in his duties occurred in September of 1536.[8] Diego had

6 ". . . por hombre de poco secreto y sería dar ocasion a que algunos dejasen de ir a decir ante el algunas cosas si supiesen por este temor."

7 AGN, Inquisición, Tomo 42, exp. 6.

8 AGN, Inquisición, Tomo 40, exp. 5-III. This fragment is published in the *Boletín del Archivo General de la Nación*, XVI (1945), 37-40.

maliciously given wrong instructions to the Indians of Atzcapozalco and
Tenayuca when their baptisms and confirmations took place. Testimonies
of the natives revealed that he had misrepresented the significance of the
holy oil and the chrism in these ceremonies. Fray Pedro de Gante made
the investigation of Diego's crime and recommended that the Indian be
brought to trial. If he was penanced we are ignorant of the fact, for the
*proceso* ends at the *información* stage.

Protection of church properties and prosecution of desecrators was
another administrative function of the Holy Office. On August 11, 1536,
Anton Pérez, a mule skinner, was denounced for having stolen stones and
other portable materials from the cathedral of Mexico. The evidence
was conclusive and Pérez was severely punished. Zumárraga required
him to do spiritual penance and submit to public humiliation, after which
he received one hundred lashes.[9]

### III. *The Apprehension of Fugitives from the Spanish Inquisition*

The *reo prófugo* was a constant concern of Zumárraga's Holy Office. The New World was a haven for those who had escaped the wrath
of the Spanish Inquisition. The escape route was usually through Portugal or the Canary Islands, where passage could be obtained by illegal
means. It was the duty of the New World Inquisitions to ferret these
people out and see that they received their just punishments.

Frequently individuals were denounced as *reos prófugos* unjustly.
When such a denunciation came, the person in question had to offer
documentary or other proof of his innocence. Often this was no easy
task, as we shall see in the trial of the merchant Jorge González,[10] who
was denounced as a fugitive from the Spanish Inquisition on August 14,
1536, by Cristóbal de Cisneros on extremely nebulous information.
Nevertheless, Zumárraga ordered the merchant arrested and the trial
proceeded. González' testimony revealed that he had been arrested by
the Inquisition in Zafra, Spain, and was taken to Llérena for questioning
in connection with a widespread campaign against Jews and other
heretics.

Jorge González insisted that he had been liberated after only a few
days, but he was unable to present any official document to substantiate
his claim. He was married but his wife had remained in Spain, and González was not sure that she had any such proof either. Zumárraga commanded the defendant to present within two years a certificate of his release from the Inquisition jail in Spain upon pain of a fine of two thousand
*castellanos* if he failed to do so.

[9] AGN, Inquisición, Tomo 42, exp. 5.     [10] AGN, Inquisición, Tomo 42, exp. 7.

González did not wait for proof to come from Spain. With the consent of Zumárraga an interrogatory was framed, and some dozen residents of the area of González' home in Spain were called in to testify. The results of these testimonies vindicated González. It appeared that there were wholesale arrests during this inquisitorial campaign and that Jorge González had merely been a victim of circumstances. Zumárraga accepted this finding as authentic and gave González a clean bill of health.

A fugitive from the episcopal Inquisition of Nombre de Dios in Panamá was tried by Zumárraga in September of 1536. Gonzalo de Ecija, a merchant, and his wife were denounced by another merchant, Francisco de Estrada, of fleeing from the sentence of the ecclesiastical judge ordinary in Panamá.[11] It developed later that Ecija had been tried in Sevilla and that his properties had been confiscated. Whether he fled to Panamá to escape sentence was obscure, but within a short period of time he was processed there by Bishop Fernando de Luque, the partner of Francisco Pizarro in the Peruvian conquest enterprise. Ecija contended that he had been branded a heretic by the *Teniente* in Nombre de Dios because he had beaten him in various games of chance. He had fled to Santo Domingo before doing the spiritual penance Luque had prescribed and paying the fine leveled against him.

Zumárraga ordered Gonzalo de Ecija to pay a fine of twenty-five *pesos de oro*, half of which was to go to the building fund of the church at Nombre de Dios and the other half to the poor ones of the hospital there. In addition Ecija was required to pay for Masses to be said in Nombre de Dios on three succeeding Fridays. Other spiritual penances rounded out the sentence.

## IV. *The Punishment of Critics of the Holy Office*

The Inquisitors felt that one of the rights of the Holy Office was to protect itself from criticism which might detract from its dignity and influence. As a consequence of this conviction, Zumárraga and his colleagues among the episcopal inquisitors set out to punish those who would attack the validity of the mission of the Holy Office and its activities. Numerous cases initiated by Zumárraga in Mexico City and Zárate in Oaxaca against critics of the Holy Office are contained in the Inquisition Archive in Mexico City. Generally these arose when citizens, and often priests, protested the arrest and trial of friends whom they believed to be completely orthodox. Such was the case with Pedro Cervero, an apothecary, who contended that friends ought not denounce each other to the Holy Office,[12] and the Antequera, Oaxaca,

[11] AGN, Inquisición, Tomo 42, exp. 9.        [12] AGN, Inquisición, Tomo 42, exp. 8.

priest, Pero Muñoz, who questioned the Holy Office's jurisdiction over a member of his parish.[13] In the Muñoz affair, his friends Marcos de Paredes and Gonzalo Martín[14] also became involved as partisans of their pastor, and were tried by the Oaxaca Holy Office. Sentences were never very harsh. Usually such fines were meted out as giving alms to monastic houses or supplying wax or consecrated oil for various churches and other religious establishments. In this way the dignity of the Holy Office was preserved.

## V. *The Sequestration and Recovery of Property and other Fiscal Functions of Zumárraga's Holy Office*

Because the Holy Office administered the properties of those who underwent trial before its judges, a treasurer and bookkeeping staff had to be employed. Immediately upon the arrest of a suspect, his property was placed under an embargo and an extensive inventory of his possessions was prepared. In cases of major heresy, when the defendant was reconciled or was relaxed to the secular arm, the properties were confiscated by Zumárraga as part of the sentence.

The treasurer of the Holy Office was empowered to collect all debts owed to the defendant and to pay out of his funds all legal debts which he had incurred prior to the embargo. When debts or other obligations were of a questionable nature, frequent lawsuits took place, the records of which were usually placed in the Inquisition trial proceedings. From these records the researcher finds fascinating data not included in actual trial documents.

Confiscated properties were placed in a type of escrow for an indeterminate period of time and then auctioned off by a *pregonero* commissioned by the Holy Office. In this interim properties were frequently recovered by the convicted or his family in view of particular circumstances. For example, Andrés Alemán, after various machinations in Sevilla where he was in exile, was able to recover some of his properties and pay certain debts, perhaps fabricated ones, out of the monies which Zumárraga's treasurer had in trust. Alemán's wife, Catalina de Caxas, was able by suit to recover that part of the properties which had been her dowry when she married Alemán.[15] Such activities entailed great administrative duties on the part of the treasurer and his staff.

Once the auctions had been held the proceeds were used in various ways. Naturally, some of the money went for the salaries and administrative expenses of Inquisition officials. The rest went for pious works.[16]

[13] AGN, Inquisición, Tomo 42, exp. 14.
[14] AGN, Inquisición, Tomo 42, exps. 15, 16.
[15] AGN, Inquisición, Tomo 42, exp. 11.
[16] For analagous materials on the finances of the Spanish Inquisition, see Lea, *The Spanish Inquisition*, II, 315-456.

Zumárraga's Holy Office relied almost entirely on fines and confiscations for its operating budget. The defendant in causes of faith nearly always paid the cost of the trial unless he was exonerated. In the case of labor sentences against Indians, the labor was auctioned off to the highest bidder and the money sequestrated as a fine. In light of the meticulous records kept by the staff of Zumárraga's Inquisition, one must conclude that his administration of properties and fines was probably scrupulously honest. This is not surprising when one considers Zumárraga's character and devotion to his duties.

# Summary and Conclusions

Until 1571 the Mexican Holy Office of the Inquisition was an episcopal institution rather than a formally established tribunal. Bishops exercised inquisitorial powers as ecclesiastical judges ordinary; where there were no resident bishops, monastic prelates became inquisitors under the authority of the papal bull known as *Omnímoda*. Both Juan de Zumárraga, the first bishop and archibishop of Mexico (1527-1548) and the Visitor General Francisco Tello de Sandoval (1544-1547) received appointments as Apostolic Inquisitors, but this special designation gave their activities no real distinction from episcopal inquisitorial activities. On the whole the episcopal Inquisition proved to be an unsatisfactory institution in the eyes of the Church and the crown, and it was replaced by a tribunal of the Holy Office of the Inquisition in Mexico City in 1571.

Zumárraga's Holy Office (1536-1543) reflected sixteenth-century Mexican society and its objectives. Early colonial Mexico was a survival of the Middle Ages; it was in effect the embodiment of Aquinas' Christian Aristotelian polity. Since both Church and state were in a sense based upon revealed dogma, the line between heresy and treason was a tenuous one. Sixteenth-century Spanish society was gripped by the fear of losing its religious orthodoxy, and the Inquisition in Spain and America was the major defensive device upon which orthodoxy rested.

The aim of Zumárraga's Inquisition was therefore to preserve and defend the Roman Catholic Faith and dogma against all individuals who held heretical views or who were guilty of lack of respect for religious principles. The total effect of this institution upon Mexican society of the 1530's is difficult to judge. It is apparent from the trial documents analyzed in the foregoing pages that Zumárraga tried only flagrant offenders. In many cases the sentences he prescribed were lenient. However, major heretics received the same punishments as they did in Spain, perhaps more rigorous in some cases. As a general rule Zumárraga was notably derelict in punishing unorthodoxy among the clergy. The principle of equal justice could hardly be exemplified in Zumárraga's treatment of the necromancer, Pedro Ruiz Calderón, or the *solicitante*, Father Diego Díaz.

Zumárraga, like many sixteenth-century intellectuals, was a segmented thinker. Although he professed to be a Christian humanist and exhibited an affinity for the ideas of Erasmus, Zumárraga was bound by Thomistic orthodoxy. In reality early sixteenth-century Mexico did not belong to the Renaissance but to Dante's World Empire. Scholars have greatly exaggerated the influence of Erasmus, More, and other humanists in early post-conquest Mexico.

In his trials of Indians for idolatry and sorcery, Zumárraga encountered a situation where philosophical eclecticism and religious orthodoxy could not easily be reconciled. Erasmism had to give way to Thomism, and the traditional patterns of European culture, which the Christian humanist hoped to avoid, were super-imposed upon the native cultures. What occurred was a fusion of the two civilizations and *indianismo* remained just beneath the surface. In religion a type of syncretism resulted in that the religion was Catholic in form, but often pagan in substance. As a lever between European and Indian cultures, the Indian Inquisition was little more than a haphazard device in the process of forced acculturation.

During the Zumárraga inquisitorial ministry the mendicant Orders, which were responsible for the instruction of the natives in the faith, were handicapped by inadequate personnel. Many outstanding friars deplored the rudimentary nature of their teaching program. In view of this, Zumárraga's Indian Inquisition appears to have been a reprehensible phase of the spiritual conquest of Mexico. Although the cacique Don Carlos of Texcoco was probably justly condemned as a heretical dogmatizer against not only the Church but all Spanish authority, one feels only pity for him in his last frantic efforts to avoid the stake. It would appear that the Grace of God was tempered by the demand for societal vengeance in this phase of inquisitorial thinking.

Besides his Indian Inquisition, three other major areas of heresy occupied the efforts of Zumárraga the Inquisitor: Lutheranism, Judaizing, and sorcery. Lutheranism never constituted a real threat to Mexican orthodoxy, although the term became almost a synonym for heresy. In spite of the numerous trials of Judaizantes between 1536 and 1540, the Jewish colony in Mexico continued to thrive until it suffered a severe setback in the late sixteenth-century when the tribunal tried the Carvajal family and other Jews. Perhaps because of his business acumen and a hardiness developed by centuries of persecution, the Mexican Jew was often able to circumvent Zumárraga's Inquisition.

Sorcery and the occult arts had been a special interest of Zumárraga's since his part in the 1527 witchcraft trials in the Pamplona region in Spain. In Mexico he pursued the sorcerers with great zeal, and although he made some progress in prosecuting offenders, he was not able to eradicate common Spanish and Indian superstitious practices and beliefs.

The crime of blasphemy was the most prevalent tried by Zumárraga, and in the majority of cases his sentences were very light. In cases of minor heresy and sexual immorality he applied the full sanctions of the Holy Office: stiff fines, spiritual penances, public humiliation, and floggings. Bigamy, simple fornication, concubinage, incest, and homosexuality fell under his jurisdiction.

In addition to the above, Zumárraga's Holy Office carried on certain trials of an administrative nature. It investigated the orthodoxy of outlying areas of the diocese, and it administered the property of those who fell under its censure. Critics of the Holy Office, both laymen and clerics, were punished by Zumárraga in order to uphold the dignity of his office.

The historian of early sixteenth-century Mexico must place Zumárraga among the five leading figures of the era. Cortés and Nuño de Guzmán were the military conquerors; Zumárraga and Quiroga were the spiritual conquerors; and Viceroy Mendoza was the administrative stabilizer of the conquest. Zumárraga's activities as Apostolic Inquisitor and real founder of the Mexican Inquisiton were comparable to those of Mendoza as founder of the viceregal system in the Spanish empire of America.

# Bibliography

I. *Essay on Source Materials*

The student of the Mexican Inquisition must gear his approach from the specific to the general. A detailed investigation of actual trials must precede any generalizations, if generalizations are to be valid. A mere scanning of indexes to bound volumes of documents in order to ascertain the names of defendants and the charges against them cannot result in deep knowledge of the Mexican Inquisition as an institution.

Work done *in absentia* through paid researchers nets the would-be author of Mexican Inquisition topics very little. A personal examination of the documents is necessary, if for no other reason because of paleographical problems. It is with these comments as a background that I urge caution in the use of José Toribio Medina, *La primitiva inquisición americana* (2 vols.; Santiago de Chile, 1914) and his *Historia del tribunal del Santo Oficio de la Inquisición en México* (México, 1954). One should also realize that the sections of Joaquín García Icazbalceta, *Bibliografía mexicana del siglo XVI* (México, 1954) and his *Obras* (México, 1896-1899) that deal with the Mexican Inquisition have some errors of fact and interpretation.

Despite a bias, the works of Henry C. Lea remain the most solid presentation of the Spanish Inquisition. As a background to the New World Inquisitions they are invaluable. Lea's *The Inquisition in the Spanish Dependencies* (New York, 1908) takes up the account at 1569, thereby avoiding the episcopal periods. Mariano Cuevas, *Historia de la iglesia en México* (4 vols.; México, 1921-1926) is an orthodox history which includes sections on the Mexican Inquisition. Julio Jiménez Rueda, *Herejías y supersticiones en la Nueva España* (México, 1944) is a survey covering the whole colonial period based on the papers of the Inquisition archive and other sources. The works of Medina, Cuevas, García Icazbalceta, Jiménez Rueda, and Lea are the only secondary sources which touch upon the Mexican Inquisition. Yolanda Mariel de Ibáñez, *La Inquisición en México durante el siglo XVI* (México, 1945) while valuable, is based on the other sources plus some archival work.

Inquisition *procesos* in the AGN have been paginated and rearranged several times. Hence there is a possible confusion in citation, especially in folio references. Citations must be based upon the Catálogo de Inquisición checked by the actual Tomo location. The bibliography that follows has been arranged in terms of manuscript materials and printed materials. Unpublished doctoral dissertations have been included in the latter category for reasons of convenience.

Manuscript materials are catalogued here in archival style rather than in strict chronological or alphabetical order. The date included in each reference refers to the year in which the trial was initiated.

II. *Manuscript Materials from Archivo General de la Nación, México [AGN], Ramo de la Inquisición*

Fragmento de una causa contra los Indios de Oquila por idólatras, 1540. Tomo I, exp. 6.

Proceso contra Diego Núñez por blasfemo, 1527. Tomo I, exp. 7.

Proceso contra Juan Bello por blasfemo, 1527. Tomo I, exp. 8.

Proceso contra Gil González de Benavides por blasfemo, 1527. Tomo I, exp. 9.

Proceso contra Juan Rodríguez de Villafuerte por blasfemo, 1527. Tomo I, exp. 9a.

Proceso contra Juan Martín Berenjel por blasfemo, 1527. Tomo I, exp. 9b.

Proceso contra Cristóbal Díaz por blasfemo, 1527. Tomo I, exp. 9c.

Proceso contra Bernabe Quemado por blasfemo, 1527. Tomo I, exp. 9d.

Proceso contra Alonso de Espinosa por blasfemo, 1527. Tomo I, exp. 9e.

Proceso contra Rodrigo Rengel por blasfemo, 1527. Tomo I, exp. 10.

Declaración de Gaspar de Plaza, ante el provisor Don Juan Rebollo, por haber escrito una carta sospechosa de herejía, 1539. Tomo I, exp. 10a.

Proceso contra Francisco González por blasfemo, 1527. Tomo I, exp. 10b.

Proceso contra Diego García por blasfemo, 1527. Tomo I, exp. 10c.

Proceso contra Francisco Núñez por blasfemo, 1527. Tomo I, exp. 10d.

Proceso contra Gregorio de Monjarás por blasfemo, 1527. Tomo I, exp. 10e.

Proceso contra Alonso de Carrión por blasfemo, 1527. Tomo I, exp. 10f.

Proceso contra Diego Morales por blasfemo, 1528. Tomo I, exp. 11.

Denuncia de una hechicera por Benito de Bejel, 1528. Tomo I, exp. 12.

Retratación de los gobernadores y alcaldes e oidores de varios pueblos de Oaxaca que habian representado en contra su Cura, 1528. Tomo I, exp. 13.

Proceso contra Andrés Griego por herejía, 1528. Tomo I, exp. 14.

Proceso contra Francisco de Agreda por blasfemo, 1528. Tomo I, exp. 15.

Proceso del Santo Oficio de la Inquisición contra Bernaldo del Castillo, estante en esta ciudad de México y condenado por el Santo Oficio como blasfemo por andar murmurando de los Inquisidores, 1538. Tomo IA, exp. 2.

Proceso contra Antón Carmona por judío, 1539. Tomo IA, exp. 10.

Denuncia contra Juan de Toledo, natural de Almagro en los reinos de Castilla, acusado de ser hijo de reconciliado y de haber dicho que los ángeles y querubines deberían comerse asados y que no estaba bien poner cruces en las calles, 1536. Tomo IA, exp. 12.

Denuncia de Francisco Alvarez contra un tal Acevedo por blasfemo, 1536. Tomo IA, exp. 13.

Proceso contra Bernaldo de Luna por blasfemo, 1527. Tomo IA, exp. 14.

Proceso contra Juan de Cuebas por blasfemo, 1527. Tomo IA, exp. 15.

Proceso contra Alonso de Corellana por blasfemo, 1527. Tomo IA, exp. 16.

Proceso contra Lucas Gallegos por blasfemo, 1527. Tomo IA, exp. 17.

Proceso contra García Hernández por judío (declaración), 1539. Tomo IA, exp. 18.

Proceso contra Beatriz Hernández por judía (declaración), 1539. Tomo IA, exp. 19.

Proceso contra Rodrigo de Soria por judío (declaración), 1539. Tomo IA, exp. 20.

Proceso contra Francisco Serrano por judío (declaración), 1539. Tomo IA, exp. 21.

Proceso contra Juan Ruiz por judío (declaración), 1539. Tomo IA, exp. 22.

Averiguación hecha por el Santo Oficio en lo de Alonso de Avila a quien se acusó de tener crucifijo debajo de su escritorio y poner los pies encima, 1537. Tomo IA, exp. 23bis.

Memoria de los hijos de quemados y reconciliados que habia en México, 1544. Tomo IA, exp. 25.

Proceso de este Santo Oficio de la Inquisición y el fiscal en su nombre contra Andrés Alemán, lapidario por luterano, 1536. Tomo II, exp. 1.

Proceso del Santo Oficio de la Inquisición contra Gonzalo Gómez vecino de Michoacán por judaizante, 1536. Tomo II, exp. 2.

Proceso del Santo Oficio de la Inquisición y el Dr. Rafael de Cervanes, fiscal en su nombre contra Marcos Ruiz por blasfemo y otros delitos, 1537. Tomo II, exp. 3.

Proceso del Santo Oficio de la Inquisición contra Rosino y Alonso Valiente por haber dicho que no es pecado mortal la simple fornicación, 1538. Tomo II, exp. 4.

Proceso del Santo Oficio de la Inquisición contra García González por blasfemo, 1538. Tomo II, exp. 5.

Proceso del Santo Oficio contra Gaspar de la Plaza por asegurar que no era pecado estar con una india, 1538. Tomo II, exp. 6.

Proceso contra Gonzalo Herradura por blasfemo, 1538. Tomo II, exp. 7.

Proceso del Santo Oficio contra Francisco de Sayavedra, por proposiciones heréticas, 1539. Tomo II, exp. 8.

Proceso del Santo Oficio de la Inquisición contra Juan de Villate por haber reprendido y reñido a su muger porque rezaba, 1539. Tomo II, exp. 9.

Proceso Criminal del Santo Oficio de la Inquisición y del fiscal en su nombre contra Don Carlos indio principal de Texcoco por idólatra, 1539. Tomo II, exp. 10.

Proceso del Santo Oficio de la Inquisición contra Juan Banberniguen por luterano, 1540. Tomo II, exp. 11.

Proceso contra Ruy Díaz por blasfemo, 1532. Tomo XIV, exp. 1.

Proceso de este Santo Oficio de la Inquisición contra Ruy Díaz por blasfemo reincidente, 1536. Tomo XIV, exp. 2.

Proceso de este Santo Oficio de la Inquisición y del Fiscal en su nombre contra Juan Porras por blasfemo, 1536. Tomo XIV, exp. 2 bis.

Proceso de este Santo Oficio de la Inquisición y del fiscal en su nombre contra Alonso de Carrión por blasfemo reincidente, 1536. Tomo XIV, exp. 3.

Proceso de este Santo Oficio de la Inquisición contra Juan de Villagómez por blasfemo, 1536. Tomo XIV, exp. 4.

Proceso de este Santo Oficio de la Inquisición y el fiscal en su nombre contra Angel de Villafaña por blasfemo, 1536. Tomo XIV, exp. 5.

Proceso de este Santo Oficio de la Inquisición y el fiscal en su nombre contra Juan Pérez Montañez por blasfemo, 1536. Tomo XIV, exp. 6.

Proceso de este Santo Oficio de la Inquisición y el fiscal en su nombre contra Francisco Martín por blasfemo, 1536. Tomo XIV, exp. 7.

Proceso del Santo Oficio de la Inquisición contra Francisco Maldonado por blasfemo, 1536. Tomo XIV, exp. 8.

Proceso del Santo Oficio contra Alonso Sánchez de Toledo por blasfemo, 1536. Tomo XIV, exp. 9.

Proceso del Santo Oficio de la Inquisición y el fiscal en su nombre contra Pedro de Sosa por blasfemo, 1536. Tomo XIV, exp. 10.

Proceso del Santo Oficio de la Inquisición y el fiscal en su nombre contra Lorenzo Hernández por blasfemo, 1536. Tomo XIV, exp. 10 bis.

Proceso del Santo Oficio contra Cristóbal de Valladolid por blasfemo, 1536. Tomo XIV, exp. 11.

Proceso del Santo Oficio contra Alonso Rodríguez de Saravia por blasfemo, 1536. Tomo XIV, exp. 12.

Proceso del Santo Oficio contra Alonso Garavito por blasfemo, 1536. Tomo XIV, exp. 12 bis.

Proceso del Santo Oficio de la Inquisición y el fiscal en su nombre contra Juan Díaz de Real por blasfemo, 1536. Tomo XIV, exp. 13.

Proceso de la Justicia del Santo Oficio de la Inquisición contra Juan Fernández del Castillo por blasfemo, 1536. Tomo XIV, exp. 14.

Proceso de este Santo Oficio de la Inquisición y el Fiscal en su nombre contra Francisco Preciado por blasfemo, 1536. Tomo XIV, exp. 15.

Proceso de este Santo Oficio de la Inquisición contra Marín Cortés por blasfemo, 1536. Tomo XIV, exp. 16.

Proceso del Oficio de la Santa Inquisición contra Hernando Díaz por blasfemo, 1536. Tomo XIV, exp. 17.

Proceso de este Santo Oficio de la Inquisición contra María de Espinosa por blasfema, 1536. Tomo XIV, exp. 17 bis.

Proceso del Santo Oficio de la Inquisición y el Dr. Rafael de Cervanes en su nombre contra Blas de Monteroso por blasfemo, 1537. Tomo XIV, exp. 18.

Proceso del Santo Oficio de la Inquisición contra Sancho de Bullo por blasfemo, 1537. Tomo XIV, exp. 19.

Proceso de la Justicia del Santo Oficio de la Inquisición contra Alvaro de Ordaz por blasfemo, 1537. Tomo XIV, exp. 20.

Proceso del Santo Oficio de la Inquisición contra Juan de Placencia por blasfemo, 1537. Tomo XIV, exp. 21.

Proceso del Santo Oficio de la Inquisición y el fiscal en su nombre contra Juan Moreno por blasfemo, 1537. Tomo XIV, exp. 22.

Proceso del Santo Oficio de la Inquisición y Dr. Rafael de Cervanes fiscal en su nombre contra Juan Fernández por blasfemo, 1537. Tomo XIV, exp. 23.

Proceso del Santo Oficio de la Inquisición contra Cristóbal Ruiz por blasfemo, 1537. Tomo XIV, exp. 24.

Proceso del Santo Oficio de la Inquisición contra Francisco Jiménes, 1537. Tomo XIV, exp. 25.

Proceso del Santo Oficio de la Inquisición contra Juan de Arroyo por blasfemo, 1538. Tomo XIV, exp. 26.

Proceso del Santo Oficio de la Inquisición contra Luis de Aguilar por blasfemo reincidente, 1538. Tomo XIV, exp. 26 bis.

Proceso del Santo Oficio de la Inquisición contra Diego Ruiz por blasfemo, 1538. Tomo XIV, exp. 27.

Proceso del Santo Oficio de la Inquisición contra Bartolomé Copada por blasfemo, 1538. Tomo XIV, exp. 28.

Proceso del Santo Oficio de la Inquisición contra Juan Fernández por blasfemo, 1538. Tomo XIV, exp. 29.

Proceso del Santo Oficio de la Inquisición contra Juan Gómez de Castilleja por blasfemo, 1538. Tomo XIV, exp. 30.

Proceso del Santo Oficio de la Inquisición contra Juan de Rivadeneyra por blasfemo, 1538. Tomo XIV, exp. 31.

Proceso del Santo Oficio de la Inquisición contra Alonso Hernández por blasfemo, 1538. Tomo XIV, exp. 32.

Proceso del Santo Oficio de la Inquisición contra Pero Sánchez por blasfemo, 1538. Tomo XIV, exp. 32 bis.

Proceso del Santo Oficio de la Inquisición contra Alonso Gómez por blasfemo, 1538. Tomo XIV, exp. 33.

Proceso del Santo Oficio de la Inquisición contra Juan de la Peña por blasfemo, 1539. Tomo XIV, exp. 34.

Proceso del Santo Oficio de la Inquisición contra José de Cayzer por blasfemo y haber resistido a la justicia del Santo Oficio, 1540. Tomo XIV, exp. 36.

Proceso del Santo Oficio de la Inquisición contra Manuel Fernández por haber blasfemado estando riñiendo con María López, panadera del Virrey, 1540. Tomo XIV, exp. 37.

Proceso del Santo Oficio de la Inquisición contra Juan Cabezas por blasfemo, 1540. Tomo XIV, exp. 38.

Proceso del Santo Oficio de la Inquisición contra Juan de Avila por blasfemo, 1541. Tomo XIV, exp. 39.

Proceso del Santo Oficio de la Inquisición contra Alonso Bueno por blasfemo, 1541. Tomo XIV, exp. 40.

Proceso del Santo Oficio de la Inquisición contra Francisco de Oyos por blasfemo, 1538. Tomo XIV, exp. 45.

Proceso del Santo Oficio de la Inquisición contra Alonso Cordero por bígamo, 1536. Tomo XXII, exp. 1.

Proceso del Santo Oficio de la Inquisición contra Pedro García quien estando casado en España contrajo aqui matrimonio con una India de Texcoco, 1536. Tomo XXII, exp. 2.

Proceso del Santo Oficio de la Inquisición y el Doctor Rafael de Cervanes, fiscal en su nombre contra Inés Hernández por bígamo, 1536. Tomo XXII, exp. 3.

Proceso del Santo Oficio de la Inquisición y el fiscal en su nombre contra Isabel Muñoz por haber sido acusada de bigamía, 1536. Tomo XXII, exp. 4.

Proceso del Santo Oficio de la Inquisición y el fiscal en su nombre contra Diego Cortés por bígamo, 1536. Tomo XXII, exp. 5.

Proceso del Santo Oficio contra Alonso de Serna por haber sido acusado de bigamía, 1536. Tomo XXII, exp. 6.

Proceso del Santo Oficio de la Inquisición contra Ana Pérez por casada dos veces, 1536. Tomo XXII, exp. 8.

Proceso del Santo Oficio de la Inquisición contra Alvar Pérez por casado dos veces y fragmentos de las causas formadas a Juana Ruiz por casada dos veces; a Juan Pérez por blasfemo; a Manuel Borullo por sospechoso de judaismo; a Juan Ruiz por las mismas sosphechas; a Diego Machuca por la misma causa, 1537-1539. Tomo XXII, exp. 9.

Proceso del Santo Oficio de la Inquisición y el fiscal en su nombre contra Nicolas Chamorro por casado dos veces, 1537. Tomo XXII, exp. 11.

Proceso del Santo Oficio de la Inquisición contra Beatriz González por casada dos veces, 1538. Tomo XXII, exp. 12.

Proceso del Santo Oficio de la Inquisición contra Baltazar Gutiérrez por blasfemo, 1538. Tomo XXII, exp. 14.

Proceso de la Justicia en nombre del Santo Oficio contra Francisco de Coyoacán por casado dos veces, 1538. Tomo XXIII, exp. 1.

Proceso del Santo Oficio de la Inquisición contra María de Vega acusada de bigamía, 1541. Tomo XXIII, exp. 2.

Información contra Cristóbal Quintero, casado dos veces, 1541. Tomo XXIII, exp. 2 bis.

Formula para gobierno de Inquisición por Don Antonio de Mendoza, 1536. Tomo XXX, exp. o.

Proceso del Santo Oficio de la Inquisición contra Juan Nizardo por no haberse querido confesar y haber roto una bula del Papa, 1536. Tomo XXX, exp. 1.

Proceso del Santo Oficio de la Inquisición contra Hernán Núñez por haber dicho que si junto a esta tierra hubiera Moros él se tornaría Moro, 1536. Tomo XXX, exp. 2.

Proceso del Santo Oficio de la Inquisición contra Maese Pedro de Sevilla por sospechoso de luterano, pues afirmó que los clerigos era mejor que fueran casados, 1537. Tomo XXX, exp. 3.

Proceso del Santo Oficio de la Inquisición contra Luis Heredero por blasfemo, 1537. Tomo XXX, exp. 4.

Proceso del Santo Oficio de la Inquisición contra Pedro Hernández de Alvor por sospechoso de ser judío, 1538. Tomo XXX, exp. 5.

Proceso del Santo Oficio de la Inquisición contra Cristóbal de la Hoz por haber renegado de Santa María, 1538. Tomo XXX, exp. 6.

Proceso del Santo Oficio de la Inquisición contra Gonzalo de Castañeda por blasfemo, 1538. Tomo XXX, exp. 7.

Proceso del Santo Oficio de la Inquisición contra Francisco Millán por sospechoso de judaizante, 1539. Tomo XXX, exp. 8.

Proceso del Santo Oficio de la Inquisición contra Cristóbal y Catalina su muger y contra Martín, hermano de Cristóbal por idólatras y ocultar ídolos, 1539. Tomo XXX, exp. 9.

Información levantada en la Villa de Santiesteban del Puerto, provincia de Pánuco, en comisión de Don Fray Juan de Zumárraga, 1539. Tomo XXX, exp. 9 bis.

Proceso del Santo Oficio de la Inquisición contra Alvaro Mateos por judaizante, 1539. Tomo XXX, exp. 9-a.

Proceso del Santo Oficio de la Inquisición contra Beatriz Gómez, muger de Mateos, por judaizante, 1539. Tomo XXX, exp. 9a.

Proceso criminal del Santo Oficio de la Inquisición contra Antonio de Cárdenas, por haber estado amancebado con una comadre suya, 1536. Tomo XXXIV, exp. 1.

Proceso del Santo Oficio de la Inquisición y el Dr. Rafael de Cervanes, fiscal en su nombre contra Sebastian Fragoso, clérigo por haber dejado el habito clerical y haber andado mucho tiempo amancebado con una mujer diciendo que era su mujer legítima, 1537. Tomo XXXIV, exp. 2.

Proceso del Santo Oficio de la Inquisición contra Lope de Sayavedra por amancebado con una prima hermana, 1538. Tomo XXXIV, exp. 3.

Proceso del Santo Oficio de la Inquisición contra Francisco Lombardo por bigamía, 1540. Tomo XXXIV, exp. 4.

Instrucción y Memoria de la que el Reverendísimo Señor Maestro Juan Infante de Barrios y Arcediano de la Catedral de México habia hacer (de orden del Señor Don Fray Juan de Zumárraga) en la Villa de Pánuco sobre la vida de Gonzalo Bernal, acusado de mal Cristiano, sobre si los indios de allí y de Santiago de los Valles continuaron en sus ritos e idolatrias y sacrificios, sobre la conducta de un padre Carmelita amancebado, sobre el cura de dicha Villa de Pánuco, Alonso Ruiz de Arévalo, que vivia con una muger casada, tenia un hijo de una criada, jugaba a los naipes y retenia bienes de la Bula de la Santa Cruzada, 1540. Tomo XXXIV, exp. 5.

Proceso de la Justicia Eclesiástica contra Antonio Anguiano por amancebado, 1534. Tomo XXXVI, exp. 1.

Proceso del Santo Oficio de la Inquisición y Dr. Rafael de Cervanes fiscal en su nombre contra Catalina de Espina por bigamía, 1537. Tomo XXXVI, exp. 2.

Información y Sentencia en el Proceso formado a María Muñoz por bigamía, 1537. Tomo XXXVI, exp. 3.

Proceso del Santo Oficio de la Inquisición contra Bernaldo del Castillo por estar amancebado con muchas indias esclavas suyas, 1538. Tomo XXXVI, exp. 4.

Proceso de la Justicia Eclesiástica contra María de Soto por bigamía, 1538. Tomo XXXVI, exp. 5.

Proceso del Santo Oficio de la Inquisición contra Martín Xuchimitl, indio de Coyoacán por haber vivido amancebado con cuatro hermanas, 1539. Tomo XXXVI, exp. 6.

Proceso del Santo Oficio de la Inquisición contra Tacatetl y Tanixtetl, indios de Tanacopán por idólatras y sacrificadores, 1536. Tomo XXXVII, exp. 1.

Proceso del Santo Oficio de la Inquisición contra los indios de Atzcapozalco por idólatras, 1538. Tomo XXXVII, exp. 2.

Proceso del Santo Oficio de la Inquisición contra Puxtecatl Tlaylotla por haber ocultar ídolos, 1539. Tomo XXXVII, exp. 3.

Proceso del Santo Oficio de la Inquisición contra Diego Díaz, clérigo de Ocuituco por haber aconsejado a dos individuos que hicieran aparecer como idólatra al indio Cristóbal, 1540. Tomo XXXVII, exp. 3 bis.

Inventario de bienes de Martín Ucelo, 1536. Tomo XXXVII, exp. 4.

Proceso del Santo Oficio de la Inquisición, contra Tlilanci, indio de Izúcar por idólatra, 1539. Tomo XXXVII, exp. 4 bis.

Proceso del Santo Oficio de la Inquisición y Dr. Rafael de Cervanes en su nombre contra Juan Franco por hechicerías, 1536. Tomo XXXVIII, exp. 1.

Proceso del Santo Oficio de la Inquisición contra Juan Franco, el cojo, por blasfemo, 1536. Tomo XXXVIII, exp. 1 bis.

Proceso hecho por el Santo Oficio de la Inquisición y Dr. Rafael de Cervanes, fiscal en su nombre contra María, esclava de Pedro Pérez, y contra la Moralla partera y María de Espinosa e María, esclava de Maestra Diego, e Margarita Pérez, y Antón, indio, por hechicerías, 1536. Tomo XXXVIII, exp. 2.

Proceso del Santo Oficio de la Inquisición y el Fiscal en su nombre contra María de Armenta por hechicerías, 1536. Tomo XXXVIII, exp. 3.

Proceso del Santo Oficio de la Inquisición contra Martín Ucelo (Ocelotl) por idólatra y hechicero, 1536. Tomo XXXVIII, exp. 4.

Proceso del Santo Oficio de la Inquisición y el Dr. Rafael de Cervanes, fiscal en su nombre contra María de Bárcena por hechicerías, 1537. Tomo XXXVIII, exp. 5.

Proceso del Santo Oficio de la Inquisición y el Dr. Rafael de Cervanes, Fiscal en su nombre contra María Marroquina, Leonor de Saravia y Francisca, negra esclava de Luis Marín por hechicerías, 1537. Tomo XXXVIII, exp. 6.

Proceso del Santo Oficio de la Inquisición y el Dr. Rafael de Cervanes, Fiscal en su nombre contra Mixcoatl y Papalotl por hechicerías, 1537. Tomo XXXVIII, exp. 7.

Proceso del Santo Oficio de la Inquisición contra María de León por maleficios y hechicerías, 1537. Tomo XXXVIII, exp. 8.

Proceso de la Santa Inquisición y el fiscal en su nombre contra Elvira Jiménez por supersticiosa, 1536. Tomo XL, exp. 1.

Proceso del Santo Oficio de la Inquisición contra Diego Tacateca de Tlapanaloa por idólatra, 1538. Tomo XL, exp. 2.

Proceso del Santo Oficio de la Inquisición contra el Doctor Cristóbal Méndez por haber mandado hacer medallas o sigilos de oro que hechas cuando el sol entraba en lo principio de ciertos signos tienen entre otras virtudes la de curar el mal de riñones, 1538. Tomo XL, exp. 3.

Proceso del Santo Oficio de la Inquisición contra Francisco Cabezas por blasfemo, 1537. Tomo XL, exp. 3-b.

Proceso del Santo Oficio de la Inquisición contra Hernando de Orellana por blasfemo y haber dicho palabras injuriosas contra el Santo Oficio, 1537. Tomo XL, exp. 3-c.

Declaración de Juan Cercado por sospechoso de judío, 1539. Tomo XL, exp. 3-d.

Declaración de Antón de Heredia por sospechoso de judío converso, 1539. Tomo XL, exp. 3-e.

Declaración de García de Morón por sospechoso de judío, 1539. Tomo XL, exp. 3-f.

Proceso del Santo Oficio de la Inquisición contra Esperanza Valenciana por supersticiosa, 1539. Tomo XL, exp. 4.

Proceso del Fiscal del Santo Oficio de la Inquisición contra el Bachiller Pedro Ruiz Calderón por nigromante, 1540. Tomo XL, exp. 5.

Fragmento del Proceso del Santo Oficio de la Inquisición contra Diego sobre si habia faltado o no su deber de interprete con las indios de Tenayuca, 1536. Tomo XL, exp., 5-II.

Proceso del Santo Oficio de la Inquisición contra Francisco de Leyva, Canónigo y Provisor de la Iglesia de Puebla de los Angeles, por haber leido el domingo 16 de Julio de 1536 en esta iglesia una carta de excomunión emplazando a todos los que tuvieran que denunciar algún delito de fe, juzgando que el Señor Zumárraga era Inquisidor General de la Nueva España, no siendo sino de su Obispado, 1536. Tomo XL, exp. 5-III.

Proceso del Santo Oficio de la Inquisición contra Gregorio Gallego y Martín de Aranda por no haber guardado el secreto que se les recomendó, 1540. Tomo XL, exp. 6.

Denuncia hecha contra Don Juan, indio Cacique del pueblo de Iguala por amancebado y idólatra, 1540. Tomo XL, exp. 7.

Información contra el Cacique de Matlatlán, Don Juan, por idólatra y amancebado, 1539. Tomo XL, exp. 8.

Proceso del Santo Oficio de la Inquisición contra Juan Moreno y Cristóbal Barrera, trompetas, por haberse negado a tocar en el recibimiento de los padres de la Inquisición, 1536. Tomo XLII, exp. 3.

Proceso del fiscal del Santo Oficio de la Inquisición contra Antón Pérez por haber hurtado piedras de la fábrica de la Catedral, 1536. Tomo XLII, exp. 5.

Información sumaria contra Nicolas Salinas, Teniente del Alguacil Mayor por haber sacado a Francisco Ramírez que se había refugiado en la Iglessia Mayor de México por cierta deuda que debia, 1536. Tomo XLII, exp. 6.

Proceso del Santo Oficio de la Inquisición contra Jorge González reo prófugo de la Inquisición de Cuenca, 1536. Tomo XLII, exp. 7.

Proceso del Santo Oficio de la Inquisición contra Pedro Cervero por ciertas palabras en contra la Inquisición, 1536. Tomo XLII, exp. 8.

Proceso del Santo Oficio de la Inquisición contra Antonio Anguiano por bígamo, 1536. Tomo XLII, exp. 8 bis.

Proceso del Santo Oficio de la Inquisición contra Gonzalo de Ecija, reo prófugo, 1536. Tomo XLII, exp. 9.

Información hecha ante Pedro Moreno, Alcalde Ordinario de Veracruz a solicitud de Cristóbal Quintero para averiguar si su muger Catalina Rodríguez habia muerto en la Ciudad de Sevilla, 1537. Tomo XLII, exp. 10.

Juicio seguido ante el Reverendísimo y Muy Magnífico Señor Don Juan de Zárate, Obispo de Oaxaca, y Juez de los Bienes Confiscados del Santo Oficio de la Inquisición, por Catalina de Caxas, muger de Maese Andrés Alemán, para que de las cantidades secuestradas a su esposo se la entrega a ella la que llevó como dote cuando se casó, 1537, Tomo XLII, exp. 11.

Proceso del Santo Oficio de la Inquisición contra Nuño Méndez por incestuoso, 1538. Tomo XLII, exp. 13.

Proceso del Santo Oficio de la Inquisición contra Pero Muñoz, clérigo, por palabras contra el Santo Oficio, 1538. Tomo XLII, exp. 14.

Proceso de la Inquisición contra Gonzalo Martín por no haber denunciado las palabras que oyó a Pero Muñoz, clérigo, 1538. Tomo XLII, exp. 15.

Proceso de la Inquisición contra Marcos de Arévalo por haber impedido la ejecución del Santo Oficio, 1538. Tomo XLII, exp. 16.

Proceso del Santo Oficio de la Inquisición contra Marcos y Francisco, indios, por haber hablado en contra de las doctrinas predicadas por los frailes, 1539. Tomo XLII, exp. 17.

Proceso del Santo Oficio de la Inquisición contra Don Baltazar, cacique de Culoacán por idólatra y ocultar ídolos, 1539. Tomo XLII, exp. 18.

Pleito seguido ante el Ilustrísimo Señor Don Fray Juan de Zumárraga en contra Diego Díaz, clérigo preso en la carcel del episcopado, por acusación presentada por Juan Ruiz, mercader, a quien no le había pagado el vino que le compró, 1542. Tomo XLII, exp. 21.

Proceso contra Diego Díaz, clérigo, por solicitante, 1542-1548. Tomo LXVIII, exp. 1.

Proceso contra Juan de Salamanca por sospechoso de judío, 1539. Tomo CXXV, exp. 1.

Denuncia que hizo Juan Hurtado contra Juan Rodriguez de Bejarano por haber dicho muchas heregías, 1543. Tomo CXXV, exp. 2.

Denuncia contra Pero Núñez por perjuro, 1539. Tomo CXXV, exp. 4.

Proceso contra Juan de Baeza por sospechoso de judío, 1540. Tomo CXXV, exp. 5.

Proceso sumarísimo contra Alonso Delgado por proposiciones luteranas, 1537. Tomo CXXV, exp. 6.

Proceso contra Inés de Casas por hechicerías, 1537. Tomo CCXI, exp. 1.

Proceso contra Diego Díaz por tener acceso carnal con madre e hija, 1538. Tomo CCXII, exp. 2.

Información levantada contra Cebrian y Antonio Lipares, marineros por sodomía, 1542. Tomo CCXII, exp. 1.

Proceso contra Pedro, indio cacique del Pueblo de Totolapa y contra Antonio su hermano, por estar amancebados con una muger que fue manceba de su padre, y con una tía suya, por tener ídolos escondidos y idolatrizar, 1540. Tomo CCXII, exp. 7.

III. *Miscellaneous Manuscript Materials*

AGN, Civil, Tomo 1271.
AGN, Hospital de Jesús, Leg. 271, exp. 11.
Archivo General de Indias, Seville [AGI], Patronato, Leg. 54, exps. 1, 2.

IV. *Printed Materials*

Adib, Víctor, "Del humanismo mexicano," *Historia mexicana*, V (1955), 109-113.
Aguayo Spencer, Rafael, *Don Vasco de Quiroga: Documentos.* México, 1940.
Alegría, Paula, *La Educación en México antes y después de la conquista*, México. 1936.
Almoina, José, "Citas clásicas de Zumárraga," *Historia mexicana*, IV (1954), 391-419.
——, "El Erasmismo de Zumárraga," *Filosofía y letras*, XXIX (1948), 93-126.
——, *Rumbos heterodoxos en México.* Ciudad Trujillo, 1948.
Anderson, Arthur J. O., and Charles E. Dibble, trans. and eds., *Florentine Codex: General History of the Things of New Spain.* Santa Fe, 1950. Vol. I. Sahagún's original text translated from the Nahuatl.
*Annales de Domingo Francisco de San Antón Muñon Chimalpahin Quauhtlehuanitzin. Sixieme et septieme relations (1258-1612).* Paris, 1889.
Arteaga Garza, Beatriz, and Guadalupe Pérez San Vicente, *Cedulario Cortesiano.* México, 1949.
Bancroft, Hubert H., *History of Mexico.* San Francisco, 1883-1888. 6 vols.
Barlow, Robert, "Las Joyas de Martín Ocelotl," *Yan*, III, (1954) 56-59.
Bataillon, Marcel, "Erasme au Mexique," *Société Historique Algérienne. Deuxieme Congres National des Sciences Historiques*, 1930. Algiers, 1932.
——, *Erasme et l'Espagne: Recherches sur l'histoire spirituelle du XVIe siecle.* Paris, 1937.
——, *Erasmo y España, Estudios sobre la historia espiritual del siglo XVI.* México, 1950. 2 vols. Expanded by Bataillon and translated by Antonio Alatorre.
Baumer, Franklin le Van, *Main Currents of Western Thought.* New York, 1952.
Bayle, Constantino, *El IV centenario de Don Fray Juan de Zumárraga.* Madrid, 1948.
——, *El Protector de Indios.* Sevilla, 1945.
Benítez, Fernando, *La Vida criolla en el siglo XVI.* México, 1953.
Blotzer, Joseph, "The Inquisition," *The Catholic Encyclopedia.* New York, 1910. VIII, 26-38.
Bonilla y San Martín, Adolfo, "Erasmo en España (Episodio de la historia del Renacimiento)," *Revue Hispanique*, XVII (1907), 379-548.
Campa, Arthur L., "The Churchmen and the Indian Languages of New Spain," *Hispanic American Historical Review*, XI (1931), 542-550.
Carreño, Alberto María, "The Books of Don Fray Juan de Zumárraga," *The Americas*, V (1949), 311-330.

——, *Un desconocido cedulario del siglo XVI*. México, 1944.

——, *Don Fray Juan de Zumárraga, primer obispo y arzobispo de México. Documentos inéditos*. México, 1941.

——, *Don Fray Juan de Zumárraga, teólogo y editor, humanista e inquisidor. Nuevos documentos*. México, 1950.

Casas, Bartolomé de las, *Colección de tratados 1552-1553*. Buenos Aires, 1924. Facsimiles.

——, *Historia de las Indias*. Madrid, c.1561.

Caso, Alfonso, *The Aztecs: People of the Sun*, tr. Lowell Dunham. Norman, 1958.

——, *El Pueblo del Sol*. México, 1953.

Castañeda, Carlos E., "Fray Juan de Zumárraga and Indian Policy in New Spain," *The Americas*, V (1949), 305-308.

Castillo, Bernal Díaz del, *Historia verdadera de la conquista de la Nueva España*. México, 1904. 2 vols.

Catálogo de Inquisición, Archivo General de la Nación. México, n.d. 14 typewritten vols.

Ceccherelli, Claudio, *El bautismo y los franciscanos en México (1524-1539)*. Madrid, 1955.

Chauvet, Fidel de J., *Fray Juan de Zumárraga, O.F.M.* México, 1948.

——, "Fray Juan de Zumárraga, Protector of the Indians," *The Americas*, V (1949), 283-295.

Clavijero, Francisco Javier, *Historia antigua de México*. México, 1917. 2 vols.

*Colección de documentos inéditos relativos al descubrimiento, conquista y colonización de las posesiones españolas en América y Oceanía*. Madrid, 1864-1884. 42 vols.

Conway, G. R. G., *An Englishman and the Mexican Inquisition*. México, 1927.

——, "Hernando Alonso, A Jewish Conquistador with Cortés in México," *Publications of the American Jewish Historical Society*, XXXI (1928), 9-31.

Cook de Leonard, Carmen, ed., *Esplendor del México antiguo*. México, 1959. 2 vols.

Coulton, George G., *The Inquisition*. New York, n.d.

Cuevas, Mariano, *Album histórico guadalupano del IV centenario*. México, 1930.

——, *Historia de la iglesia en México*. México, 1921. 4 vols.

Dávila Padilla, Agustín, *Historia de la fundación y discurso de la provincia de Santiago de México, de la Orden de Predicadores, por las vidas de sus varones insignes y casos notables de Nueva España*. Madrid, 1596.

Dusenberry, William H., "The Regulation of Meat Supply in Sixteenth Century Mexico City," *Hispanic American Historical Review*, XXVIII (1948), 38-52.

Dutton, Bertha, *Tula of the Toltecs*. Santa Fe, 1955.

Encinas, Diego de, *Cedulario indiano*. Madrid, 1945. 4 vols.

*Escritos sueltos de Hernán Cortés*. México, 1871.

Eymeric, Nicolas, *Manual de inquisidores*. Madrid, 1571.

Eymericus, Nicolas, *Directorium inquisitorum*. Rome, 1579.

Fernández del Castillo, Francisco, *Libros y libreros en el siglo XVI*. México, 1914.

Fernández de Oviedo y Valdés, Gonzalo, *Historia general y natural de las Indias, islas y tierra firme del Mar Oceano*. Madrid, 1851-1855. 4 vols.

Frasso, Pedro, *De regio patronatu indiarum*. Madrid, 1677-1679. 2 vols.

García, Genaro, *Carácter de la conquista española en América y en México según los textos de los historiadores primitivos*. México, c.1954.

———, *El Clero en México durante la dominación española.* México, 1907.

García, Granados, Rafael, *Diccionario biográfico de la historia antigua de Méjico.* México, 1952-1953. 3 vols.

García Icazbalceta, Joaquín, *Bibliografía mexicana del siglo XVI.* México, 1954.

———, *Don Fray Juan de Zumárraga, primer obispo y arzobispo de México.* México, 1947. 4 vols.

———, "La Instrucción pública en México durante el siglo XVI," *Obras de Joaquín García Icazbalceta,* I. México, 1896.

———, *Investigación histórica y documental sobre la aparición de la Virgen de Guadalupe.* México, c.1950.

———, *Obras.* México, 1896-1899. 10 vols.

Gibson, Charles, *Tlaxcala in the Sixteenth Century.* New Haven, 1952.

Gillmor, Frances, *Flute of the Smoking Mirror.* Albuquerque, 1949.

Hanke, Lewis, *Bartolomé de las Casas, pensador político, historiador, antropólogo.* Habana, 1949.

———, "The Contribution of Bishop Zumárraga to Mexican Culture," *The Americas,* V (1949), 275-282.

———, *The First Social Experiments in America: A Study in the Development of Spanish Indian Policy in the Sixteenth Century.* Cambridge, 1935.

———, "Pope Paul and the American Indians," *The Harvard Theological Review,* XXX (1937), 65-102.

———, *The Spanish Struggle for Justice in the Conquest of America.* Philadelphia, 1949.

Haring, Clarence, *The Spanish Empire in America.* New York, 1947.

———, *Trade and Navigation between Spain and the Indies in the Time of the Hapsburgs.* Cambridge, 1918.

Hernáez, Francisco, *Colección de bulas, breves y otros documentos relativos a la iglesia de América y Filipinas.* Brussels, 1879. 2 vols.

Herrera y Tordesillas, Antonio de, *Historia general de los hechos de los castellanos en las islas y tierra firme de la Mar Oceano.* Madrid, 1601. 2 vols.

*The Holy Bible,* various editions.

Holzapfel, Herbert, *The History of the Franciscan Order,* trans. Antonine Tibesar and Gervase Brinkmann. Teutopolis, Illinois, 1948.

Isidore of Sevilla, *Etymologiae.* Oxford, 1911.

Ixtlilxochitl, Fernando de Alva, *Historia Chichimeca,* México, 1944. 2 vols.

Jiménez Moreno, Wigberto, "Tula y los Toltecas según las Fuentes Históricas," *Revista mexicana de estudios antropológicos,* V (1941).

Jiménez Rueda, Julio, *Don Pedro Moya de Contreras, primer inquisidor de México.* México, 1944.

———, *Herejías y supersticiones en la Nueva España.* México, 1946.

———, "La secta de los Alumbrados en la Nueva España," *Boletín del Archivo General de la Nación,* XVI (1945), 5-32.

Junco, Alfonso, *Inquisición sobre la Inquisición.* México, 1949.

King, Edward (Viscount Kingsborough), *Antiquities of Mexico.* London, 1830-1848. 9 folio vols.

Kubler, George, *Mexican Architecture of the Sixteenth Century.* New Haven, 1948. 2 vols.

Labayru, Estanislao J. de, *Estudios y hechos de la vida del ilustrísimo y vener-*

*able vizcaíno Don Fray Juan de Zumárraga, natural de Durango, primer obispo y arzobispo de México*. Bilbao, 1890.

*La Vida Colonial*, Vol. VII of *Publicaciones del Archivo General de la Nación*. México, 1923.

Lea, Henry C., *Chapters from the Religious History of Spain Connected with the Inquisition*. Philadelphia, 1898.

————, *A History of the Inquisition of Spain*. New York, 1908. 4 vols.

————, *The Inquisition in the Spanish Dependencies*. New York, 1908.

————, *The Inquisition of the Middle Ages*. New York, 1908-1911. 3 vols.

————, *The Moriscoes of Spain: Their Conversion and Expulsion*. London, 1901.

León, Nicolás, *Documentos inéditos referentes al ilustrísimo señor Don Vasco de Quiroga*. México, 1940.

Leonard, Irving, *Books of the Brave*. Cambridge, 1949.

Leitz, Paul S., "Don Vasco de Quiroga and the Second Audiencia of New Spain," unpublished doctoral dissertation. Loyola University, Chicago, 1940.

————, "Vasco de Quiroga, Oidor Made Bishop," *Mid-America*, XXXII (1950), 13-32.

————, "Vasco de Quiroga, Sociologist of New Spain," *Mid-America*, XVIII (1936), 247-259.

*Literae apostolicae diversorum romanorum pontificum, pro officio sanctissimae inquisitionis, ab Innoc. III*. Rome, 1579.

Llorca, Bernardino, *Die spanische Inquisition und die Alumbrados (1509-1667)*. Berlin-Bonn, 1934.

————, *La Inquisición en España*. Barcelona, 1946.

Llorente, Juan Antonio, *Historia crítica de la Inquisición*. Barcelona, 1835-1836. 4 vols.

————, *The History of the Spanish Inquisition from the Time of its Establishment to the Reign of Ferdinand VII*. Philadelphia, 1826.

Longhurst, John E., *Erasmus and the Spanish Inquisition: The Case of Juan de Valdés*. Albuquerque, 1950.

————, *Luther and the Spanish Inquisition: The Case of Diego de Uceda, 1528-1529*. Albuquerque, 1953.

López de Gómara, Francisco, *Historia de la conquista de México*. México, 1943. 2 vols.

López Martínez, Nicolas, *Los Judaizantes castellanos y la Inquisición en tiempo de Isabel la Católica*. Burgos, 1954.

*Los Códigos españoles. Concordados y Anotados*. Madrid, 1872-1873. 12 vols.

Mariel de Ibáñez, Yolanda, *La Inquisición en México durante el siglo XVI*. México, 1945.

Marín Melagres, Julio, *Procedimientos de la Inquisición*. Madrid, 1888. 2 vols.

Marín-Tamayo, Fausto, *El primer conflicto colonial civil-eclesiástico (1529)*. Puebla, 1957.

Martínez del Río, Pablo, *Alumbrado*. México, 1937.

Maza, Francisco de la, *El Palacio de la Inquisición*. México, 1951.

Mecham, J. Lloyd, *Church and State in Latin America*. Chapel Hill, 1934.

Medina, José Toribio, *Historia del Tribunal del Santo Oficio de la Inquisición en México*. México, 1954.

————, *La Imprenta en México*. Santiago de Chile, 1907-1912. 8 vols.

———, *La primitiva Inquisición americana, 1493-1569.* Santiago de Chile, 1914. 2 vols.

Melody, John W., "Blasphemy," *The Catholic Encyclopedia.* New York, 1910. II, 595-596.

Méndez Plancarte, Gabriel, *Humanismo Mexicano del Siglo XVI.* México, 1946.

Mendieta, Gerónimo de, *Historia eclesiástica indiana.* México, 1945. 4 vols.

Menéndez y Pelayo, Marcelino, *Historia de los heterodoxos Españoles.* Madrid, 1911-1933. 7 vols.

Millares Carlo, Agustín, *Utopías del renacimiento,* México, 1941.

Millares Carlo, Agustín, and J. I. Mantecón, *Indice y extractos de los protocolos de notarías de México, D. F.* México, 1945. 2 vols.

Miranda, José, "Renovación Cristiana y Erasmismo en México," *Historia mexicana,* I (1951), 22-47.

Mulvihill, Daniel J., "Juan de Zumárraga, First Bishop of Mexico," unpublished doctoral dissertation. University of Michigan, 1954.

Nuttall, Zelia, "L'evêque Zumárraga et les idoles principales du Grand Temple de México," *Journal of the Society of Americanists* (1911), 153-171.

Oesterley, W. O. E. and Theodore H. Robinson, *Hebrew Religion, Its Origin and Development.* London, 1955.

Orozco y Berra, Manuel, *Historia de la dominación española en México.* México, 1938. 4 vols.

Paddock, John, *A Guide to G. C. Vaillant's Aztecs of Mexico.* México, 1956.

Pallares, Eduardo, *El Procedimiento inquisitorial.* México, 1951.

Paso y Troncoso, Francisco del, *Papeles de la Nueva España.* Madrid, 1905-1941. 7 vols.

Pérez-Bustamente, Carlos, *Compendio de historia de España.* Madrid, 1952.

Peterson, Frederick, *Ancient Mexico: An Introduction to the Pre-Hispanic Cultures.* London, 1959.

Pomar, Juan Bautista and Alonso de Zurita, *Relaciones de Texcoco y la Nueva España.* México, 1941.

*Primer libro de las actas de cabildo de la ciudad de México.* México, 1889.

"Proceso contra Diego Naghuato," *Boletín del Archivo General de la Nación,* XVI (1945), 37-40.

"Procesco contra Francisco de Sayavedra por Erasmista," *Boletín del Archivo General de la Nación,* XVIII (1947), 1-15.

"Proceso del Santo Oficio contra una India Curandera," *Boletín del Archivo de General de la Nación,* XII (1941), 211-214.

*Proceso inquisitorial del cacique de Texcoco,* Vol. I of *Publicaciones del Archivo General de la Nación.* México, 1910.

*Procesos de indios idólatras y hechiceros,* Vol. III of *Publicaciones del Archivo General de la Nación.* México, 1912.

*Procesos de Luis Carvajal (El Mozo),* Vol. XXVIII of *Publicaciones del Archivo General de la Nación.* México, 1935.

Puga, Vasco de, *Provisiones, cédulas, instrucciones de su magestad, ordenanças de difuntos y audiencia para la buena expedición de los negocios y administración de justicia y gobernación de esta Nueva España, y para el buen tratamiento y conservación de los Indios desde el Año 1525 hasta este presente 1563.* México, 1878. 2 vols.

*Recopilación de Leyes de los Reynos de las Indias.* Madrid, 1681. 4 vols.

Remesal, Antonio de, *Historia de la provincia de San Vicente de Chyapa*. Madrid, 1619.

Reyes, Alfonso, *Letras de la Nueva España*. México, 1948.

——, *The Position of America and Other Essays*. New York, 1950. Translated by Harriet de Onís.

——, "Utopías Americanas," *Sur* (Buenos Aires, 8 de Enero, 1938), 7-16.

Ricard, Robert, *La Conquista espiritual de México: Ensayo sobre el apostolado y los métodos misioneros de las ordenes mendicantes en la Nueva España de 1523-1524 a 1572*. México, 1947. Translated from the French by Angel Garibay K.

Robertson, Donald, *Mexico Manuscript Painting of the Early Colonial Period: the Metropolitan Schools*. New Haven, 1959.

Rubio Mañe, Jorge Ignacio, "El Archivo General de la Nación," *Revista de la historia de América*, Número 9 (August 1940), 63-169.

Ruiz de Alarcón, Hernando, *et al.*, *Tratado de las idolatrías, supersticiones, dioses, ritos, hechicerías y otras costumbres gentílicas de las razas aborígenes de México*. México, 1952. 2 vols.

Ruiz de Larrínaga, Juan, *Don Fray Juan de Zumárraga, primer obispo y arzobispo de México, durangués, franciscano, y servidor de la patria. Al margen de su pontificado*. Bilbao, 1948.

Russell, Bertrand, *A History of Western Philosophy*. New York, 1945.

Santillana, Giorgio de, *The Age of Adventure: The Renaissance Philosophers*. New York, 1956.

Schäfer, Ernst, *Beitrage zur Geschichte des spanischen Protestantismus und der Inquisition*. Gutersloh, 1902. 3 vols.

——, *Indice de la colección de documentos inéditos de Indias*. Madrid, 1946. 2 vols.

Scholes, France V., "Franciscan Missionary Scholars in Colonial Central America," *The Americas*, VII (1952), 391-416.

——, "The Beginnings of Hispano-Indian Society in Yucatan," *The Scientific Monthly*, XLIV (1937), 530-538.

Scholes, France V. and Eleanor B. Adams, *Don Diego de Quijada Alcalde Mayor de Yucatan, 1561-1565. Documentos sacados de los archivos de España*. México, 1938. 2 vols.

——, eds., *Proceso contra Tzintzicha Tangaxoan el Caltzontzin formado por Nuño de Guzmán, Año de 1530*. México, 1952.

——, eds., *Relación de las encomiendas de indios hechas en Nueva España a los conquistadores y pobladores de ella, año de 1564*. México, 1955.

Scholes, France V. and Ralph L. Roys, *Fray Diego de Landa and the Problem of Idolatry in Yucatan*. Washington, 1938. Reprinted from *Cooperation in Research*, Washington, 1938, 585-620.

Scott, James Brown, *The Spanish Origin of International Law. Francisco de Vitoria and his Law of Nations*. London, 1934.

Simpson, Lesley B., "Spanish Utopia," *Hispania*, XX (1937), 353-368.

——, *The Encomienda in New Spain*. Berkeley, 1950.

Solórzano Pereira, Juan de, *Política indiana*. Madrid, 1647.

Spinden, Herbert J., *Ancient Civilizations of Mexico and Central America*. New York, 1917.

Steck, Francis Borgia, *Education in Spanish North America during the Sixteenth Century*. Washington, 1943.

——, trans. and ed., *Motolinía's History of the Indians of New Spain*. Washington, 1951.

——, *El primer colegio en América: Santa Cruz de Tlatelolco*. México, 1944.

Suárez de Peralta, Juan, *Noticias históricas de la Nueva España*. México, 1949.

Thompson, J. Eric, *Mexico Before Cortez, An Account of the Daily Life, Religion and Ritual of the Aztecs and Kindred Peoples*. New York, 1933.

Toro, Alfonso, *La Familia Carvajal*. México, 1944. 2 vols.

——, *Los judíos en la Nueva España*, vol. XI of *Publicaciones del Archivo General de la Nación*. México, 1932.

Torquemada, Juan de, *Monarquía indiana*. Madrid, 1615. 2 vols.

Torquemada, Tomás, *Compilación de las instrucciones del Santo Oficio de la Inquisición*. Madrid, 1630.

Torre Revello, José, *El Libro, la imprenta y el periodismo en América durante la dominación española*. Buenos Aires, 1940.

Toussaint, Manuel, *Proceso y denuncias contra Simón Pereyns en la Inquisición de México*. México, 1938.

Tozzer, Alfred M., *Landa's relación de las cosas de Yucatan*. Cambridge, 1941.

Turberville, A. S., *The Spanish Inquisition*. New York, 1932.

Vacandard, E., *The Inquisition. A Critical and Historical Study of the Coercive Power of the Church*. New York, 1926.

Vaillant, George C., *The Aztecs of Mexico. Origin, Rise and Fall of the Aztec Nation*. Harmondsworth, Middlesex, 1950. Revised ed.

Vera, Fortino Hipólito, *Tesoro Guadalupano. Noticia de los libros, documentos, inscripciones que tratan, mencionan o aluden a la aparición de devoción de Nuestra Señora de Guadalupe*. México, 1887-1889. 2 vols.

Verrill, Alpheus H., *The Inquisition*. New York, 1931.

Warmington, Eric H. and Philip G. Rouse, *Great Dialogues of Plato*. New York, 1956.

Wicke, Charles, and Fernando Horcasitas, "Archaeological Investigations on Monte Tlaloc, México," *Mesoamerican Notes*, V (1957), 83-96.

Zavala, Silvio, "The American Utopia of the Sixteenth Century," *The Huntington Library Quarterly*, X (1947), 337-347.

——, *Ideario de Vasco de Quiroga*. México, 1941.

——, "Letras de Utopia: Carta a Don Alfonso Reyes," *Cuadernos Americanos*, II (1942), 146-152.

——, *New Viewpoints on the Spanish Colonization of America*. Philadelphia, 1943.

——, *La Utopía de Tomás Moro en la Nueva España y Otros Estudios*. México, 1937.

# Index

149

# Y

Yucatan: first bishop of, 18; inquisition in, 18

# Z

Zalaya, Pedro de, 86
Zarate, Juan López de, 124
Zavala, Martín de, 14
Zavala, Silvio, 26n, 32, 37n
Zumárraga, Juan de: administrative duties, 122-132; aim in Inquisition, 130; apostolic inquisitor, 13-15; appointment as bishop, 12n; arrival in Mexico, 12n-13n, 34; assumption of inquisitorial functions, 13; attitude on encomienda, 36; attitude on the nature of the In-dians, 28, 34-35; and blasphemers, 103-106; biographies of, 33n-34n; campaign against idolatry and superstition, 50 ff.; cases against Erasmism, 85-86; cases against Lutherans, 87-85; cases against minor heresies, 86-88; cases involving Indians, 50-75; Christian humanist, 33, 37, 131; consecration, 12n-13n; early years, 34n; and education for Indians, 35-36; evaluation of his Indian Inquisition, 74-75; Indian policy, 14, 34; and Judaizantes, 89-99; influence of Erasmus on, 37-41; influence of Thomas More on, 40-41; as inquisitor, 12-13; intellectual background, 26-41, 131; jurisdiction, 14; quarrel with audiencia, 35; sentences: *see* Inquisition, Mexican: sentences